D0148497

*Management of Knowledge
in Project Environments*

Management of Knowledge in Project Environments

Edited by

Peter E. D. Love
Patrick S. W. Fong
Zahir Irani

ELSEVIER
BUTTERWORTH
HEINEMANN

AMSTERDAM BOSTON HEIDELBERG LONDON NEW YORK OXFORD
PARIS SAN DIEGO SAN FRANCISCO SINGAPORE SYDNEY TOKYO

Elsevier Butterworth-Heinemann
Linacre House, Jordan Hill, Oxford OX2 8DP
30 Corporate Drive, Burlington, MA 01803

First published 2005

Copyright © 2005, Elsevier Limited. All rights reserved

The right of Peter E. D. Love, Patrick S. W. Fong and Zahir Irani to be
identified as the editors of this work has been asserted in accordance
with the Copyright, Design and Patents Act 1988

No part of this publication may be reproduced in any material form (including
photocopying or storing in any medium by electronic means and whether or
not transiently or incidentally to some other use of this publication) without
the written permission of the copyright holder except in accordance with the
provisions of the Copyright, Designs and Patents Act 1988 or under the terms
of a licence issued by the Copyright Licensing Agency Ltd, 90 Tottenham
Court Road, London, England W1T 4LP. Applications for the copyright
holder's written permission to reproduce any part of this publication should be
addressed to the publisher

Permissions may be sought directly from Elsevier's Science and Technology
Rights Department in Oxford, UK: phone: (+44) (0) 1865 843830;
fax: (+44) (0) 1865 853333; e-mail: permissions@elsevier.co.uk. You may
also complete your request on-line via the Elsevier homepage
(www.elsevier.com), by selecting 'Customer Support' and then
'Obtaining Permissions'

British Library Cataloguing in Publication Data
A catalogue record for this book is available from the British Library

Library of Congress Control Number: 2004116789

ISBN 0 7506 6251 4

For information on all Elsevier Butterworth-Heinemann
publications visit our website at www.elsevier.com

Typeset by Charon Tec Pvt. Ltd, Chennai, India
www.charontec.com
Printed and bound in Great Britain

Working together to grow
libraries in developing countries

www.elsevier.com | www.bookaid.org | www.sabre.org

ELSEVIER   BOOK AID
             International   Sabre Foundation

Contents

Contributors

F. Ackermann, Department of Management Science, University of Strathclyde, UK

T. Brady, CENTRIM, Freeman Centre, University of Brighton, UK

M. Bresnen, Management Centre, University of Leicester, UK

S. Cicmil, Bristol Business School, University of the West of England, UK

L. Edelman, Bentley College, USA

C. Eden, Department of Management Science, University of Strathclyde, UK

D. J. Edwards, Department of Building and Construction Engineering, Loughborough University, UK

P. S. W. Fong, Department of Building and Real Estate, Hong Kong Polytechnic University, China

M. Gustafsson, Research Manager, Research Institute for Project Based Industry, Finland

J. Hall, Haskayne Business School, University of Calgary, Canada

S. Howick, Department of Management Science, University of Strathclyde, UK

J. Huang, Nottingham University Business School, UK

Z. Irani, Department of Information Systems and Computing, Brunel University, UK

J. Liebowitz, Department of Information Technology, Johns Hopkins University, USA

P. E. D. Love, School of Management Information Systems, Edith Cowan University, Australia

N. Marshall, CENTRIM, Freeman Centre, University of Brighton, UK

S. Newell, Bentley College, USA

A. Prencipe, Faculty of Economics, University G. d'Annunzio, Italy

J. Sapsed, CENTRIM, Freeman Centre, University of Brighton, UK

H. Scarborough, Warwick Business School, University of Warwick, UK

J. Swan, Warwick Business School, University of Warwick, UK

F. Tell, Department of Management and Economics, Linköping University, Sweden

K. Wikström, Industrial Economics and Management, Åbo Akademi University, Finland

T. Williams, Department of Management Science, University of Strathclyde, UK

Forewords

Over the years there has been a shift in emphasis in research into project management, from focusing on the management of the individual project, to focusing on creating an environment in which projects can thrive.

In the 1970s, the focus of project management research was on developing tools and techniques, particularly critical path analysis, but also earned value analysis. In the 1980s, the focus was on success factors on projects. Before you can choose appropriate tools to manage the project, you need to know what factors will influence success. In the 1990s, the focus switched to success criteria. Before you can chose appropriate success factors, and hence appropriate tools, you need to know how the project will be judged successful at the end, and have the entire team, indeed all the stakeholders, focusing on the same end objectives, both project outcomes and business benefits. This research led to a measured improvement in project performance, with success rates doubling for one third of projects to two thirds of projects, (and failure rates halving from two thirds to one third). Clearly the research of the last three decades of the 20th century made an important contribution to project performance, but it was not enough, it was not the whole story.

Another part of the story is the context in which the project takes place. Senior management in the parent organization must ensure that they create an environment in which projects can thrive. They must govern the set of relationships between the management of projects taking place in the organization, the organization itself, themselves as client, and other stakeholders to ensure that projects can successfully deliver business benefit and help achieve corporate strategy. Project governance, governing that set of relationships, is not just the role of projects management; their role is primarily to successfully deliver project outputs. Senior management must create and govern the supportive project environment.

Part of that environment is the management of knowledge. Many project-based organizations from both the high-tech and engineering industries recognize that their ability to deliver projects successfully gives them a competitive advantage. So being able to manage project management knowledge, to be able to remember how to deliver projects successfully and to improve that knowledge, is key to the organization's success. But in project-based organizations, knowledge management is problematic, with new knowledge created on temporary projects and used on other projects. In the functional organization there is a classic three-step process of knowledge management: variation, selection, retention. New ideas are created in the function, successful ideas are chosen for reuse, and the knowledge stored within the function where it can be reused. In project-based organizations, new ideas are created on temporary projects, but the project cannot select and retain new ideas. Further, wherever those new ideas are stored, they are not immediately available to new projects. The project-based organization needs to think about how it is going to select new knowledge, where it is going to store it, and it needs to create a fourth step of knowledge management, distribution of knowledge to new projects.

A book on knowledge management within project-based organizations is therefore a welcome addition to the literature. The book contains chapters by many recognized experts from the project management literature. It builds on a special issue of *The International Journal of Project Management* (Volume 21, Number 3, April 2003), which was edited by Peter Love. The book contains some revised papers, but also many new chapters by significant contributors to the field. It contains many important topics, such as the sharing of knowledge across boundaries, the creation of a learning environment in project-based firms, and learning from project failure.

The book will be a valued addition to my library.

Professor J Rodney Turner
Professor of Project Management
Graduate School of Management Lille

Project-based work currently faces some of its greatest opportunities and challenges. The opportunities are clear to see; the huge increase in interest in project management presents clear evidence that more and more firms recognize it as a viable and effective means to achieve organizational goals. The flexibility, responsiveness, and innovativeness that projects offer modern organizations demonstrate again and again that project-based work is not the latest management fad, but represents a very real sea-change in the manner in which organizations must do business if they are to be successful in a fast-paced, global marketplace. For additional evidence of the role of project management, one only needs to examine the myriad of businesses and industries that are embracing these techniques. Industries as diverse as heavy manufacturing, financial services, insurance, and utilities have all adopted project management techniques as they seek the twin advantages of internal operating efficiency, coupled with rapid external response of business opportunities. It would not be an exaggeration to suggest that in many ways, project management offers the key to competitive advantage in the modern commercial world.

At the same time, the challenges confronting organizations that are intent on using projects cannot be ignored. The very features that make project management special – creation of a temporary organization within the firm, one-off activity sequences, and essential uniqueness – also place the firm in a very difficult and almost contradictory position. How can we institutionalize and make these practices systematic, when by its very nature, project management represents a unique undertaking, one that is not long-term process driven, but in every sense temporary? How do we capture, organize, and manage the knowledge we derive from past project experiences in order to create an effective database designed to help future project managers and their subordinates make optimal decisions? In short, how can we learn from the past and best apply relevant project-based knowledge to help manage future project challenges?

The above is not an easy question to address but one, I am convinced, that we will need to come to terms with quickly if we are to continue the upward trend in the use of project management techniques in modern organizations. As a result, it is with real satisfaction that I have read this book, *Management of Knowledge in Project Environments*, edited by Peter Love, Patrick S.W. Fong and Zahir Irani. They have assembled an excellent set of contributors who approach the challenge of knowledge management from a variety of perspectives – all interesting and right on target. The book can be read either as a whole, coherent work or perused for the implications embedded in each individual chapter. Either way, the authors have produced a work that is extremely timely and offers an excellent, up-to-date and useful treatment of an important and under-researched area in project management. For me, a key hurdle that any book on project management must clear is whether it can be equally useful for a practitioner or academic audience. That is: is the work relevant, readable, and cutting edge? *Management of Knowledge in Project Environments* handles these demands superbly. I am sure that readers will gain enormous insight and profit from the work.

Dr Jeffrey K Pinto, PhD
Andrew Morrow and Elizabeth Lee Black
Chair of Management Technology,
Sam and Irene Black School of Business,
Penn State Erie

Introduction

Managing through projects has become a standard way of doing business and now can be seen to form an integral part of many organization's business strategies (Björkegren, 1999; Prencipe and Tell, 2001; Korppi-Tommola, 2003). Factors that have influenced the emergence of project management as an approach for conducting business related activities include global competition, compression of the product life cycle, new product development, corporate downsizing, outsourcing, increased customer focus, and innovations in information and communications technology. In response to such influences and prompted by the need to remain competitive, businesses need to learn to manage more effectively the knowledge that they acquire and accumulate from their projects (Davenport et al., 1998; Joyce and Stivers, 2000; Fernie et al., 2003). This will, however, require a culture change, as there will be a need to instil learning through reflection. If knowledge is managed effectively, it can be used to reduce project time, improve quality and customer satisfaction, and minimize 'reinventing the wheel'. The management of knowledge, whether explicit or tacit, is a necessary prerequisite for project success in today's dynamic and changing global environment.

Knowledge and learning

The concepts of knowledge management (KM) (e.g. Nonaka, 1991; Nonaka and Takeuchi, 1995; Spender, 1996; Davenport and Prusak, 1998; Davenport et al., 1998) and the learning organization (e.g. Senge, 1990; Huber, 1991; Garvin, 1993) have significantly influenced the way in which organizations transform themselves in the wake of the external and internal change being imposed upon them (Sethi and King, 1998).

A plethora of definitions for KM and the learning organization can be found in the literature. Davenport and Prusak (1998), for example, define knowledge as a fluid mix of frame experience, values, contextual information and expert insight that provides a framework for evaluating and incorporating new experience and information. Alavia and Leidner (1999) define KM as 'a systemic and organizationally specified process for acquiring, organizing and communicating both tacit and explicit knowledge of employees so that others may make use of it to be more effective and productive'. Garvin (1993) defines a learning organization as 'an organisation skilled at creating, acquiring and transferring, knowledge and modifying its behaviour to reflect new knowledge and insights' (p. 80). In a similar vein, Watkins and Golembiewski (1995) suggest that a learning organization is one that 'involves creating systems which put in place long term capacities to capture knowledge, to support creation, and empower continuous transformation' (p. 88). Clearly, the underlying objectives of KM and the learning organization are akin, as they seek to improve business performance, and deal with data–information–knowledge and the processes for acquiring, refining, storing and sharing the content in an organizational setting. Knowledge management is therefore best viewed as a subset of the learning organization (King and Ko, 2001).

Using knowledge gained to learn from failures or successes that have occurred in projects is vital for the long-term sustainability and competitiveness of businesses. Learning from project experiences can engender 'communities of practice' within organizations, and possibly between organizations where a strategic alliance exists, whose purpose is to create a cycle of application, assessment, reflection and renewal. A culture that is able to harness knowledge as a transferable asset and can be used to enhance future projects, and in certain cases expand the scope of an organization's project capability, can and should be created.

The amount of new knowledge needed to generate a project depends on the novelty and uniqueness of the product being created (Pohjola, 2003). However, it is often argued that the processes involved in delivering the final outcome are similar, even though a project (the project team composition, the product to be produced, etc.) is unique (Love et al., 1999). Most projects, therefore, do not need to start from scratch inasmuch as they can utilize existing processes and learn from the experiences acquired from previous projects. The effectiveness of this cycle will invariably be dependent upon the mechanisms for learning that are implemented throughout a project's life cycle. However, a well-designed organization structure, incentive schemes and management processes are crucial in assisting organizations to shape their knowledge assets into competences (Willem and Scarbrough, 2002).

As knowledge is created and captured, learning can take place and the knowledge that is applied can then be embedded within individual, organizational and interorganizational processes (Liebowitz and Megbolugbe, 2003). According to Liebowitz and Megbolugbe (2003) the effects of learning will create new knowledge, which will then recycle through data–information– knowledge process transformation and iteration (p.189). The recursive relationship that exists between project data, information and knowledge can enable businesses to reflect on and use the knowledge gained to plan for future project successes. Implicitly, this point is reinforced by Spiegler (2000), who states: 'Yesterday's data are today's information, which will become tomorrow's knowledge, in turn, will recycle down the value chain back into information and into data.'

Projects are always required to be completed within a specified period, which makes the reuse and harnessing of knowledge a necessity. Without the reuse of existing knowledge or the ability to create new knowledge from existing solutions and experiences, project organizations have to create solutions to every problem, which is clearly inefficient. With the reuse of knowledge, project organizations can learn to ameliorate project planning and operations so that deliverables can be achieved. The reuse of knowledge and learning can become more problematic when personnel leave a project before its completion, or the project is a temporary assemblage of experts who are geographically dispersed with diverse expertise or backgrounds, or where they use technology in different ways (Kasiv et al., 2003). Such project organizations are disbanded once the project is completed and these experts are then absorbed back into their own organizations and engage in other projects. Research undertaken by Love et al. (2003) found that project reviews are rarely undertaken in the construction sector where such disbandment takes place, and when they are, they are invariably used to determine who was to blame for events that have gone wrong. Construction is not dissimilar to other sectors that operate in project-based environments.

Projects do not have any organizational memory, as they are temporary in nature. In comparison with organizations, which are supported by structure and routines to absorb knowledge, projects do not support any natural transfer mechanism. Deliberate management efforts and incentives are crucial to the creation, capture and transfer of knowledge. For instance, lessons learned have to be socialized consciously among individuals before they leave the project. Absence of KM will make projects unable to contribute to any improvement of the organizational business processes.

The management of knowledge in project-based organizations is becoming a prerequisite to sustain a competitive advantage. Without management support and effort to manage knowledge during a project's life cycle, knowledge assets can lost once a project is completed. This results in organizational knowledge fragmentation and loss of organizational learning (Kotnour, 2000). The identification of critical knowledge and the ability to utilize it is a challenge for every project organization (Kasiv et al., 2003). Successful project management is based, on the one hand, on accumulated knowledge and, on the other hand, on individual and collective competences. The following chapters examine how the management of knowledge, particularly the sharing of knowledge and the importance of learning through reflection, can lead to project success and improved business performance.

References

Alavi, M. and Leidner, D. (1999) Knowledge management systems: issues, challenges and benefits. *Communications of the Association of Information Systems* 1(7). http://cais.isworld/articles/1-7/article

Björkegren, C. (1999) Learning for the next project. In Easterby-Smith, M., Araujo, L. and Burgoyne, J. (eds) *Organisational Learning 3rd International Conference*, Lancaster, UK, 6–8 June, pp. 107–123.

Davenport, T. and Prusak, L. (1998) *Working Knowledge: How Organizations Manage What They Know*. Boston, MA: Harvard Business School Press.

Davenport, T. H., DeLong, D. W. and Beers, M. C. (1998) Successful knowledge management projects. *Sloan Management Review* 39(2): 43–57.

Davenport, T. H. and Prusak, L. (1998) *Working Knowledge: How Organizations Manage What They Know*. Harvard Business School Press, Boston, MA.

Fernie, S., Green, S. D., Weller, S. J. and Newcombe, R. (2003) Knowledge sharing: context, confusion and controversy. *International Journal of Project Management* 21: 177–187.

Garvin, D. A. (1993) Building a learning organization. *Harvard Business Review* 71(4): 78–91.

Huber, G. P. (1991) Organisational learning: the contributing processes and the literature. *Organization Science* 2(1): 88–115.

Joyce, T. and Stivers, B. P. (2000) Leveraging knowledge in small firms. *Journal of Cost Management* (May/June): 6–10.

Kasiv, J. J. J., Vartianinen, M. and Hailikar, M. (2003) Managing knowledge and knowledge competencies in projects and project organisations. *International Journal of Project Management* 21: 571–582.

King, W. R. and Ko, D.-G. (2001) Evaluating knowledge management and the learning organisation: an information/knowledge value chain approach. *Communications of the Association of Information Systems* 5(14). http://cais.isworld/articles/5-14/article

Korppi-Tommola, S. (2003) Knowledge management in projects. *TU-22.165 Seminar in Industrial Management*. Helsinki: Department of Industrial Engineering and Management, Helsinki University of Technology. http://www.tuta.hut.fi/studies/Courses_and_schedules/Teta/TU22.165/papers/korppi-tommola.pdf

Kotnour, T. (2000) Organisational learning practices in the project management environment. *International Journal of Quality and Reliability Management* 17(4/5): 393–406.

Liebowitz, J. and Megbolugbe, I. (2003) A set of frameworks to aid the project manager in conceptualizing and implementing knowledge management initiatives. *International Journal of Project Management* 21: 189–198.

Love, P. E. D., Smith, J. and Li, H. (1999) The propagation of rework benchmark metrics for construction. *International Journal of Quality and Reliability Management* 16(7): 638–658.

Love, P. E. D., Irani, Z. and Edwards, D. (2003) Learning to reduce rework in projects: analysis of firms' learning and quality practices. *Project Management Journal* 34(3): 13–25.

Nonaka, I. (1991) The knowledge creating company. *Harvard Business Review* 69(6): 96–104.

Nonaka, I. and Takeuchi, H. (1995) *The Knowledge Creating Company*. New York: Oxford University Press.

Pohjola, M. (2003) Knowledge management in projects. *TU-55.165 Seminar in Industrial Management*. Helsinki: Department of Industrial Engineering and Management, Helsinki University of Technology. http://www.tuta.hut.fi/studies/Courses_and_schedules/Teta/TU22.165/papers/pohjola.pdf

Prencipe, A. and Tell, F. (2001) Inter-project learning: processes and outcomes of knowledge codification in project-based firms. *Research Policy* 30(9): 1373–1394.

Senge, P. (1990) The leader's new work: building learning organisations. *Sloan Management Review* 32(1): 7–23.

Sethi, V. and King, W. R. (1998) *Organizational Transformation Through Business Process Reengineering*. Upper Saddle River, NJ: Prentice-Hall.

Spender, J. C. (1996) Making knowledge the basis of a dynamic theory of the firm. *Strategic Management Journal* 17: 45–62.

Spiegler, I. (2000) Knowledge management: a new idea or recycled concept? *Communications of the Association for Information Systems*: 3(14). http://cais.isworld/ articles/3-14/article

Watkins, K. E. and Golembiewski, R. (1995) Rethinking organisation development for learning organisations. *International Journal of Organisational Analysis* 3(1): 86–101.

Willem, A. and Scarbrough, H. (2002) Structural effects on inter-unit knowledge sharing: the role of coordination under different knowledge sharing needs. In *Proceedings of the 3rd European Conference on Organisational Knowledge, Learning and Capabilities*, Athens, Greece, 5–6 April. http://www.alba.edu.gr/OKLC2002/Proceedings/pdf_files/ID350.pdf

Chapter 1

Conceptualizing and implementing knowledge management

Jay Liebowitz

Introduction

Knowledge management (KM), in many ways, is more of an art than a science (Liebowitz, 1999). Knowledge management is the process of creating value from an organization's intangible assets. Simply put, KM refers to sharing and leveraging knowledge within an organization and outwards toward customers and stakeholders. According to Liebowitz (2004), however, many organizations do not have a systematic approach to sharing and leveraging knowledge internally and externally.

In any growing field, the art often precedes the science until various methodologies, techniques, processes and tools are developed to underpin the field. This has certainly been the case with KM, as there has been a blurring of the true meaning of data, information, knowledge, expertise, wisdom and beyond (Liebowitz, 1999). In addition, the early contemporary works in KM promised improved knowledge-sharing techniques to increase innovation, improve customer service, retain expertise and enhance learning. As a result, many organizations appointed chief knowledge officers or chief learning officers to develop a KM strategy to spearhead knowledge initiatives. Several organizations, such as Dell and the National Aeronautics and Space Administration (NASA), preferred a codification approach, which emphasizes a systems approach to capturing and sharing knowledge, often emanating from their information technology (IT) department. Others, such as Hewlett-Packard,

Hallmark and the US Federal Aviation Administration, felt that a personalization approach to accentuate people-to-people connections was a better fit for their organization (Zack, 1999). Often both approaches have been used by organizations, but one generally dominates.

Knowledge management has such strategic value that organizations should include it as one of the key pillars of their human capital strategy (Liebowitz, 2004). Liebowitz (2004) suggested that KM strategy should be used to complement other strategic initiatives such as competency management, performance management and change management. It has been estimated that about half of the Federal civil servants in the US government are eligible to retire in the next five years, about 71 per cent of whom are senior executives (Liebowitz, 2004). In the coming years in the US government, there will be a severe knowledge bleed effect resulting from retirements. Knowledge management can play a significant role in addressing some of these human capital concerns (Liebowitz, 2004). Knowledge management can help to capture, share and leverage knowledge before it leaves the organization. Newly appointed chief human capital officers in the US government have undertaken the task of developing human capital plans for their agencies (Liebowitz, 2004).

A key question is whether KM will be the 'management fad of the day', and fall peril to the demise similar to business process re-engineering efforts. It has been estimated that about 70 per cent of business process re-engineering efforts have been failures in organizations (Love and Gunasekaran, 1997). Many people feel that KM may also become a similar victim if science and rigour in the discipline are not accomplished (Liebowitz, 1999). Knowledge management sceptics believe that knowledge cannot be managed; however, there are those who believe that it is possible to manage the environment in which knowledge exists. Others, such as Davenport and Glasser (2002), have suggested that KM is too amorphous, although it has an excellent altruistic value; however, the returns on investment for KM efforts are difficult to calculate. Liebowitz (2004) has suggested that KM is often viewed as being a 'no brainer' philosophy that is adopted by businesses; that is, taking advantage of learning what others know and have experienced is essential in today's competitive, fast moving, global environment.

Thus, a mystique of doubt and optimism surrounds KM. Part of this mystique is attributed to the evolution of the field as it develops. Certainly, to convert the doubters to believers, there must be a great degree of rigour imparted into the KM field. This chapter will examine some of these areas, and will suggest how KM can form an integral part of an organization's fabric and strategy for managing projects.

A knowledge framework

A framework that organizations can use to conceptualize KM is presented in Figure 1.1. Here, data refer to discerned elements, and when processed or patterned in some way, they are transformed into information. Once the information becomes actionable, it is transformed into knowledge. When knowledge is then learned and embedded into individual and organizational processes, the value of knowledge to the individual and organization increases in worth. The environmental factors affecting this knowledge cycle relate to domain context, organizational culture and individual value system, management

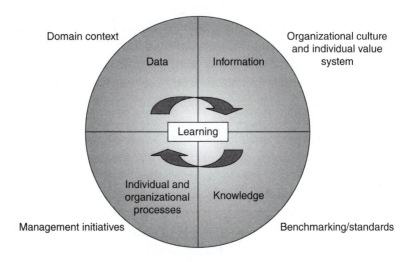

Figure 1.1   *Conceptual view of the knowledge framework.*

initiatives and benchmarking/standards. Knowledge must have context if it is to be useful to an organization. In addition, the promotion or inhibition of knowledge will be affected by the organizational culture, as well as the individual's value system. How knowledge is internalized and then externalized is related to an individual's worldviews. Management initiatives and standards will also affect the creation of knowledge in the organization.

Suppose a project manager is currently concerned with testing a satellite that their team is building, for possible vibration problems. The project manager could receive some test data showing the results of the vibration testing experiment. By looking at some of the trends in the data, various patterns could be revealed (i.e. information). By examining these patterns, the project manager decides also to consult an available organizational 'lessons learned' database and discovers that a previous satellite experienced the same types of vibration testing problems that their satellite is experiencing. The project manager acts on this new information through their knowledge to determine the criticality of the testing results and what should be done to resolve these problems. At this point, this information is transformed into knowledge. As this knowledge is shared with others, either via word of mouth or through the lessons learned system, this knowledge will be embedded into the working processes of future project teams involved with testing.

The domain context in this example deals with satellite vibration testing. Certain standards are typically used to ensure the 'safety and health' of the satellite. If the organizational culture lacks a pervasive knowledge-sharing flavour, then the creation and exchange of vibration testing knowledge may be at risk of not being codified and transferred to other project teams that need these lessons learned. However, if the organization promotes the active capture, analysis and dissemination of lessons learned, then those project teams involved with vibration testing will be better informed. Coupled with the organizational culture and climate, the synergistic effect of management initiatives could influence how the knowledge is shared throughout the organization; that is, if there are competing management initiatives that shift work priorities on a frequent basis, then there may be more risk of not capturing and sharing the necessary knowledge with all appropriate project teams.

Knowledge is often gained through experience. Experiential learning typically generates rules of thumb (heuristics). These rules of thumb are pieces of knowledge that can be in the form of lessons learned, anecdotes, cases, rules, guidelines or the like. In the project management or business environment, a general rule of thumb may be to take an estimate for the software development schedule and budget and double it. In the university setting, a rule of thumb is never to miss the first committee meeting. Usually the chair of the committee is selected at the first committee meeting of the year, and whoever is absent is unanimously selected as the chair (mainly because most people prefer not to have that responsibility and added workload).

Knowledge without context is futile. For example, Americans enjoy having a 'comfort zone' or personal space when speaking to others. Comfort zone refers to the physical distance between a person and others when speaking at an informal gathering (Kramer, 2001). In Asia and Latin America, the intimate distance or personal space is much closer than that in the USA. These cross-cultural differences influence the universality and generality of applying knowledge. These cross-cultural differences also impact the management of projects in organizations, as international team members must respect each other's culture and customs, yet are able to move the project along within time, cost and schedule constraints. For example, NASA often works with international partners on space projects, so having the ability to respect each other's practices is a necessity. Hence, context is an important part in producing knowledge.

Knowledge can be distilled from successes as well as failures. In project management, lessons learned and best practices abound. For example, NASA has a Lessons Learned Information System (LLIS), which has over 1300 lessons relating to project management, systems engineering and other areas. NASA project managers are now required to capture, access and apply lessons learned from the LLIS to their projects. Both successes and failures should populate a lessons learned repository to allow knowledge to be internalized and created in the context of various project environments.

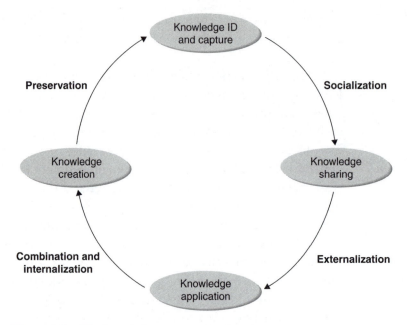

Figure 1.2   *The knowledge management cycle.*

The knowledge management cycle

The KM cycle consists of four major stages, as shown in Figure 1.2, and is used to support the framework presented in Figure 1.1. Knowledge is identified and captured, shared with others, applied in combination with existing pertinent knowledge, and then created in the form of new knowledge, which is then captured and continues as noted in Figure 1.2.

Nonaka and Takeuchi's (1995) Socialization–Externalization–Combination–Internalization (SECI) model can be included as part of the KM cycle. Once key knowledge has been identified and codified in some way, a socialization effect occurs resulting in knowledge sharing. Knowledge resulting from this knowledge-sharing experience becomes externalized, resulting in an application of the knowledge. This knowledge is then combined with other knowledge that the individual possesses, as well as internalized along with the individual's worldviews and value hierarchy. This should hopefully result in new knowledge being created, which then needs to be preserved as it becomes captured and the cycle begins again.

Knowledge management strategy and implementation

Now that a KM framework has been built, we can better understand how to develop a KM strategy and resulting implementation plan. Several researchers and practitioners have been studying techniques and methodologies for developing KM strategies and implementation plans (Apostolou and Mentzas, 2003; Liebowitz and Megbolugbe, 2003). According to Chourides et al. (2003), for KM to be successful, an organization must have a strategy and individuals must be persuaded to contribute to its formulation and implementation. The KM strategic plan has greater focus on the knowledge needs of the organization and an evaluation of capabilities. Apostolou and Mentzas (2003) developed the Know-Net KM approach, which includes the interplay among strategy, assets, process, systems, structure, individuals and teams, across organizations and within the organization itself. They use a systems thinking approach to KM that looks at the interlinking, feedback and control between these areas. Similarly, Sveiby (2001) discusses his knowledge-based theory of the firm and indicates nine important knowledge strategy questions:

- How can we improve the transfer of competence between people in our organization?
- How can the organization's employees improve the competence of customers, suppliers and other stakeholders?
- How can the organization's customers, suppliers and other stakeholders improve the competence of the employees?
- How can we improve the conversion of individually held competence to systems, tools and templates?
- How can we improve individual competence by using systems, tools and templates?
- How can we enable the conversations among the customers, suppliers and stakeholders so they improve their competence?
- How can competence from the customers, suppliers and other stakeholders improve the organization's systems, tools, processes and products?

- How can the organization's systems, tools, processes and products improve the competence of the customers, suppliers and other stakeholders?
- How can the organization's systems, tools, processes and products be effectively integrated?

O'Dell et al. (1999) performed benchmarking studies on KM strategies. They found organizations using KM strategies as a matrix of KM as a business strategy, transfer of knowledge and best practices, customer-focused knowledge, personal responsibility for knowledge, intellectual asset management, and innovation and knowledge creation. In project management terms, the work of O'Dell et al. implies that successful project teams need to have a shared vision for the project, as well as a sharing of responsibilities to achieve the project's goal. Levett and Guenov (2000) developed a methodology for KM implementation that looks at a four-phase approach of case-study definition, capturing KM practice, building a KM strategy, and implemention and evaluation. April (2002) developed guidelines for building a knowledge strategy looking at the interlinking of assets or resources, complementary resource combinations and the strategic architecture of the company. Nickerson and Silverman (1998) examined intellectual capital management strategies and proposed a strategy integration analysis methodology that uses six steps: assemble a multidisciplinary team, identify and select a target market and position, identify investments and technology, identify unique or idiosyncratic technologies that form the basis of competitive advantage by comparing the firm's technology and intellectual position with that of potential competitors, choose optimal organizational and intellectual capital management configuration based on the preceding four steps, and evaluate expected profitability of this integrated strategy. Other researchers and practitioners, such as McElroy (2003), Liebowitz and Megbolugbe (2003), Mertins et al. (2001), Hult (2003) and Davenport and Probst (2002), have been involved in writing case studies dealing with KM strategy and implementation.

From the American Productivity and Quality Center's Knowledge Management Benchmarking studies (2000), the key features of successful implementation of KM are:

- An important senior champion or group saw the strategic value of KM and endorsed what became a significant investment in it.
- Communities of practice are a central part of the KM strategy. Sponsorship, membership, roles and responsibilities, accountability and measurement, and supporting tools are the elements that must be in place to develop and evolve communities.
- Functional silos are the most significant cultural barrier to KM implementation. Solicit senior leadership vision and active support to break down these barriers.
- The importance of making connections – of people to people and of people to information – is the driver to use IT in KM initiatives.
- As KM becomes more structured and widespread, the need for measurement steadily increases.

Seeley and Dietrick (2001) emphasize that building a KM strategy should use the following components: governance, culture, content management, technology, application and measurement. Earl (2001) discusses a knowledge mapping, cartographic approach to KM where knowledge networking and incentives to share knowledge are critical success factors. AT&T and Bain and Company have used this approach. Chauvel and Despres (2002), in their 1997–2001 review of survey research in KM, found that surveys are typically used in KM research. Liebowitz (2004) indicates the importance of KM as a key pillar in an organization's human capital strategy. Holsapple (2003) talks about the importance of performing a knowledge audit as a first step in developing a KM strategy for an organization.

An essential output of the knowledge audit process is the knowledge map, which provides insights for improving business and organizational processes. A knowledge map portrays the sources, flows, constraints and sinks (losses or stopping points) of knowledge within an organization. Well-developed knowledge maps help to identify intellectual capital, socialize new members and enhance organizational learning (Wexler, 2001). Knowledge maps have been used for a variety of applications, even for developing a knowledge map of KM software tools (Noll et al., 2002). By developing a knowledge map, the organization can (Grey, 1999):

- encourage reuse and prevent reinvention, saving search time and acquisition costs
- highlight islands of expertise and suggest ways to build bridges to increase knowledge sharing
- discover effective and emergent communities of practice where learning is happening
- provide a baseline for measuring progress with KM projects
- reduce the burden on experts by helping staff find critical information/knowledge quickly.

Some of the key principles in knowledge mapping are: establish boundaries and respect personal disclosures, recognize and locate knowledge in a wide variety of forms, and locate knowledge in processes, relationships, policies, people, documents, conversations, suppliers, competitors and customers (Hylton, 2003). The types of question that should be asked to develop a knowledge map include (Grey, 1999):

- What type of knowledge is needed to do your work?
- Who provides it, where do you get it, how does it arrive?
- What do you do, how do you add value, what are the critical issues?
- What happens when you are finished?
- How can the knowledge flow be improved, what is preventing you doing more, better, faster?
- What would make your work easier?
- Who do you go to when there is a problem?

Typically, information is collected for the knowledge map by using the following methods (Grey, 1999):

- conduct surveys, interviews and focus groups
- observe the work in progress
- obtain network traffic logs, policy documents, organization charts, process documentation
- explore the common and individual file structures
- concentrate on formal and informal gatherings, communications and activities

- gather from internal/external sources
- move across multiple levels (individual, team, department, organization).

Knowledge management strategy implications for projects

Most of the KM researchers and practitioners stress three major components of a KM strategy: people, process/culture and technology. The mantra in the KM field is that 80 per cent of KM is people and process/culture, and the other 20 per cent is technology (Liebowitz, 1999). The technology is used as an enabler for sharing knowledge (the organization's intranet, lessons learned information system, expert locator system, online communities, etc.), but the tough part of KM is the people, process and culture aspects. For example, why would an individual want to share his or her expertise (i.e. his or her 'competitive edge') with others? As a project manager or team member, why should they perform KM as they already have a full plate of other responsibilities?

In both of these cases, it becomes quite clear that the people and process aspects become paramount when trying to build and nurture a knowledge-sharing culture. With respect to the first question of sharing what one knows, there should be a recognition and reward structure within the organization to encourage people to perform knowledge-sharing. The World Bank, for example, has a set of learning and knowledge-sharing proficiencies whereby each employee is evaluated at their annual job performance review as to how well they have achieved these, and other, proficiencies. Knowledge sharing needs to be encouraged and built into the daily working activities. Knowledge management processes need to be embedded into normal work processes so that they do not seem to be a burden on the individual. At NASA, for example, capturing and applying lessons learned is a requirement for all NASA projects. Sharing of lessons learned, mentoring, applying knowledge capture/retention activities, exchanging stories and experiences at staff meetings, and other approaches could be used to help to embed KM throughout everyone's job.

Ultimately, the goal is to use KM to 'work smarter, not harder', and hopefully to stimulate innovation, improve worker productivity, increase customer satisfaction and maximize employee fulfilment.

For KM to work, it must be aligned and integrated with the strategic goals of the organization. If it seems disjointed and not synchronized with the business and strategic organizational goals, then KM will be doomed to fail. The KM plan must also be well-conceived and designed, and should be congruent with the organization's culture. For example, in the NASA environment, most of the employees were scientists, engineers and technologists. They preferred a codification approach (i.e. systems-orientated approach) to KM rather than the personalization approach, partly because of their personalities, educational backgrounds and technical orientations. Thus, the KM strategy should probably be dominated by the codification approach, as well as applying KM personalization approaches (e.g. knowledge-sharing forums whereby experienced project managers exchange 'war stories' with up-and-coming project leaders).

To maximize the effectiveness of KM, senior management support (both financially and morally) must be very strong. Since KM has a long-term vision and deals with intangible assets, some managers may be reluctant to invest resources in this area, especially if budgets are tight and there are more pressing short-term needs. Thus, top management support is critical in paving the way for KM. Various organizations are integrating KM as part of their human capital strategy. In the future, more organizations will probably do the same as KM should be a critical part of one's human capital strategy. The following case study examines how NASA applied a KM strategy within the organization.

Case study: NASA's strategic plan for knowledge management

The environment at NASA has a heavy project management-based orientation. As the Columbia Accident Investigative Board's report (www.caib.us) indicated, the organizational culture of NASA must reflect the best practices of a learning organization. These practices need to extend to all projects throughout NASA. Knowledge management should be a key component in creating a knowledge-sharing culture at NASA and transforming the agency into a learning, adaptive organization.

Towards making this goal a reality and recognizing the importance of KM, NASA had developed its own strategic KM plan (NASA Knowledge Management Team, 2001). NASA has been active in KM through its work at its ten NASA centres (Liebowitz et al., 2003). The plan reflects three priority areas where KM can help NASA's ability to deliver its missions (NASA Knowledge Management Team, 2001), which are:

- to sustain NASA's knowledge across missions and generations (KM will identify and capture the information that exists across the Agency)
- to help people to find, organize and share the knowledge NASA already has (KM will help to manage efficiently the Agency's knowledge resources)
- to increase collaboration and to facilitate knowledge creation and sharing (KM will develop techniques and tools to enable teams and communities to collaborate across the barriers of time and space).

NASA's KM strategic plan is built upon three key areas: people, process and technology. In terms of people issues, some of the following desired attributes of the 'new' environment would be encouraged (NASA Knowledge Management Team, 2001):

- recognize the value of both generalists as well as experts
- reward people with bonuses or awards for broadly sharing or making knowledge reusable by others
- create or augment position descriptions for people whose job is primarily to share or distribute knowledge
- institute ground rules (procedures) for sharing discoveries so that professionals can feel secure in getting proper credit for their contributions
- help people to maintain and disseminate corporate knowledge through informal and formal methods

- publish and recognize successes in KM that help to increase mission success or create expectations of sharing
- encourage collaboration and sharing across centres.

In terms of process, KM can contribute towards NASA's strategic goals by (NASA Knowledge Management Team, 2001):

- developing a set of collaborate tools for virtual teams and communities to share information and knowledge
- applying KM services to help to capture and manage scientific and engineering knowledge as it moves from one researcher to another
- using KM to disseminate knowledge across internal and external audiences
- embedding KM into the daily working activities of the NASA employees.

Learning from successes and failures is also a critical part of KM activities at NASA. The NASA LLIS (http://llis.nasa.gov) serves this purpose in providing over 1300 NASA-related lessons in project management, systems engineering and other areas (there is even a public version of the LLIS called 'Public Lessons Learned System' at http://llis.nasa.gov). There is a user-profiling feature that allows the user to indicate his or her areas of interest, and as new lessons are entered into the LLIS and fit the user's interest profile, these lessons are sent via e-mail to the user showing URL links to the lessons. In addition to the LLIS, lessons learned must be captured and used throughout the NASA project life cycle, as indicated in NASA Procedures and Guidelines 7120.5B: Program and Project Management. In this manner, project teams will become accustomed to accessing and capturing lessons learned during their project's life cycle. Pharmaceutical companies are also very interested in learning from past projects as the drug development process can take twelve to fifteen years, and few researchers are involved from start to finish so staff turnover can complicate the management of knowledge (Zimmermann, 2003; Schindler and Eppler, 2003).

With regard to the technology component in NASA's KM strategic plan, the thrust is to use technology as an enabler to sharing knowledge. Web portals, lessons learned databases, document-sharing systems, expert systems, intelligent agents, data-mining tools, collaboration tools, improved intranets, expertise locator systems, web-based online searchable video repositories and other technologies should be applied to improving knowledge capture and sharing at NASA.

In terms of implementing KM initiatives, many organizations typically try in the first year to educate people on KM, develop some quick-win KM pilots and build the technology infrastructure to enable knowledge sharing to take place. In the second and succeeding years, the organizational infrastructure to support KM is further developed (such as having knowledge stewards or knowledge capture managers on key projects), the KM pilot efforts expand into full-length projects, processes are established to embed KM into daily work activities (e.g. capturing and applying lessons learned, starting each staff meeting with five to ten minutes of 'storytelling'/ knowledge sharing and developing a formal mentoring programme), and the recognition and reward structure is adjusted to incorporate learning and knowledge-sharing proficiencies.

For example, when Liebowitz (2002) was the first knowledge management officer at NASA Goddard Space Flight Center, a knowledge management working group was established, comprised of representatives across all directorates, human resources, IT, library, public affairs and selected others. The first year was devoted to creating an awareness of KM throughout the organization, via briefings, tutorials, quick-win pilot efforts, knowledge-sharing forums and online communities, and using creative learning groups to improve connections between people. The technology infrastructure, specifically the intranet, was being revised to improve the look and supporting functionalities for information and knowledge sharing to take place. At the end of the first year, a new position, the knowledge capture/retention manager, was established on two major projects. This individual was responsible for promoting a knowledge-sharing environment, through codifying key expertise and processes, developing lessons learned, establishing knowledge-sharing forums where experienced project managers would meet up-and-coming project leaders and exchange their 'war stories', and initiating other KM activities.

Towards the beginning of the second year, KM was being considered as a key component of the organization's human capital strategy, processes were being developed to facilitate KM as part of everyday working life, and the recognition and reward system was being reviewed, possibly to include learning and knowledge-sharing proficiencies as part of everyone's annual performance plan.

Conclusions

Knowledge management has a critical role to play in project-based environments. This chapter described some conceptual frameworks behind KM, and discussed some KM strategy and implementation issues. NASA was used as a short case study to demonstrate how KM can be applied in a project-based environment. The use of lessons learned, capturing and sharing key knowledge, and providing mechanisms to encourage the management and sharing of knowledge are important elements that can enhance project management and systems engineering. In the years ahead, those organizations that apply the tenets of KM should be able to increase innovation and customer satisfaction, while improving the retention of expertise and strengthening a sense of community among employees, project teams, customers, suppliers and other stakeholders.

References

American Productivity and Quality Center (2000) *Successfully Implementing Knowledge Management. Best Practice Report.* Houston, TX: American Productivity and Quality Center.

Apostolou, D. and Mentzas, G. (2003) Experiences from knowledge management implementations in companies of the software sector. *Business Process Management Journal* 9(3): 354–381.

April, K. (2002) Guidelines for developing a k-strategy. *Journal of Knowledge Management* 6(5): 445–456.

Chauvel, D. and Despres, C. (2002) A review of survey research in knowledge management: 1997–2001. *Journal of Knowledge Management* 6(3): 207–223.

Chourides, P., Longbottom, D. and Murphy, W. (2003) Excellence in knowledge management: an empirical study to identify critical factors and performance measures. *Measuring Business Excellence* 7(2): 29–45.

Davenport, T. H. and Glasser, J. (2002) Just-in-time delivery comes to knowledge management. *Harvard Business Review* (July): 5–9.

Davenport, T. and Probst, G. (2002) *Knowledge Management Case Book: Siemens' Best Practices*, 2nd edn. Berlin: John Wiley & Sons/ Publicis Corporate Publishing.

Earl, M. (2001) Knowledge management strategies: toward a taxonomy. *Journal of Management Information Systems* 18(1): 215–233.

Grey, D. (1999) Knowledge mapping: a practical overview. March. http://www.it-consultancy.com/extern/sws/knowmap.html

Holsapple, C. (2003) *Handbook on Knowledge Management*. Berlin: Springer.

Hult, G. T. (2003) An integration of thoughts on knowledge management. *Decision Sciences* 34(2): 189–195.

Hylton, A. (2003) A knowledge management initiative is unlikely to succeed without a knowledge audit. *Proceedings of the Knowledge Management Aston Conference*, Operational Research Society/ Aston Business School, Birmingham, UK, 14–15 July, pp. 10–18.

Kramer, M. (2001) *Business Communications in Context*. Englewood Cliffs, NJ: Prentice-Hall.

Levett, G. and Guenov, M. (2000) A methodology for knowledge management implementation. *Journal of Knowledge Management* 4(3): 258–269.

Liebowitz, J. (1999) *The Knowledge Management Handbook*. Boca Raton, FL: CRC Press.

Liebowitz, J. (2002) *A look at NASA Goddard Space Flight Center's Knowledge Management Initiatives*. IEEE Software. Los Alamitos, CA: IEEE Computer Society, May/June.

Liebowitz, J. (2004) *Addressing the Human Capital Crisis in the Federal Government: A Knowledge Management Perspective*. Burlington, MA: Butterworth-Heinemann/Elsevier.

Liebowitz, J., Holm, J. and Day, R. (eds) (2003) *Making Sense of Rocket Science: Managing Knowledge at NASA*. Washington, DC: US Government Printing Office (in press).

Liebowitz, J. and Megbolugbe, I. (2003) A set of frameworks to aid the project manager in conceptualizing and implementing knowledge management initiatives. *International Journal of Project Management* 21(3): 189–198.

Love, P. E. D. and Gunasekaran, A. (1997) Process re-engineering: a review of enablers. *International Journal of Production Economics* 50(2/3): 183–197.

McElroy, M. (2003) *The New Knowledge Management*. Burlington, MA: Butterworth-Heinemann/Elsevier.

Mertins, K., Heisig, P. and Vorbeck, J. (2001) *Knowledge Management: Best Practices in Europe*. Berlin: Springer.

NASA Knowledge Management Team (2001) *Strategic Plan for Knowledge Management, 18 March*. Washington, DC: NASA.

Nickerson, J. and Silverman, B. (1998) Intellectual capital management strategy: the foundation of successful new business generation *Journal of Knowledge Management* 1(4): 320–331.

Noll, M., Frohlich, D. and Schiebel, E. (2002) Knowledge maps of knowledge management tools: information visualization with BibTechMon. *Practical Applications of Knowledge Management 2002 Conference Proceedings*, Vienna, Austria, 2–3 December. Berlin: Springer, pp. 14–27.

Nonaka, I. and Takeuchi, H. (1995) *The Knowledge Creating Company*. Oxford: Oxford University Press.

O'Dell, C., Wiig, K. and Odem, P. (1999) Benchmarking unveils emerging knowledge management strategies. *Benchmarking: An International Journal* 6(3): 202–211.

Schindler, M. and Eppler, M. (2003) Harvesting project knowledge: a review of project learning methods and success factors. *International Journal of Project Management* 21(3): 219–228.

Seeley, C. and Dietrick, W. (2001) *Crafting a Knowledge Management Strategy*. KM Review Special Report. London: Melcrum Publishing.

Sveiby, K. E. (2001) A knowledge-based theory of the firm to guide in strategy formulation. *Journal of Intellectual Capital* 2(4): 344–358.

Wexler, M. (2001) The who, what, and why of knowledge mapping. *Journal of Knowledge Management* 5(3): 249–263.

Zack, M. H. (1999) Managing codified knowledge. *Sloan Management Review*. Cambridge, MA: MIT Press, pp. 45–58.

Zimmermann, K. (2003) Learning from success and failure. *KM World* (October). www.kmworld.com

Chapter 2

Knowledge integration processes and dynamics within the context of cross-functional projects

Sue Newell and Jimmy Huang

Introduction

A growing emphasis on the value and potential of organizational knowledge is reflected in the increasing amount of research output on this subject, as well as the growing number of firms that initiate and implement knowledge management (KM) programmes as a way of systematically mobilizing and utilizing their knowledge assets. While one stream of research addresses the need to externalize tacit knowledge to ensure its accessibility (e.g. Marwick, 2001), another stream characterizes the underlying activities through which knowledge is acquired (Huber, 1991), created (Nonaka and Takeuchi, 1995), shared (Brown and Duguid, 1991) and applied (Blackler, 1995). For the purpose of brevity, the authors refer to the latter stream of research as knowledge-related activity research.

Grant's (1996) theory of knowledge integration is an example of an attempt to synthesize these two streams of research. Grant (1996) noted that 'the primary role of the firm, and the essence of organizational capability, is the integration of knowledge' (p. 375). There are two building blocks in Grant's theory of knowledge integration: the need for specialization to achieve economies of scope, or differentiation (Lawrence and Lorsch, 1967) and the linking mechanisms to streamline and co-ordinate the specialized workforce, often referred to as integration (Lawrence and Lorsch, 1967). The importance and relevance of knowledge integration to a firm's competitiveness have been well-established. The question, however, as to how established theory can be applied to examine new and emerging organizational forms remains unanswered.

To address this issue, this chapter focuses on the dynamics and effectiveness of knowledge integration within cross-functional projects. Knowledge integration can be defined as 'an ongoing collective process of constructing, articulating and redefining shared beliefs through the social interaction of organizational members' (Huang, 2000, p. 15). Exploring knowledge integration in cross-functional projects is important because firms are increasingly relying on this form of organization. This is primarily because such projects do not require a drastic modification of existing organizational structures, yet have proved to be helpful to firms in their attempts to manage complex organizational tasks (De Meyer, 1998; Turner and Keegan, 1999). However, although cross-functional project teams are often formed on the premise that this will allow for the pooling of specialized expertise from different organizational units, current conceptualization of how knowledge is integrated within this specific context remains limited (Huang et al., 2001). Exploring these processes of knowledge integration within cross-functional projects is therefore important. However, it is crucial to recognize that cross-functional knowledge integration within the context of a project team is not limited to a focus on the dynamics occurring within the team boundary. It is equally vital to understand the dynamics of knowledge integration beyond the team boundary, in particular in relation to knowledge integration with stakeholder groups. This is illustrated by the cases discussed later in this chapter.

Cross-functional project teams

The popularity of employing cross-functional project teams is clear in many organizations today (Turner and Keegan, 1999). While the tasks performed by cross-functional project teams vary from one organization to another, three distinctive yet interrelated types of tasks can be identified. First, cross-functional teams are often used where the focus is on creativity and innovation. Triggered by the need for innovation, teams are often formed to generate new ideas or solutions that did not previously exist in the organization. Cross-functional project teams formed for new product development would be a typical example (Clark and Fujimoto, 1991). Secondly, such teams are used to generate consensus through collective input, investigation and negotiation. For example, cross-functional teams are formed for strategic planning which needs to take into account the different interests of organizational units or divisions. Even though this type of task also often demands creativity, resolving internal politics to form an agreement characterizes the key focus (Bishop, 1999). Thirdly, such teams are used for managing strategic change initiatives. For example, a strategy change initiative might include implementing new technological solutions, such as enterprise resource planning (ERP) (Markus et al., 2000) and group decision support systems (Gopal and Prasad, 2000), and process innovations, such as business process re-engineering (BPR) (Davenport, 1992) and KM (Gupta and Govindarajan, 2000). Because strategic change initiatives often involve multiple stakeholder groups, such as project sponsors, users and external consultants (Lee and Lee, 2000), the project scale and degree of complexity can often outstrip the previous two types. In addition to the need for the continuous generation of new ideas and ongoing settlements over political battles, this type of project has relatively low recurrence in the same organization. One of the issues related to this type of project is that organizations often fail to generate insightful lessons from their implementation experience, because they do not see the value of it, or they simply need to move on to different tasks (Huang et al., 2001). Given the underlying difficulty, challenge and complexity of strategic change projects the authors chose this type of project to focus their investigation of knowledge integration.

Knowledge integration

Stemming from the need for differentiation and integration (Lawrence and Lorsch, 1967), the theory of knowledge integration (Grant, 1996) emphasizes the economic value of specialization and the effectiveness of integration. In particular, competitiveness depends on the diversity and strategic value of specialized knowledge, as well as an organization's capacity to integrate the knowledge in an effective manner. An organization's knowledge integration capacity is determined by two crucial mechanisms: direction and organizational routines (Grant, 1996). The underlying assumption is that rather than having all specialists master all subject matters, direction enables the communication between specialists by codifying tacit knowledge into explicit rules (Demsetz, 1991), and organizational routines reduce the need for communicating the explicit knowledge.

In addition to these two mechanisms, Grant (1996) argues that an organization's competitiveness derived from knowledge integration is determined by three issues: the efficiency of integration, the scope of integration and the flexibility of integration. Based on Grant's argument, the level of efficiency depends on the extent to which common knowledge exists between participants, the level of co-ordination and organizational structure. According to Demsetz (1991), common knowledge, or knowledge redundancy in Nonaka and Takeuchi's (1995) terms, refers to the common understanding of a subject area shared by organizational members who engage in communication. For example, to facilitate the discussion of developing a trading system between a technologist and trader, it is crucial for the trader to have some basic understanding about the technology, and for the technologist to know something about the trading process. Undoubtedly, then, the lower the level of common knowledge that exists, the harder the integration between organizational members. Despite the importance of common knowledge, the level of co-ordination can only be improved through repetition. Based on the need for repetition, it is clear that when common knowledge is created, different specialists need to practise continuously to enhance the quality of their co-ordination. This is reflected in the notion of collective mind, which facilitates 'seamless co-ordination' between specialists, so ensuring the consistency of performance (Weick and Roberts, 1993). Moreover, the level of efficiency depends on how the organizational structure aligns with the nature of the tasks performed by members. For instance, a bureaucratic structure reduces the need for communication and can maximize the efficiency of integration in a stable environment. By contrast, when the level of environmental change is high, an organic structure supports the increasing demands for communication and permits the improvement of integration efficiency (Wright and Snell, 1998).

The scope of integration refers to the level of complexity underlying the integration of differentiated knowledge. Referring to the discussion on integration efficiency, it is clear that the greater the scope of integration, the lower the level of integration efficiency that can be expected. This is because the need for a sufficient level of common knowledge may not be fulfilled when the scope of integration widens. In addition, when the scope of integration expands, the need for a higher level of co-ordination is required. Hence, without prior experience in a large-scale co-ordination project, organizations may potentially suffer from a low level of integration efficiency. Finally, according to Grant (1996), the degree of integration flexibility is determined by an organization's capacity for reconfiguring existing knowledge as a means of promoting continuous innovation. The significance of integration flexibility is reflected in his statement that: 'hypercompetitive conditions ultimately result in all positions of competitive advantage being eroded by imitative and innovative competition' (p. 382).

Synthesizing the discussion on cross-functional project teams with the discussion on the requirements to derive competitiveness from knowledge integration, it becomes clear that the expectations about what cross-functional project teams can achieve tend to be overambitious. While prior studies have provided useful insights, it is also apparent that the current conceptualization of how the efficiency, scope and flexibility of knowledge integration influence the implementation of cross-functional projects remains limited. To shed some light on this issue, a comparative study of four cases was conducted, in particular to address the two proposed research questions: (1) How are the efficiency, scope and flexibility of knowledge integration shaped in the context of cross-functional project teams? (2) What are the opposing forces that facilitate and inhibit the development of knowledge integration efficiency, scope and flexibility in cross-functional project teams? The following section outlines the methodological foundation of the study.

Methodological concerns and issues

The research design was essentially a comparative case study (Yin, 1994). This was considered appropriate for this research since it allowed 'why' and 'how' research questions to be addressed. In particular, the aim of the research was to unravel the complexity of knowledge integration in cross-functional project teams.

Data collection

Four sources of evidence collected from each case were on-site observation, semistructured interviews, informal dialogues (including conversing via e-mail or telephone, or conversation without any prior arrangement) and documentation to ensure the richness of the findings and for the purpose of triangulation (Yin, 1994). Before interviewing, an average of two months' on-site observation in each case organization was conducted to familiarize the research contexts.

Data analysis

The analytical strategy (Yin, 1994) consisted of two main techniques, including 'open coding' (Strauss and Corbin, 1990) and 'conceptually clustered matrix' (Miles and Huberman, 1994). While the former was used to categorize the data into various categories and concepts in each case, the latter was used to generate cross-case comparison. Specifically, building upon the outcome of open coding, conceptually clustered matrices were developed to display key themes to represent the efficiency, scope and flexibility of integration (Grant, 1996), and to cross-examine concepts generated from open coding to ensure the validity of the findings.

Case background

Restructured in 1997, Dynamic Investment Bank (DBank) provides a range of financial products, including foreign exchange, currency options and interest rate derivatives. Operating in major financial centres, including London and New York, a total of 1500 employees generated more than US $2 billion gross profits in 2000. The overall structure of DBank is characterized by a hierarchy that consists of several parallel functions. Technology and Business Divisions account for more than 65 per cent of the total workforce. The rest of the employees are organized in various supporting functions, such as administration, accounting and legal. The business and technology divisions are divided into various small teams that specialize in a specific range of financial products and supporting technology. Various business and technology teams are grouped, according to the nature of trading, into the front, middle and back offices.

Innovation Engineering Limited (IEngineering) is a major league multinational player in the engineering industry, designing and manufacturing standard and custom-built products and providing consulting services for corporate clients from over 70 countries worldwide. More than 60 000 employees across the globe generated sales turnover in excess of US $8 billion during 2000 alone. IEngineering's employees are based in four main product divisions, namely Power Generation, Transport, Infrastructure, and Gas and Oil, each organized on a global basis. In addition to the centralized head office functions, each product division has its own support functions, such as finance, accounting and human resources, that report directly to Head Office.

Trustworthy Retailing Limited (TRetailing) is one of the largest retailers in the UK, and has more than 1350 stores throughout the UK and the Republic of Ireland's high streets and out-of-town shopping centres. New stores in continental Europe and south-east Asia were being added as the initial step of its global operation strategy. With a total workforce of just under 60 000, TRetailing has yielded more than £3.5 billion of sales in 2000. In addition to the central supporting functions, such as marketing, human resources and information technology (IT), the headquarters is organized based on three main product categories: healthcare, beauty and leisure. All stores in the UK are grouped into 13 different regions, and report directly to the designated regional office.

Global Oil Company (GOil) is one of the largest companies in the world, and has continuously undergone numerous mergers and acquisitions during the past decade. 100 000 employees worldwide have contributed to the revenue of about £100 billion in 2001. Specialized in exploration, refinery, chemicals and retailing, GOil is perceived as one of the strongest players in its fields. In contrast to the above three case organizations, GOil had a flat structure that consisted of more than 100 business units worldwide. Strong emphasis on technology and innovation had helped GOil to cut down its operational costs by more than a quarter during the past decade.

Case findings

The findings generated from the cross-case comparison are presented in this section. Table 2.1 summarizes some of the key features of the projects.

The four projects represent two distinct foci, namely intrinsic and extrinsic innovation, to represent the differences in the role of internal and external knowledge in relation to the project implementation. This distinction does not imply that intrinsic innovation does not have any influence from an organization's external environment, or vice versa. Rather, the purpose is to indicate that extrinsic innovation requires external knowledge, which can only be acquired through 'grafting' (Huber, 1991). For example, IEngineering used an IT consulting firm to facilitate the ERP implementation, whereas DBank had recruited more than 100 new staff to fill the vacuum of component-based development (CBD) knowledge. By contrast, while intrinsic innovation can be initiated through grafting, such organizational innovation can also be achieved by using the organization's existing knowledge. Compared with extrinsic innovation, an organization is less dependent on external knowledge for intrinsic innovation. For example, TRetailing appointed a management consultant team to conduct the

Table 2.1   Key features of the studied projects

	DBank	IEngineering	TRetailing	GOil
Project	Component-based development	Enterprise resource planning	Business process redesign	Knowledge management
Project nature	Technology-led process innovation	Technology-led process innovation	Process innovation	Process innovation
Starting date	1997	1996	1997	1996
Project duration	Ongoing	3 years	2 years	Ongoing
Project objectives	To enhance technology leadership by revolutionizing software development	To enable information sharing across all units. To improve efficiency and reduce product cost	To embed continuous change into work practice. To improve HQ's support to all regions and stores	To learn from past experience. To transfer the learning outcome for future reuse
Involvement of external consultants	No	Yes	Yes	No
Stakeholders	Business users and technologists	All divisions	All divisions	All business units
Steering group	No	Yes	Yes	No

initial process analysis. When the process analysis was completed, an internal team took over the implementation of the BPR programme. Likewise, members of GOil carried out all activities related to the implementation of its KM programme.

All project teams had an average of twelve to fourteen core members who were selected from a variety of organizational units to ensure organization-wide representativeness. Ensuring organization-wide representation means that organizational members are more likely to accept the innovation, because each group will have a project team member who represents their interests (Steensma and Tetteroo, 2000). This is particularly vital for organization-wide projects where there is a need to obtain acceptance across the organization.

Two of the case organizations used a steering group as a control mechanism to monitor the progress of the project. In the IEngineering case, the steering group continuously provided help and support to the ERP team, facilitating the

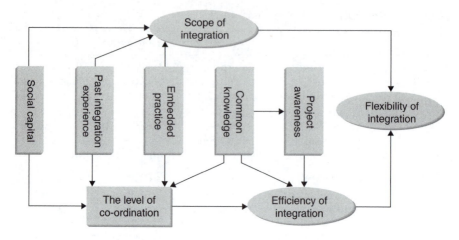

Figure 2.1 *The model of knowledge integration – efficiency, scope and flexibility – in the context of cross-functional project teams.*

removal of obstacles and the obtaining of sufficient resources. However, in the TRetailing case, the steering group provided virtually no help to rescue the struggling BPR team. While both steering groups were composed of senior managers, the focus and interests of the members varied between the two cases. In particular, in the TRetailing case, the steering group members were more concerned with their own departmental interests than the broader interest of the organization.

The following discussion links findings derived from the study to the theoretical framework of knowledge integration (Grant, 1996), and summarizes the findings based on the relationship between integration efficiency, scope and flexibility, and the promoting and opposing forces that affect this integration. Figure 2.1 provides a summary of these relationships.

Efficiency of integration

Although common knowledge was found to be essential across all cases, the analysis revealed some interesting similarities and differences in how the required level of common knowledge was created. In terms of similarities, common knowledge was primarily created within the project team, before being diffused throughout the organization. However, differences were found in how the project teams created common knowledge through building project awareness, and how stakeholders shared such knowledge within and beyond their divisions. Even though all teams had organized workshops and training courses to promote their projects and educate the users, the results suggested that it was individuals' attitudes towards learning the knowledge that most strongly influenced the effectiveness of creating common knowledge. For example, in the IEngineering case, a large number of users had attended various ERP-related workshops and seminars before the implementation decision. A collective demand was created across various divisions to ensure that ERP would be adopted. In contrast to the proactive learning in IEngineering, business users in DBank refused to attend any training, because the need to understand technology was perceived as part of the technologists' job.

Furthermore, it was found that the effectiveness of building common knowledge was strongly associated with the availability of objective measures. For example, in the GOil case, the team had faced difficulties in convincing some users about the value of KM, because there was no measurement available for calculating its costs and benefits. As one member from the KM team noted, 'you can't measure how much a nut contributes to a washing machine, can you?' Similar problems were faced by the BPR team in the TRetailing case. As some interviewees noted, why should users change something with which they were familiar and that allowed them to achieve their targets to something with which they were unfamiliar? By comparison, the level of effectiveness was relatively high in the technology-led process innovation cases at IEngineering and DBank, for two reasons. First, users did not need to understand the design of a technology and thus could not use it. Secondly, the creation of common knowledge could be underpinned by tangible benefits, such as better support from the new technology (Davis, 1989). In particular, in the IEngineering case, the cost savings achieved from the ERP implementation were reflected in an increase in the year-end bonus. It is clear that common knowledge is vital for communication (Demsetz, 1991), yet the perceived value of this common knowledge appears to be the driving force behind its creation. Where those involved see little value in gaining common knowledge, they are unlikely to attempt to learn this knowledge.

Two themes that were found to shape the level of co-ordination were the case organizations' past experience in cross-functional collaboration and the organizations' embedded practice that permitted or inhibited the building, nurturing and maintaining of social capital (Nahapiet and Ghoshal, 1998). In each of the four cases, the creation of common knowledge was primarily built upon the perceived value of and benefits derived from being involved in the project. This is reflected in the notion of intellectual buy-in suggested by Huang et al. (2001). However, the creation of common knowledge alone did not necessarily lead to the level of 'emotional attachment' (Lembke and Wilson, 1998), required to overcome resistance. The need to influence stakeholder groups at the emotional level was found to be strongly related to the organization's past experience in implementing cross-functional projects. Thus, DBank and TRetailing had limited experience in carrying out large-scale cross-functional projects. These two cases had much more difficulty in achieving emotional attachment with the stakeholders compared with the other two cases. As noted by Robey et al. (2000), collaboration requires practice.

The emotional dimension of collaboration explains only part of the importance of social capital as it affects cross-functional project work. As illustrated by Nahapiet and Ghoshal (1998), social capital, in addition to its relational dimension, has structural and cognitive dimensions. The structural dimension refers to the network ties and configuration between various organizational groups. Where an organization's practice does not require frequent cross-functional collaboration, this sub-stantially undermines the need for and development of net-work ties. This was particularly evident in the DBank case. Referring to the scale of the project and the organization's size, in the GOil, TRetailing and IEngineering cases, it is clear that only limited strong ties can be developed purely by the project team members. Yet, through a process of referral (Burt, 1992) the strong ties had been extended, allowing the teams to expand their social networks to a broader network. This was seen to be crucial for implementing this type of project, where organization-wide representation was vital.

In relation to the cognitive dimension, the findings suggest that social capital, specifically the development of shared narratives and codes, requires a facilitating organizational structure. This is because various different tasks performed by different organizational units have led to the development of group-specific subcultures (Schein, 1996). Shared narratives and codes across these different groups are not developed, unless frequent cross-functional communication and collaboration are encouraged. Compared with Grant's (1996) view that efficiency of knowledge integration lies in a structure that minimizes the need for communication, the findings have shown the opposite. The reason for this difference is likely to be because the focus of the study has here focused on cross-functional projects, which are tasked with performing a series of non-routine tasks. Grant (1996), in contrast, was focusing on routine organizational operations. Rather than deriving integration efficiency from routinization and minimizing the need for communication, it seems that the level of efficiency in the context of cross-functional project work depends on how common knowledge is created, how social capital is managed and how an organization's structure facilitates the development of social capital.

Scope of integration

As suggested by Grant (1996, p. 381), 'the greater the scope of knowledge integrated, the harder it is for competitors to replicate the integration capability'. Referring to cross-functional implementation projects, it is evident that there were differences in such capability across the cases. In the cross-functional project context, findings generated by this study suggest that an organization's past experience in integrating knowledge that is wide in scope, for example, experience gained from implementing previous organization-wide projects, is an important influence. Compared with TRetailing and DBank, which had limited experience in large-scope integration, GOil and IEngineering had gained substantial experience from past projects. For example, in GOil, before the KM programme, various corporate-wide initiatives, such as creating a common operating environment and a virtual teamwork project, were successfully implemented. Similarly, in the IEngineering case, experience was gained from projects, such as total quality management and a common IT platform project.

Clearly, the examination of integration scope cannot be isolated from the understanding of integration efficiency. In particular, the four cases demonstrated that an organization's capacity to integrate functionally specific knowledge with a broad scope is influenced by its past experience as well as the structure through which cross-functional collaboration is encouraged and rewarded. Specifically, where social capital had been developed through previous cross-functional collaboration it was found to be easier to integrate knowledge with a broad scope. However, knowledge integration cannot be perceived as merely an intellectual activity (Huang et al., 2001), so that the understanding of how an organization copes with wide-scope knowledge integration should not be understood simply by considering an organization's past experience. Rather, it is equally important to take into account how the development of social capital is promoted and managed in the organization and facilitated by the organizational structure and practice. For example, cross-functional projects of various scales had previously been undertaken in IEngineering and these previous experiences had benefited the organization by laying a strong foundation in comprehensive social networks. In contrast, the overemphasis on specialization in DBank had reduced the opportunity for its workforce to develop the required social capital to facilitate CBD implementation.

Flexibility of integration

As suggested in the earlier discussion, the flexibility of integration is closely related to how continuous innovation is exploited and nurtured. In other words, the level of flexibility is shaped by an organization's capacity to build one innovation initiative on top of another. The need to draw on past innovation for future innovation is reflected in the notion of infusion (Cooper and Zmud, 1990), which portrays how organizations increase their effectiveness by synthesizing lessons learned from past innovation experience. Referring to the GOil and IEngineering cases, it is clear that their strong emphasis and dependence on innovation to survive had facilitated the development of integration flexibility. However, this does not suggest that DBank and TRetailing had under-emphasized the need for continuous innovation. As one manager from TRetailing noted, 'we are suffering from initiative overload and inability to cope with change consistently and successfully'. A similar experience was also found in the DBank case. Nevertheless, it was clear in the DBank and TRetailing cases that, even though innovations had been continuously initiated, there was little synergy generated from these initiatives.

Observed differences between the levels of integration flexibility across the four cases can be explained using the distinction between adaptive and generative modes of learning as proposed by Senge (1990). According to Senge (1990), an organization cannot learn effectively simply by concentrating on fixing problems with quick solutions. Such adaptive learning is insufficient. Rather, it is vital to promote generative learning by constantly evaluating the way in which solutions are created. Findings derived from the GOil and IEngineering cases suggest that integration flexibility is developed through generative learning. For example, a KM programme was initiated in IEngineering when the implementation of ERP was almost completed. The reason for this new initiative was that those involved recognized the limitations of the ERP solution. They recognized that the free flow of information enabled by ERP did not necessarily lead to the sharing of tacit knowledge. To improve the sharing of this tacit knowledge, various product-related innovation communities were formed under the KM initiative. In contrast, evidence collected from the DBank and TRetailing cases suggested that the capacity to enhance integration flexibility had been undermined by the fire-fighting mode of adaptive learning. In particular, in the TRetailing case, interviewees commonly agreed that BPR did not generate the expected outcome largely because stakeholders were not equipped with the understanding that a fundamental change was needed. Given that adaptive learning appeared to be the norm in this organization, differences in perceiving the need for innovation between the project team and stakeholder groups seemed to be inevitable. Even though business users in the DBank case considered that the implementation of CBD was crucial to support their trading, they did not perceive the necessity of acquiring basic technological knowledge, which is crucial to maximize the benefit of CBD.

Moreover, differences in the way in which external consultants contributed to the level of integration efficiency were evident between the TRetailing and IEngineering cases. Instead of facilitating the BPR implementation, the external consultant team was appointed by TRetailing simply to carry out the evaluation study. It was not involved in the actual implementation because the company wanted to save on the consultancy fee. Since the internal team had limited knowledge about the concept of BPR, the evaluation report produced by the external consultants proved to be useless. It was therefore perhaps unsurprising to find that the adaptive mode of learning became the dominant style in the BPR team. In contrast, the external consultant team appointed by IEngineering had been a long-term strategic partner of IEngineering. Past experience in collaborating on large-scale projects had enhanced the integration flexibility, which benefited not only IEngineering, but also its strategic partner.

The relationship between integration efficiency, scope and flexibility

As shown in Figure 2.1 and elaborated above, three forces, namely social capital, past integration experience and embedded practices, appeared collectively to influence the level of co-ordination achieved and the way in which the scope of integration was accommodated. The influence of these three forces, as evident in the comparison of the four cases, suggests that to develop higher levels of co-ordination and fulfil the demand of larger integration scope requires more than just the development of teamwork within the project team itself. It is equally crucial for team members to engage with other stakeholder groups through utilizing their social capital. The importance of social capital is reflected not only in the need for developing teamwork, but also in aligning different stakeholders to ensure that stakeholders are committed to the project by prioritizing the project on their agenda (Huang et al., 2001). Compared with Grant's conceptualization, which underemphasizes the role of social capital, findings elaborated in the study address the concept that knowledge integration within the context of cross-functional project implementation is in essence a continuous process through which social capital facilitates the connection, disconnection and/or reconnection between different stakeholder groups. In addition, an organization's past integration experience is found to be a prerequisite condition, formed based on the collective results of past project implementation experience. Finally, embedded practices reflect an organization's structure, which may either facilitate or impede knowledge integration.

In terms of the efficiency of integration, the results shown here have coincided with Grant's (1996) conceptualization that the level of co-ordination, common knowledge and organizational structure are paramount. However, findings generated by this study also suggest that in the context of cross-functional project implementation the way in which team members mobilize their social capital and diffuse project awareness through creating common knowledge across different stakeholder groups is equally crucial. In terms of the relationships between the integration elements, Grant indicates that an organization's ability to integrate knowledge cross-functionally is determined primarily based on the collective effect of integration efficiency, scope and flexibility. Findings illustrated here differ from Grant's probably because of the kinds of projects examined here, that is, broad, organization-wide projects that are more complex and demand higher levels of knowledge integration than anything previously undertaken within each organization. Under these conditions, where an organization has very limited experience to apply to their current actions, the results generated by this study suggest that the utilization of social capital and the creation of common knowledge within and beyond the project team are essential. In particular, when the scope of a cross-functional project is greater than all projects implemented before, identifying, acquiring and sharing knowledge required by the project is largely determined by how the potential of social capital, specifically 'referral', is maximized (Nahapiet and Ghoshal, 1998).

Conclusions

The above discussion has explored the efficiency, scope and flexibility of knowledge integration in the context of four cross-functional projects. It is clear that while the scope of the four projects spanned virtually all organizational divisions, the creation of common knowledge between the team and stakeholders was found to be difficult. As noted above, the creation of common knowledge is driven by the way in which stakeholders perceive the value of the project. Yet, the awareness of value derived from the project does not fully explain the complexity of integration efficiency, because the development, nurturing and maintenance of social capital are equally crucial. In particular, organizational structure and practice can significantly promote or oppose members' opportunities to develop and manage their social capital. When such opportunities are limited, the efficiency of knowledge integration between the project team and stakeholders is significantly minimized. It has been demonstrated that an organization's past experience in implementing large-scale projects plays a key role in determining the level of integration efficiency and scope. Moreover, it is evident that the way in which organizations can build on their past innovation to initiate new innovation shapes the development of integration flexibility.

Contributions made by the study are reflected in not only applying the theory of knowledge integration to examine cross-functional projects, but also synthesizing the findings with other conceptualizations. Cross-functional project teams, however, represent only one of many new organizational forms. Others, such as virtual teams and interorganizational teams, also call for more empirical studies. Furthermore, instead of focusing on projects that have a relatively long lifespan, other research can potentially extend the knowledge integration theory by observing short-term and non-recurrence teams. Managers can learn from this study to evaluate the effectiveness of forming cross-functional project teams, in particular by assessing how past experience and organizational context facilitate or inhibit the implementation. While the benefits of involvement need to be clearly specified, the understanding of the existing network structure is equally beneficial. Since the emotional influence of organizational members on performance is often understated, managers will need to encourage the development of emotional attachment between various stakeholder groups by promoting the importance of cross-functional collaboration.

References

Bishop, S. (1999) Cross-functional project teams in functionally aligned organisations. *Project Management Journal* 30(3): 6–12.

Blackler, F. (1995) Knowledge, knowledge work and organisations: an overview and interpretation. *Organisation Studies* 16(6): 1021–1046.

Brown, J. and Duguid, P. (1991) Organisational learning and toward a unified view of working, learning and innovation. *Organization Science* 2(1): 40–56.

Burt, R. (1992) *Structural Holes: The Social Structure of Competition.* London: Harvard University Press.

Clark, K. and Fujimoto, T. (1991) *Product Development Performance: Strategy, Organization, and Management in the World Auto Industry.* Boston, MA: Harvard Business School Press.

Cooper, R. B. and Zmud, R. W. (1990) Information technology implementation research: a technological diffusion approach. *Management Science* 36(2): 123–139.

Davenport, T. (1992) *Process Innovation: Reengineering Through Information Technology.* Boston, MA: Harvard Business School Press.

Davis, F. (1989) Perceived usefulness, perceived ease of use, and user acceptance of information technology. *MIS Quarterly* 13(3): 319–340.

De Meyer, A. (1998) Manufacturing operations in Europe: where do we go next? *European Management Journal* 16(3): 262–271.

Demsetz, H. (1991) The theory of the firm revisited. In Williamson, O. and Winter, S. (eds) *The Nature of the Firm.* Oxford: Oxford University Press.

Gopal, A. and Prasad, P. (2000) Understanding GDSS in symbolic context: shifting the focus from technology to interaction. *MIS Quarterly* 24(3): 509–546.

Grant, R. (1996) Prospering in dynamically-competitive environment: organisational capability as knowledge integration. *Organization Science* 7(4): 375–387.

Gupta, A. and Govindarajan, V. (2000) Knowledge management's social dimension: lessons from Nucor Steel. *Sloan Management Review* 41(3): 71–80.

Huang, J. (2000) Knowledge integration processes and dynamics: an empirical study of two cross-functional programme teams. Unpublished PhD Thesis. Warwick: Warwick Business School, University of Warwick.

Huang, J., Newell, S. and Pan, S. L. (2001) The process of global knowledge integration: a case study of a multinational investment bank's Y2K program. *European Journal of Information Systems* 10(3): 161–174.

Huber, G. (1991) Organisational learning: the contributing processes and the literatures. *Organization Science* 2(1): 88–115.

Lawrence, P. and Lorsch, J. (1967) *Organization and Environment: Managing Differentiation and Integration*. Boston, MA: Harvard University Press.

Lee, Z. and Lee, J. (2000) An ERP implementation case study from a knowledge transfer perspective. *Journal of Information Technology* 15(2): 281–288.

Lembke, S. and Wilson, M. (1998) Putting the 'team' into teamwork: alternative theoretical contributions for contemporary management practice. *Human Relations* 51(7): 927–944.

Markus, M. L., Tanis, C. and Fenema, P. C. (2000) Multi-site ERP implementation. *Communications of the ACM* 43(4): 42–46.

Marwick, A. D. (2001) Knowledge management technology. *IBM Systems Journal* 40(4): 814–830.

Miles, M. B. and Huberman, A. M. (1994) *Qualitative Data Analysis: An Expanded Sourcebook*. London: Sage.

Nahapiet, J. and Ghoshal, S. (1998) Social capital, intellectual capital, and the organisational advantage. *Academy of Management Review* 23(2): 242–266.

Nonaka, I. and Takeuchi, H. (1995) *The Knowledge-Creating Company: How Japanese Companies Create the Dynamics of Innovation*. Oxford: Oxford University Press.

Robey, D., Khoo, H. M. and Powers, C. (2000) Situated learning in cross-functional virtual teams. *IEEE Transactions on Professional Communication* 43(1): 51–66.

Schein, E. H. (1996) Three cultures of management: the key to organisational learning. *Sloan Management Review* 38(1): 9–20.

Senge, P. (1990) *The Fifth Discipline, The Art and Practice of the Learning Organisation*. London: Century Business.

Steensma, H. and Tetteroo, A. (2000) Attitudes toward cross-functional quality project groups: net utility and procedural justice. *Total Quality Management* 11(1): 123–128.

Strauss, A. and Corbin, J. (1990) *Basics of Qualitative Research: Grounded Theory Procedures and Techniques*. London: Sage.

Turner, R. and Keegan, A. (1999) The versatile project-based organisation: governance and operational control. *European Management
Journal* 17(3): 296–309.

Weick, K. and Roberts, K. (1993) Collective mind in organisations:
heedful interrelating on flight decks. *Administrative Science
Quarterly* 38(3): 357–381.

Wright, P. and Snell, S. (1998) Toward a unifying framework for
exploring fit and flexibility in strategic human resource management. *Academy of Management Review* 23(4): 756–772.

Yin, R. (1994) *Case Study Research: Design and Methods*. London: Sage.

Chapter 3

Co-creation of knowledge by multidisciplinary project teams

Patrick S. W. Fong

Introduction

This chapter examines the underlying processes and their interrelationships in knowledge creation in multidisciplinary project teams. While some organizations are beginning to seek more sophisticated organizational structures, or train personnel in many managerial, creative or teamwork skills, many are still likely to have difficulty in being continuously innovative. They may be highly effective in exploiting existing knowledge in the short term, but there is likely to be relatively little long-term learning and knowledge creation, particularly if individuals and knowledge are isolated and fragmented (Dachler, 1992). Bringing the collective knowledge of members in teams to bear on serving customers or clients is practically important because knowledge is a source of competitive advantage (Prahalad and Hamel, 1990). Knowledge-creating skills in particular are important as they are required to create new products or processes, or to enhance existing ones (Leonard-Barton, 1995). Learning must be integrated with current tasks, not only to meet present goals, but also to develop and retain knowledge for future organizational needs.

Knowledge creation and new product development teams

Several researchers have described new product development as a knowledge-intensive activity (Iansiti and MacCormack,

1997). New product development often involves cross-functional linkages, where different participants join a team with differing viewpoints. Such teams are often characterized according to the risk and synergy resulting from their interaction with other team members (Jassawalla and Sashittal, 1998). Morrison and Kennedy (1996) suggest that this interaction brings in the need to organize, integrate, filter, condense and annotate the collaborative data and other relevant information that these team members contribute.

Creating new knowledge and perspectives is fundamental to new product development. A new product can be considered as 'a package of features and benefits, each of which must be conceived, articulated, designed and "operationalized", or brought into existence' (Dougherty, 1996, p. 425). The development of a constructed facility can be viewed as a new product development, with customers or end-users purchasing or using the facility. They would assess their own needs and affordability before they purchase. The development of a new product entails the application of knowledge to new problem-orientated situations, thus requiring uncertainty reduction (Cyert and March, 1963). The same applies to construction projects, with each project unique in itself in terms of design and construction. With the many constraints that the construction industry faces (due to limited space, increasing project complexity, limited budgets, tight programmes and the constant demand for facility innovation), project teams are faced with challenges to utilize diverse knowledge and create new knowledge in order to meet stringent requirements and fulfil ever-changing needs. Project team members have to incorporate new information into their understanding to solve the technical challenges that they face. Thus, learning is inherent in the work that they do (Mohrman et al., 1995).

Several researchers investigating product innovation have emphasized the importance of a team approach in successful product development (e.g. Clark and Fujimoto, 1991). Project team members with diverse skills, knowledge and experiences are required to work together to resolve the issues or problems encountered in a project. Although there is extensive literature covering teams (e.g. Cohen and Bailey, 1997) and the benefits that they can bring to organizations (e.g. Ancona and Caldwell, 1992), a focus on the processes of knowledge creation from a multidisciplinary project team perspective is compelling as research specifically addressing this issue appears to be very limited (Newell and Swan, 2000). Senge (1990) suggests that creating knowledge at the team level is essential for long-term team effectiveness, innovation and productivity. In addition, a team can be viewed as a socially constructed phenomenon or linking mechanism that integrates individuals and organizations (Horvath et al., 1996). For consistency reasons, no distinction has been made between the term 'team' and 'group'. Instead, both words are used interchangeably throughout the chapter.

Knowledge creation: interrelationships between explicit and tacit knowledge

The issue of knowledge has been debated for several centuries (Nonaka and Takeuchi, 1995). Knowledge has only recently been viewed as a collective phenomenon in organizational contexts. Two conflicting theoretical perspectives about knowledge have emerged during the course of this research. The first perspective, as highlighted by Wernerfelt (1984), focuses on the resource-based view, where knowledge is professed as a set of strategically important commodities that exist independently of their creators and are context independent, that is, the firm's primary role is as knowledge applicator. The second perspective, from Berger and Luckmann (1966), views knowledge as a set of shared beliefs that are constructed through social interactions and embedded within the social contexts in which knowledge is created, that is, the firm's primary role is as knowledge creator. This view of knowledge elaborates the social construction perspective held by this study of trying to understand knowledge-creation processes and investigate the phenomenon of knowledge creation in multidisciplinary project teams. The literature on knowledge creation at team levels is rather limited, particularly in relation to multidisciplinary project teams. Recognition of this fact has led this research to emphasize the multidisciplinary team context in order to fill a theoretical gap.

The present framework for examining the knowledge-creation processes within multidisciplinary project teams is based on Nonaka and Takeuchi's (1995) organizational knowledge-creation theory. Nonaka and Takeuchi's theory is utilized because it is one of the few knowledge-creation theories available that examines the interrelationships between explicit and tacit knowledge. As illustrated in Figure 3.1, the processes of organizational knowledge creation give rise to cycles that feed off each other.

How organizations view knowledge creation seems to be dependent on their organizational culture. Nonaka and Takeuchi (1995) explain that the superiority of the Japanese in continuous innovation has been due to their strong emphasis on socialization (i.e. sharing tacit knowledge directly) and internalization (i.e. individuals' own participation in learning by doing). In contrast, the Western focus is more on externalization,

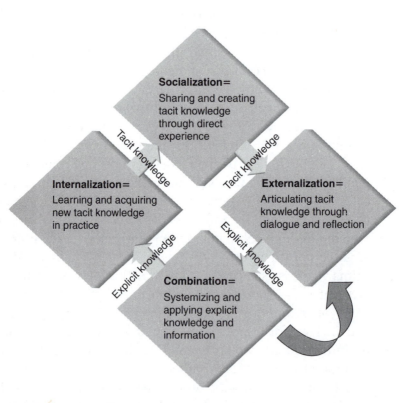

Figure 3.1   *Knowledge-conversion processes (adapted from Nonaka and Takeuchi, 1995; Nonaka and Konno, 1998).*

with a strong emphasis on explicit knowledge and combination. This is due to the epistemological difference whereby 'Westerners tend to emphasise explicit knowledge and the Japanese tend to stress tacit knowledge' (Nonaka and Takeuchi, 1995, p. 243). Moreover, in Japanese society, knowledge is mainly created on a group level through dialogue, whereas in Western organizations the link between individual learning and organizational learning is less obvious. This stems from the ontological difference between their focus on individual and group, whereby 'Westerners are more focused on individuals, while the Japanese are more group-oriented' (Nonaka and Takeuchi, 1995, p. 243). They add that in the West, work at the group level is devoted to carrying out predefined tasks rather than maintaining dialogue through which tasks are newly defined and further developed. Conversely, Japanese firms are less adapted to managing large, complex systems, requiring extensive articulation and transfer of knowledge to the environment through products, patents and people.

However, Nonaka and Takeuchi's (1995) knowledge-creation model has some limitations that lessen its suitability for the study of knowledge creation in multidisciplinary project teams. Their primary distinction between tacit and explicit knowledge is problematic, as tacit or unarticulated knowledge is always a precondition for explicit knowledge (Polanyi, 1962). Tuomi (1999) also criticizes the model for taking culture and language for granted. The difficulty of discussing the role of language as a 'repository of culturally shared meaning' (Tuomi, 1999, p. 340), critical for any knowledge-creation theory, may make its use difficult for multidisciplinary project teams. It is also not clear what happens when the knowledge-creating spiral expands outside a team: is knowledge still created in the same way (Tuomi, 1999)? As Tuomi points out (1999, p. 328), 'there is no model of social activity within the [knowledge-creation] model – the motives for knowledge creation, and their relations to individual or organizational needs, remain obscure. Why some knowledge is created, and why some knowledge is not, remains an open question'. Furthermore, Tuomi (1999) finds that although Nonaka and Takeuchi (1995) stress that the process of knowledge creation is 'social', their underlying focus is on individual and intra-personal knowledge. He adds that 'as their concept of knowledge is intra-personal, truth becomes a necessary aspect of knowledge, grounding intra-personal knowledge into interpersonal reality' (Tuomi, 1999, p. 333).

To overcome some of the shortcomings in Nonaka and Takeuchi's knowledge-creation model, if one accepts the social construction perspective of knowledge as a set of shared beliefs constructed through social interaction amidst certain social circumstances, then both individual and social levels require acknowledgement and integration. Specifically, by adding the social construction and communication elements to Nonaka and Takeuchi's model, three modes of knowledge creation can be distinguished. They are knowledge sharing, knowledge integration and collective project learning.

In this chapter, knowledge sharing is viewed as a multitude of processes taking place directly without language (socialization) and with language (externalization). Designing a facility requires collaborative interaction of individuals from different professional backgrounds. Their diverse expertise represents different interests and issues. Those different experiences, mental models and motivations can be expressed only partly in explicit language. Thus, socialization is a valuable mode of sharing knowledge in teams without language through imitation, observation and sharing experiences face to face. Nonaka (1994) emphasizes that socialization is also an important way to further trust between partners. Saint-Onge (1996) refers to socialization as a way of creating a sufficient level of congruence to enable individuals to understand each other and work together towards their common goals from different perspectives. Besides sharing without language, sharing work-related expertise requires the use of language. Social constructionists regard language as a co-ordination of action and therefore a fundamental tool in knowledge creation (Burr, 1995). The commonly used tool in externalization is dialogue. Dialogue triggers the unconscious elements of knowing and not-knowing, as well as revealing gaps in knowledge compared with what the community knows (Ayas, 1996).

An important aspect of knowledge integration is the willingness to combine knowledge from within and outside the team. The more differentiated the knowledge inputs needed in a task, the higher the knowledge diversity and the greater the scope for knowledge integration. Design, involving art, engineering, finance and business, is a process of knowledge integration, and a facility's design emerges from the collaboration of project participants and stakeholders. Leonard-Barton (1995) views creation of new knowledge by combining previously unconnected elements or by developing ways of combining previously associated elements.

Innovation teams are likely to engage in effective knowledge sharing and integration to achieve their predefined goals, but do their processes include activities to ensure the future creation of knowledge as well? Nonaka and Takeuchi (1995) suggest that large Western organizations are not good at internalizing learning from their activities at the team level. There is a strong emphasis on converting tacit knowledge to explicit knowledge, but less is done to support the further generation of tacit knowledge. Learning usually has a more open-ended and long-term focus.

Case studies

Cases derived from the construction industry are used to explore the underlying processes of knowledge creation in a multidisciplinary project team setting, while determining the interrelationships between these processes. Evidence for the case studies relied on three main sources collected over a period of fourteen months: documentation and organizational records, interviews and, finally, direct observation.

Two project teams – infrastructural and residential – with diverse design concepts, discipline and knowledge bases, skills and possibly attitudes towards knowledge creation, were considered. Both cases shared common involvement in the construction of two large-scale projects on a green-field site. In addition, the nature of the work was information and knowledge intensive, requiring the teams to develop new or use existing technologies, techniques and processes to achieve their work goals. The nature of project team at work was both intellectual and interactive. It was intellectual in that it required the team to find novel or hidden solutions to complex problems, and it was interactive as it required constant co-operation between all participants in the design development process. However, these two projects differed in many respects. The nature of the tasks was different, as were the personnel involved and the ways in which design knowledge was created. It was hoped that the selection of the cases would give further insight into the multiple and divergent phenomena fuelling the different modes of knowledge creation during design development. All the while, the study viewed knowledge as a dynamic phenomenon.

The selection of the residential development project recognizes the large reservoir of idiosyncratic knowledge developed by the case organization over the years. It also recognizes the crucial innovating dynamics behind the need to compete on the market with other residential developments. The infrastructure project presented alternative opportunities for knowledge creation and learning, unique in several respects. First, it was a complex operation, distinguished by an extraordinary multiplicity of consultants being employed. Secondly, it was rare to find such a project, usually managed by government, in private hands. Finally, the technical challenges presented in this project made it an interesting arena for knowledge creation and absorption within the team.

Knowledge creation in multidisciplinary project teams

Beyond modifying Nonaka and Takeuchi's (1995) model of knowledge conversion processes, a major and significant finding from the case studies was that the collaborative nature of multidisciplinary project teams was essential in creating new knowledge. With a traditional focus on professional specialization, many facility projects may be managed with tasks being executed in parallel or in sequence, or by certain project team members in isolation.

The first process in knowledge creation involves boundary crossing, with two types of boundary identified as affecting the progress and success of multidisciplinary knowledge creation. The importance of boundary crossing is reflected in solving the 'boundary paradox' (Quintas et al., 1997), where team members are able to exchange and combine knowledge (Nahapiet and Ghoshal, 1998). The interactions across these boundaries can either foster or hinder knowledge creation. The first boundary identified was between team members of different disciplines. The second boundary existed between client, consultant and contractor. The expertise boundaries could be crossed, not only through knowledge redundancy among team members, but also through boundary objects. The most prominent project boundary objects were drawings and personal conversations among team members. The second hierarchical boundaries could be crossed through team members consciously breaking down any barriers by valuing the expertise of others. The example set by the project managers was also helpful in this regard. It must be stressed that crossing boundaries does not necessarily guarantee the creation of knowledge. It is seen, however, as a prerequisite for the four remaining processes to occur.

The second process relates to knowledge sharing, with project team members of differing knowledge domains more likely to discuss their uniquely distinct information and knowledge than those who possess information in common. It seemed to be an advantage to have a diverse pool of knowledge for team members to access and share in discussion. Despite the existence of little competition among team members, external competition could act as a double-edged sword in the knowledge-sharing process. Sharing important market or design knowledge could lead to imitation by competitors, possibly even resulting in project poaching. In addition, the type of communication appeared more influential in the transfer of tacit knowledge than in that of explicit knowledge. For tacit knowledge to be effectively transmitted, interpersonal communication seemed of the utmost importance.

The third process to be considered is that of knowledge generation, in which teams create knowledge by generating new or 'emergent' knowledge through interaction and communication. New or emergent knowledge, not possessed before discussion, can develop through group discussion and interaction (Kogut and Zander, 1992). The development of emergent knowledge is vital for creativity and innovation. It is generated through various means, including those of social networks, printed sources, and customer and competitor feedback.

Social networks were identified as the most important vehicle for information and knowledge exchange, with team members heavily reliant upon colleagues, friends and ex-colleagues as rich resources for generating design knowledge. The use of printed data in the design process appeared to be limited, viewed as time-consuming and used mainly to cross-check solutions offered. Social networks tended to recommend published materials, helping to reduce research time and enhance usability. However, they could potentially restrict the generation of new knowledge, improving on existing situations or learning from projects, as team members might resort to antecedent project approaches or activities. Comprehension of customer needs, insight into competitor products and an inspection of completed facilities all seemed to stimulate knowledge generation.

Fourth is knowledge integration, realized by marrying the differing perspectives and knowledge of various disciplines in the design decision-making process. It enables different stakeholder views to be incorporated so that they can be considered and integrated. Facilities design requires multidisciplinary skills and knowledge input. Various team members brought different sets of assumptions about optimal ways to proceed, prioritizing different values and perspectives ultimately to best meet stakeholder requirements as well as arrive at satisfactory design solutions. Project documentation and various design objects were used as tools to integrate the range of knowledge input from project participants.

The fifth process involves collective project learning, in which professionals with extensive experience in self-directed learning learn from the projects in which they are engaged. Project team members had constantly to absorb new technology and techniques to remain competitive. Experts in self-directed learning, they created an environment maximizing opportunities for individual enquiry and learning. Problem solving being central to their work, they also recognized that failure was an opportunity for learning and understanding. Understanding failure is a primary mechanism in learning how new technology and systems operate, optimally avoiding repetitive mistakes. Therefore, considerable effort should be made to support an individual's critical problem-solving and reflection processes. Individuals then develop personal strategies based on their own thinking and learning preferences.

The project teams encouraged team learning activities, independent of any directives. Small subteams typically pooled their resources for learning, acquiring the necessary skills and knowledge to solve problems in an open and permissive environment. Individuals shared their information-seeking strategies so that the subteam might learn in as many different ways as possible. The larger project teams followed more formal processes and procedures for sharing and interacting. The smaller teams contributed directly to the work of the larger project teams, but they were not formally recognized in the organizational structure of the projects. They spontaneously grouped and regrouped, navigated by the team members themselves. Most formations were temporary, lasting only until the immediate goals were accomplished.

Interproject learning can be seen as gaining knowledge from a project and transferring it directly or indirectly to other subsequent or concurrent projects. It can happen both concurrently or sequentially. In concurrent transfer, a project transfers knowledge to another project before the tasks of the current project are completed. Sequential transfer occurs when knowledge and experience from a completed project are transferred to a subsequent project. This transfer is identified not from interviews, but from direct observation in team meetings. Once knowledge and experience have been gained from a completed project, they become part of the team members' knowledge and expertise and are hard to identify separately. Central to interproject learning is a certain degree of repetitiveness between projects, whether in similarities between tasks or in similar principles. The most widely observed strategy in interproject learning occurred in team members engaged in multiple projects, rather than where knowledge was codified in any format.

Considering the above generic findings from the two case studies presented above, a knowledge-creation model specific for multidisciplinary project team settings is presented in the next section of this chapter.

Interrelationships between the five processes of knowledge creation

Knowledge creation in multidisciplinary project teams starts with the prerequisite boundary-crossing process, which then leads to the three knowledge processes of knowledge sharing, knowledge generation and knowledge integration. Collective project learning is central to the three knowledge processes. This shows that the knowledge-creation processes within multidisciplinary teams are not linear. Instead, they are interwoven, occurring throughout the projects, as shown in Figure 3.2.

It was found in both cases that the project teams needed to cross boundaries imposed both by the range of diverse professional disciplines and also by the hierarchical divisions of client, consultant and contractor before genuine work, problem solving or pertinent knowledge creation could occur. Without boundary crossing, team members could focus simply on their own disciplinary work without due regard for or collaboration with other disciplines. In crossing these two boundaries,

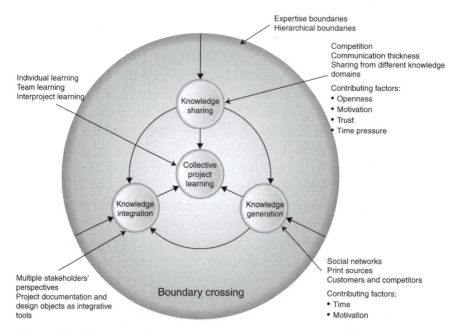

Figure 3.2   *The interrelationships between multidisciplinary knowledge-creation processes.*

they could initiate the three knowledge processes through joint problem solving. Once the design issues and problems influencing several disciplines had been identified, knowledge could be shared using their own experience and perspectives. This shared knowledge could include both positive and negative experiences. In this process, they might also examine various issues such as assumptions and constraints. If the team members possess insufficient knowledge to resolve the situation, or if the situation is not familiar, they can then proceed to the next circular process of knowledge generation, where knowledge from various sources is elicited to fill the knowledge gaps. This happens frequently in design situations, where team members may not have the necessary expertise or experience to generate the pertinent knowledge. Individuals draw on their own resources to generate new knowledge. Once the required knowledge has been elicited, knowledge integration will happen by combining all knowledge. In this respect, the knowledge-sharing and generation processes are repetitive until sufficient knowledge is found to solve the issue at hand. In some situations where the design problems are familiar, team members can reuse existing knowledge. This implies that generation of new knowledge is not necessary. However, owing to changing customer needs, unique design inputs and new technologies or regulations, continuous improvements and initiatives may often be required to generate new knowledge rather than reuse existing knowledge. Once team members have sourced new or emergent knowledge, they need to integrate their collective knowledge. This involves combining, modifying and negotiating among team members so that not only their needs but also those of stakeholders are fulfilled. Drawing this balance is an intricate process, requiring full appreciation of the multiple perspectives held by all stakeholders, including project team members.

The knowledge-creation process does not stop here. Through the processes of knowledge sharing, generation and integration, a lot of the emergent knowledge accessed by individual team members or the team as a whole will be learnt, absorbed and turned into valuable experience that may be used again in the future. Collective project learning is the nucleus of all three knowledge processes (i.e. sharing, generation and integration). In addition, collective project learning can occur within individuals and teams, as well as at interproject levels.

Conclusions

This chapter has developed a model of knowledge creation within multidisciplinary project teams. It places primary emphasis on the processes rather than the outcomes of multidisciplinary knowledge creation as put forward by previous researchers. In the proposed model, the five processes of knowledge creation are identified, including the processes of boundary crossing, knowledge sharing, knowledge generation, knowledge integration and collective project learning. The interrelationships of these five processes are elaborated to enable a thorough understanding of them. It must be stressed that these knowledge-creation processes within multidisciplinary teams are not linear. Instead, they are interwoven, occurring throughout projects. Through these interwoven processes, new or emergent knowledge is created within the project team, or existing knowledge is combined to give new insights. This model provides a critical comparison with existing organizational knowledge-creation models and has tried to embrace past literature related to team processes and knowledge creation.

References

Ancona, D. G. and Caldwell, D. F. (1992) Bridging the boundary: external activity and performance in organisational teams. *Administrative Science Quarterly* 37: 634–665.

Ayas, K. (1996) Design for learning and innovation. *Long Range Planning* 29(6): 898–901.

Berger, P. L. and Luckmann, T. (1966) *The Social Construction of Reality: A Treatise in the Sociology of Knowledge.* Garden City, NY: Doubleday.

Burr, V. (1995) *An Introduction to Social Constructionism.* London: Routledge.

Clark, K. and Fujimoto, T. (1991) *Product Development Performance: Strategy, Organization, and Management in the World Auto Industry.* Boston, MA: Harvard Business School Press.

Cohen, S. G. and Bailey, D. (1997) What makes teams work: group effectiveness research from the shop floor to the executive suite. *Journal of Management* 23(3): 239–290.

Cyert, R. and March, J. (1963) *A Behavioral Theory of the Firm.* Englewood Cliffs, NJ: Prentice-Hall.

Dachler, H. P. (1992) Management and leadership as relational phenomena. In von Cranach, M., Doise, W. and Mugny, G. (eds) *Social Representations and the Social Bases of Knowledge. Swiss Monographs in Psychology* 1: 169–178.

Dougherty, D. (1996) Organizing for innovation. In Clegg, S. R., Hardy, C. and Nord, W. R. (eds) *Handbook of Organization Studies.* London: Sage, pp. 424–439.

Horvath, L., Callahan, J. L., Croswell, C. and Mukri, G. (1996) Team sensemaking: an imperative for individual and organizational learning. In Holton, E. F. (ed.) *Proceedings of the Academy of Human Resource Development*, Minneapolis, MN, USA, 29 February–3 March, pp. 415–421.

Iansiti, M. and MacCormack, A. (1997) Developing products on Internet time. *Harvard Business Review* 75(5): 108–117.

Jassawalla, A. R. and Sashittal, H. C. (1998) An examination of collaboration in high-technology new product development processes. *Journal of Product Innovation Management* 15(3): 237–254.

Kogut, B. and Zander, U. (1992) Knowledge of the firm, combinative capabilities, and the replication of technology. *Organization Science* 3(3): 383–397.

Leonard-Barton, D. (1995) *Wellsprings of Knowledge: Building and Sustaining the Sources of Innovation.* Boston, MA: Harvard Business School Press.

Mohrman, S. A., Mohrman, A. M., Jr and Cohen, S. G. (1995) Organizing knowledge work system. In Beyerlein, M. M., Johnson, D. A. and Beyerlein, S. T. (eds) *Advances in Interdisciplinary Studies of Work Teams.* Greenwich, CT: JAI Press, pp. 61–91.

Morrison, R. and Kennedy, J. (eds) (1996) *Advances in Databases: Proceedings of the 14th British National Conference on Databases*, BNCOD 14, Edinburgh, UK, 3–5 July. New York: Springer.

Nahapiet, J. and Ghoshal, S. (1998) Social capital, intellectual capital, and the organisational advantage. *Academy of Management Review* 23(2): 242–266.

Newell, S. and Swan, J. (2000) Trust and inter-organisational networking. *Human Relations* 53(10): 1287–1328.

Nonaka, I. (1994) A dynamic theory of organisational knowledge creation. *Organization Science* 5(1): 14–37.

Nonaka, I. and Takeuchi, H. (1995) *The Knowledge-Creating Company: How Japanese Companies Create the Dynamics of Innovation.* Oxford: Oxford University Press.

Nonaka, I. and Konno, N. (1998) The concept of Ba: Building a foundation for knowledge creation. *California Management Review* 40(3): 40–54.

Polanyi, M. (1962) *The Tacit Dimension.* New York: Doubleday.

Prahalad, C. K. and Hamel, G. (1990) The core competence of the corporation. *Harvard Business Review* 68(3): 79–91.

Quintas, P., Lefrere, P. and Jones, G. (1997) Knowledge management: a strategic agenda. *Long Range Planning* 30(3): 385–391.

Saint-Onge, H. (1996) Tacit knowledge: the key to the strategic alignment of intellectual capital. *Planning Review* 24(2): 10–14.

Senge, P. M. (1990) *The Fifth Discipline: The Art and Practice of the Learning Organization.* New York: Currency Doubleday.

Tuomi, I. (1999) *Corporate Knowledge – Theory and Practice of Intelligent Organisations.* Helsinki: Metaxis.

Wernerfelt, B. (1984) A resource-based view of the firm. *Strategic Management Journal* 5(2): 171–180.

Chapter 4

Influences of knowledge sharing and hoarding in project-based firms

Jeremy Hall and Jonathan Sapsed

Introduction

The sharing and application of knowledge have been widely identified as key sources of sustained competitive advantage. Yet, in spite of recent advances in our understanding of how to manage knowledge (Dixon, 2000; Szulanski, 2003), its capture and transfer remain acute problems for project-based firms and organizations (DeFillippi and Arthur, 1998; Gann and Salter, 2000; Prencipe and Tell, 2001; Keegan and Turner, 2002). This is particularly so in the context of incentives to share or hoard knowledge (Gupta and Govindarajan, 2000), an area on which this chapter focuses. So, drawing on theory from several sources and empirical research from four different industrial settings, this chapter presents an analytical framework represented by a matrix that suggests determinants of knowledge transfer behaviour within project-based firms. All these organizations operate dissimilar and discontinuous projects, and thus illustrate a particularly challenging knowledge transfer environment. The authors argue that the tendency to share or hoard knowledge depends on organizational incentives and motivational characteristics, which are in turn shaped by industrial and organizational circumstances. It is concluded that an understanding of these underlying characteristics and circumstances will facilitate better utilization of explicit knowledge management (KM) tools such as intranets, expert systems and 'lessons learned' reporting.

Knowledge management

Managers and academics have recognized knowledge as a key source of competitive advantage (Kogut and Zander, 1992; Grant, 1996; Teece, 1998; Boisot, 1998; Zack, 1999). Knowledge is a potentially significant resource to the firm as it may possess valuable, rare, inimitable and non-substitutable characteristics (Barney, 1991), particularly if it has a tacit dimension (Polanyi, 1962; Wernerfelt, 1984; Peteraf, 1993; Nelson, 1994) or is specific to a venture, that is, contingent on particular and temporary circumstances of time and place (Hayek, 1945; Jensen and Meckling, 1992). As a result there has been widespread adoption of KM systems (Osterloh and Frey, 2000), defined by Sarvary (1999) as '… the infrastructure necessary for the organization to implement the Knowledge Management process'. Such systems include information technology (IT), internal governance mechanisms, organizational culture and incentive schemes. Yet the promised returns of KM remain elusive. A particular difficulty concerns the key function of knowledge transfer, the application of knowledge acquired in one situation to another (Singley and Anderson, 1989; Szulanksi, 1995, 1996; Bartezzaghi et al., 1997). This chapter investigates the problems of transferring knowledge in project-based firms, an environment where transfer is especially acute because of dissimilarity and discontinuity between successive projects. Based on four case studies in different industrial settings, the authors argue that the tendency to share or hoard knowledge (Gupta and Govindarajan, 2000) depends on organizational incentives which are in turn shaped by industrial and organizational circumstances.

The challenges of knowledge transfer

In addition to identifying the benefits of effective KM, the recent and extensive studies on knowledge transfer have identified considerable difficulties. Dixon (2000) identifies five types of knowledge transfer: serial transfer within the same team, near transfer to a team in a different location, far transfer of non-routine tasks, strategic transfer of complex knowledge and expert transfer. Yet for all these types of transfer, there are resisting forces. Szulanski (2003) describes five types of 'stickiness' that may be encountered during the phases of transfer: initiation stickiness, the difficulty in recognizing opportunities to transfer and in acting upon them, implementation stickiness, ramp-up stickiness and integration stickiness, where the knowledge becomes routinely used by a recipient. For the purpose of this discussion, the sources of knowledge transfer difficulties are categorized into four broad areas:

- *Resource constraints*: March (1991) argues that the tasks of exploration and exploitation of knowledge often compete for scarce resources. Such competition may lead to conflict between daily versus long-term pressures (Cross and Baird, 2000), while downsizing or high employee turnover may damage the organization's learning capacity (Fisher and White, 2000; Cross and Baird, 2000). Such circumstances can lead to conflicting pressures, goal incongruence and knowledge hoarding.
- *Capabilities*: Szulanski's (1995, 1996, 2003) work on stickiness in the transfer of best practice within firms has shown the importance of preparedness and prior knowledge in the recipient of knowledge transfer, or 'absorptive capacity' (Cohen and Levinthal, 1990) to receive and process the knowledge successfully. Szulanski argues that an intimate relationship between source and recipient reduces barriers to transfer, but that the capability to receive is crucial.
- *Contingencies*: KM policies are highly influenced by the nature of the knowledge and the circumstances under which the firm operates (Das, 2003; Uzzi and Lancaster, 2003). For example, Argote et al. (2003) note that environmental factors such as turbulence and competitiveness shape learning processes and organizational design. Knowledge management strategies must therefore be tailored to environmental circumstances.
- *Motivational factors*: Incentives (Hansen et al., 1999) and egos (Brown and Starkey, 2000) play a key role in the

knowledge-sharing process. Lord and Ranft (2000), for example, found that formal vertical reporting channels and incentive systems linked to performance are positively related to knowledge sharing and transfer, which in turn were positively related to divisional performance. Zack (1999) argues:

'... effective knowledge creation, sharing, and leveraging requires an organizational climate and reward system that values and encourages cooperation, trust, learning, and innovation and provides incentives for engaging in those knowledge-based roles, activities, and processes' (p. 55).

O'Dell and Grayson (1998) argue that structural barriers such as organizational designs that promote 'silo' behavior within departments and functions, 'cultures of expertise', and the 'not invented here' syndrome may hinder knowledge sharing if there is an absence of reward systems.

While all these factors are clearly influential, it is the authors' contention that they are not easily separable but rather highly related. For example, contingencies such as industrial characteristics and the nature of the knowledge used often shape resource allocation, which in turn prioritizes incentive schemes. Birkinshaw et al. (2002) argues that system-embedded knowledge (i.e. knowledge that is a function of the social and physical system in which it exists) is a strong predictor of organizational structure. The success of KM systems is thus contingent upon the fit between the reward systems and the organizational roles, structure (formal and informal), along with sociocultural factors such as culture, power relations, norms, management philosophy and reward systems (Zack, 1999), as well as industry dynamics.

Knowledge transfer in project-based firms

The problems of knowledge transfer are particularly acute in project-based firms (Gann and Salter, 2000; Prencipe and Tell,

2001; Keegan and Turner, 2002). Managers in many of these organizations have tried to implement KM solutions by converting tacit knowledge and work routines into explicit, codified knowledge (Nonaka and Takeuchi, 1995) that may be categorized and made available through a digital network, but with limited success (Marshall and Sapsed, 2000). Furthermore, many companies have found that the codification of good practice and lessons learned is incomplete (Blackler, 1995; Dutta, 1997; McDermott, 1998). The problem of applying knowledge and insights gained in one project to others appears to have more to do with the knowing embodied in people, rather than disembodied knowledge in expert systems or intranets (Cook and Brown, 1999). For example, knowledge transfer is much easier when the same project teams are reassembled for subsequent projects (Bartezzaghi et al., 1997).

Knowledge transfer as an agency problem

Transferring knowledge between projects is an intrinsically difficult task because of discontinuity and the limits of knowledge codification and disembodiment. The authors contend that the difficulties are exacerbated if incentives are inadequate, inconsistent or poorly aligned with the firm's resource constraints, capabilities and/or contingencies. Such problems of goal incongruence can be conceptualized as an agency problem (Jensen and Meckling, 1976) where unclear goals and incentives can inhibit knowledge transfer. In this context the conflict is between the strategic benefits accruing to the organization as a whole from knowledge transfer, and the operational costs associated with knowledge capture that are borne by the individual projects. Motivational approaches and associated control mechanisms must therefore be aligned.

Eisenhardt (1985, 1989a) suggests three approaches for aligning control mechanisms to the task. The first is behavioural-based control, which is appropriate if the job is simple and routine or if complex firms can gain knowledge about behaviours and invest in measurement systems. Another mechanistic approach is outcome-based control, where rewards are based on evaluations (e.g. profits or sales). Although simpler (and thus less costly), the problem of this approach for knowledge transfer in project-based firms is the difficulty in discounting the costs of the knowledge gained by attribution to potential benefits. The third option is social control for situations where the task is not easily programmed and outcomes are not measurable. The goal of social control is to align employees' preferences to coincide with those of management. Henceforth, these first two types are referred to as mechanistic–behavioural and mechanistic–outcomes based, whereas the third is social. (A similar concept to social control is clan control, defined by Schein, 1985, p. 443, as: '... a pattern of basic assumptions – invented, discovered, or developed by a given group as it learns to cope with its problems of external adaptation and internal integration – that has worked well enough to be considered valid and, therefore, to be taught to new members as the correct way to perceive, think, and feel in relation to those problems'.)

Intrinsic and extrinsic motivation

Within the context of knowledge transfer, Osterloh and Frey (2000) make the important distinction between extrinsic (i.e. pay for performance) and intrinsic (i.e. undertaken for one's need satisfaction) motivational approaches. The latter they argue is crucial when tacit knowledge is to be transferred between teams, as explicit motivation (i.e. pricing systems) are unlikely to work because the transfer of tacit knowledge cannot easily be observed or attributed to an individual. They further note that inappropriate organizational forms can hinder knowledge transfer. For example, extrinsic incentives may crowd out intrinsic motivation. Thus, it is proposed that the tendency to hoard knowledge will be reduced if control mechanisms match the nature of the task and motivational factors (Figure 4.1).

Methodology

As the subject is exploratory in nature, qualitative methodologies were used (Robson, 1993). Four case studies in different settings (Yin, 1984; Eisenhardt, 1989b) were conducted

Motivation

		Extrinsic	Intrinsic
Control mechanisms	**Social**	Hoard	Share
	Mechanistic	Share	Hoard

Figure 4.1 *The propensity to hoard or share: control mechanisms and motivation.*

between 1999 and 2001. The first case is a UK-based consulting engineering firm, the second a UK-based aircraft simulator manufacturer, the third a Canadian-based specialized supplier in the oil and gas industry, and the fourth a major management consultancy with offices in most major business centres. Semistructured interviews addressing KM policies, practices, tools and incentive structures designed to foster knowledge transfer were conducted. To address triangulation standardized protocols were used (Stake, 1995) and multiple sources within the company (senior and middle-level managers and practitioners) were interviewed, as suggested by Denzin (1984) and Yin (1984). Although all four firms are project-based organizations, operate internationally and are considered leaders in their respective fields, the incongruous industry categories illustrate a broad range of KM techniques. The fact that each organization operates under different circumstances allows for a useful contrast (Eisenhardt, 1989b) in how KM is conducted.

Case study firm A: Consulting engineers

Industry contingencies

Firm A is an international engineering consultancy with knowledge and expertise across a broad range of civil engineering sectors, providing design and management services for projects as diverse as maritime structures, roads, railway stations and bridges, as well as mechanical and electrical engineering-intensive structures for commercial or industrial use. Over the past few decades, the consulting engineering industry has enjoyed substantial and sustained growth due to high demand. Paradoxically, the industry suffers from a decline in new talent: in spite of opportunities in globally distributed project-based firms, consulting engineering does not appear to be an attractive career.

Firm level

According to firm A's technical director, a major problem with KM is that much of the important organizational knowledge resides with individual senior engineers, while junior engineers waste substantial amounts of time trying to access a senior engineer with the know-how to help solve a problem on a current project. The senior engineers' knowledge arises from experience of successive projects and its management is left almost entirely to individuals. Many keep indexed personal libraries of technical documentation, notes on lessons learned and drawings, but these are not accessible beyond the individuals. This problem has become particularly acute as the senior engineers are increasingly reaching retirement age and little knowledge is being transferred from the retiring engineers to their junior successors. There is a perception that this knowledge has been gained at the company's expense and it has some rights over it. As a technical director commented: 'Most of the things I've learned, I've learned because I've made mistakes … In fact, all of my experience has come out of this firm's turnover at some time or another'.

Senior management proposes to resolve these problems through the introduction of an intranet real-time project reporting system, where problem solving and lessons learned are captured and codified as they occur. One senior manager expected that the intranet would effectively replace the need for identifying and consulting people for everyday problems. However, this approach is counter to the manager's sophisticated understanding of knowledge transfer between people, which he maintains is primarily through storytelling. Despite the acknowledgement of the limitations of codification, KM strategies tend to revert to exercises in codification.

The current reality in firm A is that practitioners rarely use the intranet, particularly as there are few points of access around the organization.

The problem of retiring directors is being tackled through softer approaches. Senior management convenes brainstorming sessions typically involving a retiring director, the succeeding director and others with experience of working in the retiring director's market domain. The goal of the exercise is to capture information on all useful contacts gained in the particular market, the nature of projects completed, problems and notable successes, and the location of documents. An opportunity for reflection is incorporated through actionable items following the meeting and a subsequent follow-up meeting two weeks later. Although a softer approach, this project is also aimed at the urgent codification of the tacit knowledge of the retiring director. It was felt that a gradual handing over or mentoring period would not work, as the retiring director had no real incentive to share the knowledge or even the working of his filing system with his successor. This reveals the truly ingrained culture of retaining knowledge in the company: senior engineers would sooner take their knowledge with them into retirement than share it.

Case study firm B: Aerospace simulator manufacturer

Industry contingencies

The aerospace industry has traditionally emphasized performance over cost, primarily as a result of government influence (Hayward, 1994). However, circumstances changed after the collapse of the Soviet Union and the industry underwent major downsizing and consolidation. An emphasis on reducing costs through increased flexible manufacturing processes, subcontracting and systems integration replaced lucrative megaprojects and 'cost-plus' pricing policies (Chinwoth and Mowery, 1995; Velocci, 1996). It is under this industrial turbulence that firm B, a UK subsidiary of a multinational aerospace conglomerate and a major supplier of simulators for military and civil aviation, was attempting to develop knowledge capture and transfer systems.

Firm level

Like most aerospace companies, firm B emphasized its strong technical orientation, with expertise in software, mechanical and aeronautical engineering and systems integration capabilities. A co-operative approach with airframe manufacturers, customers, suppliers and other simulation manufacturers is required. For example, they need to liaise with aircraft manufacturers to ensure that their products replicate the aircraft feel and performance; the inside of a simulator has identical parts to a real aircraft. Meeting these criteria is particularly difficult when a new aircraft is being introduced, as customers need trained, certified pilots to operate the new aircraft before they are in operation.

More recently, budgetary and time constraints have become critical. Management believed that capturing and transferring 'lessons learned' from project to project is one technique that will allow them to meet these constraints, particularly for software activity where costs tend to overrun. Managing knowledge is therefore critical. According to a senior manager: 'The commercial environment is extraordinarily tough, and you cannot afford to have a lot of non recurring costs for every design …'.

Firm B operates a lessons learned programme, where a review is conducted at certain breakpoints and made available to project managers. It is an open process with full disclosure encouraged, positive and negative. However, the programme is not linked to the employee appraisal process, and is thus often an academic exercise rather than a potential source of valuable knowledge. One project manager believed that the programme documents are not commonly accessed; sometimes project managers request a previous lessons learned document simply to use as a formatting guideline. The problem is therefore more concerned with transfer than capture:

The actual gathering of the knowledge is good … But from then on, I'm not sure that the information then is spread out correctly ... it's almost, 'we've done the lessons learned, that goes to your engineering manager and he makes sure it's signed and then puts it in the bookcase' ...   although it's available, it's not actually used by other programmers ... I think the lessons learned are only carried into other programmes by the people who then move into those programmes (project manager).

Although firm B possesses a high degree of technical proficiency, it is apparent that the company is run by the accountants rather than by the technicians, while the organizational structure is designed to facilitate financial control. Given the narrow financial constraints imposed upon the industry, project accountability is very tight, with minimal overhead costing. For example, employees are sometimes discouraged from asking others for information, as a manager may question how this use of time will be accounted for. For example, one employee stated the following scenario:

We are very much structured with how much it costs for me to sit down with somebody for an hour ... my programme manager's paying for that and if someone is coming over to talk to me about a subject, they had better bring across an hour's worth of pay ....

If unexpected specialized expertise is needed, it has to be accounted for as an additional 'consultancy' expense, even if it comes from within the firm. Although management offer a reward scheme called 'Solutions' where employees receive a financial award for proposing improvements to the overall business, one project manager said that it was concerned with specific improvements and not knowledge capturing and transferring activities. The senior manager further stated that KM issues are not included in project performance measurements: 'You need a mature organization to do that, and this time it was challenging enough to deliver it to schedule and within budget'. The company's appraisal process is only concerned with the individual's ability to meet specified objectives, and has little consideration for knowledge capturing or transferring activities beyond financial accountability. Indeed,

according to one project manager, the capturing of information is actually cost based:

> ... the finance people have got all the information they
> want. They gather it and they know what's going on. But
> the whole company is set up to do that – it's not really set
> up to exchange any new information .... I think maybe the
> whole problem of communication within the company is
> the fact that everybody's got their little purse that they
> have to control ....

Case study firm C: Oil and gas service company

Industry contingencies

Firm C is a US-owned, Canadian-based supplier of physically
and technically complex products and services for the North
American oil and gas industry. Over the years the industry has
had to deal with high-capital investments in a fluctuating
commodity market. Environmental issues, health and safety
risks, human rights issues and other stakeholder concerns
have played a key role in the patterns of innovation (Sharma
and Vredenburg, 1998). Accumulating expertise to cope with
these pressures has been a central feature of KM within the
industry and the company.

Firm level

Although the company is geographically and functionally
segmented with cross-functional teams, firm C is culturally
divided into two distinct camps, the university-trained engineering group and the field operations group. Engineering is
responsible for the design and application of well treatments
and equipment fabrication. Within engineering, employee
turnover is consistently low (less than 5 per cent annually)
and postgraduate professional training is facilitated through
professional associations and communities of practice. A senior manager describes the engineers as 'a tight-knit group,
much like a family ... and they take great pride in their work'.

In contrast, recruitment of the field operations group is less formal: 'Recruiting is based on the Wrigley's concept: if you can chew gum and walk, you have a job' (senior manager). Once hired, they receive technical training by the company and are then sent to remote project sites where they continue to learn from their supervisors and gain experience. Although well compensated, the work is physically challenging and isolated. Labour turnover among field operations is as high as 40 per cent in the first six months, but drops to less than 4 per cent once they have been with the organization for more than a year. (The turnover rates are not considered unusual for this group owing to exceptionally competitive compensation packages offered by the oil and gas service firms during busy seasons.)

Although a technical business, there is no formal research and development. Knowledge is carried by individuals on a given project and transferred to the organization by both formal and informal mechanisms. One informal mechanism is a mentoring programme that was implemented in response to organizational growth and triggered by a senior manager who felt that the culture had 'degraded' to a point where it had become necessary to 'legislate caring' for fellow workers. Other informal mechanisms include project debriefings, which transpire only if a substantial problem has occurred. Mitigating loss of organizational intelligence was also cited as a primary objective behind policies such as internal promotion and interdepartmental transfers that facilitate knowledge pollination between cost centres.

Formal mechanisms include the annual business plan process and frequent technical and safety training. Firm C also operates a proprietary software system that incorporates over 7000 databases using conventional platforms (e.g. Excel, Lotus Notes, SAP) and a specialized treatment report system, which is mandatory for all 100-plus projects running on a given day. The latter is widely recognized as the firm's most timely and accurate source of information and is the most overt mechanism for capturing and transferring knowledge. The reports ideally trickle back to engineering, which uses them for 'historical matching', examining the requirements of new jobs and comparing them with solutions that worked in similar situations. Everyone has access to most information and employees are encouraged to use the system regularly to reference safety manuals, training materials, job opportunities, critical incident reports, and so on. The large set of databases, however, is admittedly cumbersome and navigating the system can be difficult, as employees are not always directed quickly to the specific information they require. Employees are also encouraged to use the system to document mistakes. (They are required by law to use the system if there is a lost time accident or a significant safety violation.) However, it was admitted that disciplinary procedures are inconsistent and an employee may be discouraged from documenting errors, thereby defeating opportunities to learn from the process.

Management realized that knowledge capture and transfer mechanisms would only work if they were linked to the incentives programme. It thus operates a bonus system that is tied to how well the employees use the above mechanisms. Funds for the bonuses come from an overhead of 3.7 per cent added to every project, and could be a substantial proportion of an employee's compensation package. However, it should be noted that these rewards are discretionary, and thus not necessarily an exact measure of how well the mechanisms are being employed.

Case study firm D: Management consultants

Industry contingencies

Firm D is a major international management consultancy, with 6000 consultants and practices dedicated to numerous business sectors and corporate functions. A main pressure in the industry is the ability to access knowledge and talent. Recruiting is competitive, and there are comparatively high employee turnover rates. According to Hansen et al. (1999), KM is critical to the industry, with two approaches, 'codification' versus 'personalization'. The former is a '… people-to-documents' approach' (p. 107) used by the consulting firms that have grown from accounting concerns. The second, a 'personalization' strategy is used by more specialized consulting firms and emphasizes networks of people and dialogue between individuals rather than via databases. Company D follows the latter strategy, and distinguishes itself from its competitors through a bespoke, rather than standardized approach to client studies. Greater knowledge is claimed to be the basis for their competitive advantage, which in turn is reflected in their substantial fees.

Firm level

All work is project based and targeted at specific client needs. Projects generate a considerable amount of knowledge that can be valuable to other projects, and the company thus promotes the sharing of knowledge. Explicit mechanisms include a wide range of electronic tools and databases as well as their own journal, while personal expertise is exploited through the firm's system of office transfers in the execution of client studies. Individuals with specific areas of expertise may be identified through an electronic yellow-pages system, which documents the firm's worldwide expertise, and the experts are expected to respond to a colleague's request within twenty-four hours. Consultants are encouraged to use this resource and internal evaluations look for evidence that attempts have been made to bring in the company's experts outside the local office. A North American-based manager revealed that he receives enquiries from colleagues throughout the world on a daily basis, half of whom he has had no prior contact with. The reach of knowledge sharing thus goes beyond 'know-who'.

Another powerful mechanism is the use of project review reports, which document 'lessons learned' as well as articulating new insights gleaned from projects. Given sufficient interest, these reports may then be developed into 'practice documents' and made available through a worldwide database to all employees. Approximately 4800 copies are requested from the various consulting teams each week. The pressure to write practice documents is described as 'a culture of codification of knowledge ... People do not want to discuss anything that is not in the pack' (European Manager).

The pressure to codify knowledge enforces a discipline on postproject discussions. About 70 per cent of the firm's consultants have authored practice documents, some of which generate sufficient interest that the company allocates funding for a research initiative, extending and consolidating the company's knowledge in an area perceived to be important across the firms' activities of interest. The leadership and management of these initiatives are considered an important career-step at the top end of the promotion ladder. 'To become a director you need a major initiative with your imprimatur' (North American manager). Only 20 per cent of the company's consultants achieve this level. Although tacit knowledge is acknowledged in the firm, it is also considered as slightly ephemeral and of limited use until it is codified and made available to colleagues. This supports a 'one-firm' ethos which is central to the company's internal and external cultural message.

Knowledge development is an explicit and critical part of the personnel appraisal process, and there are four levels to staff development in this regard. The first level is through transferring tacit knowledge to the immediate team, the second is through codifying it via practice documents, the third is a more general development project, and the fourth is the leadership of large initiatives. Consultants demonstrate their expertise and build reputations through moving up this hierarchy of knowledge development. Such knowledge demonstrations are critically important for new recruits as there is a very high attrition rate. New employees are told early in their career if they are likely to be 'partner material'. Those that are not are encouraged to leave as they are 'too good' to be a junior consultant indefinitely. Compiling concise, insightful practice documents is a powerful means by which consultants can establish a reputation.

To hoard or share?

Figure 4.2 illustrates the results of the study with respect to motivation and control mechanisms. Company D's KM appears to rely largely on incentives. The company's social

Motivation

		Extrinsic	Intrinsic
Control mechanisms	**Social**	**Hoard** Consulting engineers	**Share** Management consultants
	Mechanistic	**Share** Oil & gas	**Hoard** Aerospace simulator

Figure 4.2 *The propensity to hoard or share: control mechanisms and motivation (case studies).*

control mechanisms capitalize on career ambitions and egos (Brown and Starkey, 2000) and are appropriate for the intrinsic nature of its employees' motivational needs. This in turn encourages knowledge codification. The more a consultant's new knowledge and expertise are codified and disseminated, the more likely that the consultant's reputation will be enhanced and be rewarded. In addition, the social nature of the organization's incentives to codify, develop and disseminate personal knowledge helps to perpetuate the model, consistent with O'Dell and Grayson (1998), who state that reward for sharing knowledge is required to sustain such a culture. The corporate culture thus reflects a propensity for knowledge sharing and receiving, and offers the strategic benefits associated with KM without jeopardizing project completion.

Firm C explicitly rewards codification of knowledge through a bonus system that is controlled hierarchically (i.e. supervisors review and approve bonus allocations). The company's KM system thus uses mechanistic controls aligned to extrinsic motivational factors to encourage knowledge sharing. The fact that firm C's employees are less culturally homogeneous than firm D's seems to demand that they rely less heavily on social control mechanisms. While the management and engineering groups may be motivated to pursue knowledge capture and transfer activities through a social control system, the organization has chosen an outcome-orientated approach where bonuses are allocated based on corporate and regional success. A more mechanistic approach is in place to manage the predominantly transient field operators, who are rewarded specifically for completing knowledge capture documentation.

Firm B appears to be using mechanistic controls that inhibit the strategic KM objectives of the firm. The company's financial control system, adopted to compete in an industry that had undergone significant restructuring, was focused on the overriding pressure to avoid cost overruns (i.e. extrinsic motivation) and neglected intrinsic motivational factors such as project-to-project knowledge sharing. There was thus little room for organizational slack and no clear reward system for transferring knowledge, even though management fully realized the benefits of not repeating mistakes. The difficult industrial context faced by the firm highlights the restrictive features such as downsizing (Fisher and White, 2000) and high employee turnover (Cross and Baird, 2000), which can generate conflicts between short-term and long-term pressures (Cross and Baird, 2000) and competition for scarce resources (March, 1991). Firm B is therefore in the difficult position of evaluating both the cost and the potential benefits of a more effective knowledge transfer system. It is suggested that their financial control model is perhaps incomplete rather than entirely inappropriate: there are insufficient incentives in place that indicate to employees the appropriate balance between extrinsic (i.e. budgetary pressures) and intrinsic motivations (i.e. strategically valuable knowledge). Managers will ultimately be concerned with the mechanics by which their performance is judged, and will seek information about the responsiveness of the system in rewarding performance (Fama, 1980).

Firm A is characterized as social and extrinsic in its incentives with the effect of hoarding knowledge. The consulting engineers' personal career paths were aligned with the company's objectives since accumulating expertise in silos (O'Dell and Grayson, 1998) was consistent with the diversified horizontal market strategy of the organization. Extrinsic motivation concerned with career progress and professional prestige (Brown and Starkey, 2000) supported the logic of personal hoarding of specialized knowledge. However, what is also clear from the case is that the strategy and incentive system were incongruent with the demographic trends in the industry.

The system was top-heavy, favouring the senior engineers and denying the younger recruits the channels to learning and knowledge that would make the profession more attractive for younger people. This case demonstrates how industry contingencies can influence internal KM systems in a dynamic sense and how the firm may need to adjust the reward system to fit the new priorities.

The ability to capture and transfer knowledge has been widely accepted as a strategically valuable capability, particularly in project-based firms, yet fraught with difficulties. There are inherent reasons – what Winter (1987) would call the 'state variables' – why this should be so in project-based firms, in terms of discontinuity and the novelty of projects, as well as the limits to disembodied knowledge. However, the authors have argued that in addition to these issues, the tendency to share or hoard knowledge is dependent on the organizational incentives and how they are perceived by individual employees. This is first through the control systems identified in agency theory, whether they are mechanistic (behavioural or outcomes based) or social (Eisenhardt, 1985). The control system, in conjunction with the nature of the motivation for the individual (i.e. either extrinsic or intrinsic), is thus a major determinant in knowledge-sharing or knowledge-hoarding behaviour. However, it should also be noted that there are considerable contingencies that influence control and reward mechanisms; knowledge sharing is thus a multifaceted issue and cannot be understood through isolated factors. Incentives must therefore align with the firm's specific resource constraints, capabilities and industrial setting to facilitate knowledge sharing. Firm-specific KM systems should come as no surprise, given the unique nature of valuable resources.

Conclusions

This chapter has presented four case studies of project-based firms and through exploratory, open-ended interviews with practitioners and managers at various levels has identified key KM issues, control systems, motivational influences and industrial circumstances. Each of the cases was analyzed across the stated dimensions and was characterized as occupying one quadrant in the matrix. The point here is not that any one firm should be a perfect fit, but that the framework is a useful analytical tool in rapidly eliciting the important determinants of knowledge-hoarding or knowledge-sharing behaviour. Once the key influences have been determined, the company may begin to isolate its structural constraints from what it may control. One can imagine instances where firms could migrate around the matrix given the diagnosis and willingness to change. The analytical framework should thus be seen as a conceptual aid to understanding the incentive processes of knowledge capture and transfer, which the authors argue should be considered together with the tools and processes of documentation and distribution. Ultimately, explicit KM tools such as intranets, lessons learned reports and expert systems are destined to underperform or fail if the underlying incentive and motivational characteristics are not understood.

References

Argote, L., McEvily, B. and Reagans, R. (2003) Managing knowledge in organisations: an integrative framework and review of emerging themes. *Management Science* 49(4): 571–583.

Barney, J. (1991) Firm resources and sustained competitive advantage. *Journal of Management* 17(1): 99–121.

Bartezzaghi, E., Corso, M. and Verganti, R. (1997) Continuous improvement and inter-project learning in new product development. *International Journal of Technology Management* 14(1): 116–138.

Birkinshaw, J., Nobel, R. and Ridderstrale, J. (2002) Knowledge as a contingency variable: do the characteristics of knowledge predict organisational structure? *Organization Science* 13(3): 274–289.

Blackler, F. (1995) Knowledge, knowledge work and organisations: an overview and interpretation. *Organisation Studies* 16(6): 1021–1046.

Boisot, M. (1998) *Knowledge Assets: Securing Competitive Advantage in the Information Economy*. Oxford: Oxford University Press.

Brown, A. and Starkey, K. (2000) Organisational identity and learning: a psychodynamic perspective. *Academy of Management Review* 25(1): 102–120.

Chinworth, M. and Mowery, D. (1995) Cross-border linkages and the US defense industry: outlook and policy challenges. *Technovation* 15(3): 133–152.

Cohen, W. M. and Levinthal, D. (1990) Absorptive capacity: a new perspective on learning and innovation. *Administrative Science Quarterly* 35(1): 128–152.

Cook, S. and Brown, J. (1999) Bridging epistemologies: the generative dance between organisational knowledge and organisational knowing. *Organization Science* 10(4): 381–400.

Cross, R. and Baird, L. (2000) Technology is not enough: improving performance by building organisational memory. *MIT Sloan Management Review* 41(3): 69–78.

Das, A. (2003) Knowledge and productivity in technical support work. *Management Science* 49(4): 416–431.

DeFillippi, R. J. and Arthur, M. B. (1998) Paradox in project-based enterprize: the case of film making. *California Management Review* 40(2): 125–138.

Denzin, N. (1984) *The Research Act*. Englewood Cliffs, NJ: Prentice-Hall.

Dixon, N. M. (2000) *Common Knowledge: How Companies Thrive by Sharing What They Know*. Cambridge, MA: Harvard Business School Press.

Dutta, S. (1997) Strategies for implementing knowledge-based systems. *IEEE Transactions on Engineering Management* 44(1): 79–90.

Eisenhardt, K. M. (1985) Control: organisational and economic approaches. *Management Science* 31(2): 134–149.

Eisenhardt, K. M. (1989a) Agency theory: an assessment and review. *Academy of Management Review* 14(1): 57–74.

Eisenhardt, K. M. (1989b) Building theories from case study research. *Academy of Management Review* 14(4): 532–551.

Fama, E. (1980) Agency problems and the theory of the firm. *Journal of Political Economy* 88: 288–307.

Fisher, S. and White, M. (2000) Downsizing in a learning organisation: are there hidden costs? *Academy of Management Review* 25(1): 244–251.

Gann, D. and Salter, A. (2000) Innovation in project-based, service-enhanced firms: the construction of complex products and systems. *Research Policy* 29(7/8): 955–972.

Grant, R. M. (1996) Toward a knowledge-based theory of the firm. *Strategic Management Journal* 17: 109–122.

Gupta, A. and Govindarajan, V. (2000) Knowledge management's social dimension: lessons from Nucor Steel. *Sloan Management Review* 42(1): 71–81.

Hansen, M., Nohria, N. and Tierney, T. (1999) What's your strategy for managing knowledge? *Harvard Business Review* (March/April): 106–116.

Hayek, F. (1945) The use of knowledge in society. *American Economic Review* 35: 9–31.

Hayward, K. (1994) *The World Aerospace Industry: Competition and Collaboration*. London: Duckworth.

Jensen, M. and Meckling, W. (1976) Theory of the firm: managerial behavior, agency costs, and ownership structure. *Journal of Financial Economics* 3: 305–360.

Jensen, M. and Meckling, W. (1992) Specific and general knowledge and organisational structure. In Werin, L. and Wijkander, H. (eds) *Contract Economics*. Oxford: Blackwell, pp. 251–274.

Keegan, A. and Turner, J. R. (2002) The management of innovation in project-based firms. *Long Range Planning* 35(4): 367–388.

Kogut, B. and Zander, U. (1992) Knowledge of the firm, combinative capabilities, and the replication of technology. *Organization Science* 3(3): 383–397.

Lord, M. and Ranft, A. (2000) Organisational learning about new international markets: exploring the internal transfer of local market knowledge. *Journal of International Business Studies* 31(4): 573–590.

McDermott, R. (1999) Why information technology inspired but cannot deliver knowledge management. *California Management Review* 41(4): 103–117.

March, J. (1991) Exploration and exploitation in organisational learning. *Organization Science* 2: 71–87.

Marshall, N. and Sapsed, J. (2000) The limits of disembodied knowledge: challenges of inter-project learning in the production of complex products and systems. *Proceedings of the Knowledge Management: Concepts and Controversies Conference*, Warwick University, UK, 10–11 February.

Nelson, R. (1994) Why do firms differ, and how does it matter? In Rumelt, R. P., Schendel, D. E. and Teece, D. J. (eds) *Fundamental Issues in Strategy*. Cambridge, MA: Harvard Business School Press, pp. 247–270.

Nonaka, I. and Takeuchi, H. (1995) *The Knowledge-Creating Company*. New York: Oxford University Press.

O'Dell, C. and Grayson, C. (1998) If only we knew what we know: identification and transfer of internal best practices. *California Management Review* 40(3): 154–174.

Osterloh, M. and Frey, B. (2000) Motivation, knowledge transfer, and organisational forms. *Organization Science* 11(5): 538–550.

Peteraf, M. (1993) The cornerstones of competitive advantage: a resource-based view. *Strategic Management Journal* 14: 179–192.

Polanyi, M. (1962) *Personal Knowledge – Towards a Post-critical Philosophy*. London: Routledge and Kegan Paul.

Prencipe, A. and Tell, F. (2001) Inter-project learning: processes and outcomes of knowledge codification in project-based firms. *Research Policy* 30(9): 1373–1394.

Robson, C. (1993) *Real World Research*. Cambridge: Blackwell.

Sarvary, M. (1999) Knowledge management and competition in the consulting industry. *California Management Review* 41(2): 95–107.

Schein, E. (1985) *Organizational Culture and Leadership*. San Francisco, CA: Jossey-Bass.

Sharma, S. and Vredenburg, H. (1998) Proactive corporate environmental strategy and the development of competitively valuable organisational capabilities. *Strategic Management Journal* 19: 729–753.

Singley, M. and Anderson, J. (1989) *The Transfer of Cognitive Skill*. Cambridge, MA: Harvard University Press.

Stake, R. (1995) *The Art of Case Research*. Newbury Park, CA: Sage.

Szulanski, G. (1995) Unpacking stickiness: an empirical investigation of the barriers to transfer best practice inside the firm. *Academy of Management Journal*, Special Issue: Best Papers Proceedings, 437–446.

Szulanski, G. (1996) Exploring internal stickiness: impediments to the transfer of best practice within the firm. *Strategic Management Journal* 17: 27–43.

Szulanski, G. (2003) *Sticky Knowledge: Barriers to Knowing in the Firm*. London: Sage.

Teece, D. (1998) Capturing value from knowledge assets: the new economy, markets for know-how, and intangible assets. *California Management Review* 40(3): 55–79.

Uzzi, B. and Lancaster, R. (2003) Relational embeddedness and learning: the case of bank loan managers and their clients. *Management Science* 49(4): 383–400.

Velocci, A. (1996) Small vendor a model for lower tier suppliers. *Aviation Week and Space Technology* (3 June): 71–72.

Wernerfelt, B. (1984) A resource-based view of the firm. *Strategic Management Journal* 5: 171–180.

Winter, S. (1987) Knowledge and competence as strategic assets. In Teece, D. J. (ed.) *The Competitive Challenge: Strategies for Industrial Innovation and Renewal*. Cambridge, MA: Ballinger.

Yin, R. (1984) *Case Study Research: Design and Methods*. Beverly Hills, CA: Sage.

Zack, M. H. (1999) Managing codified knowledge. *Sloan Management Review* 40(4): 45–58.

Chapter 5

A community perspective on managing knowledge in project environments

Mike Bresnen, Linda Edelman, Sue Newell, Harry Scarbrough and Jacky Swan

Introduction

The importance of managing knowledge for competitive advantage has received a considerable amount of attention in the past decade. Until fairly recently, however, comparatively little attention has been directed towards examining the specific problems associated with managing knowledge in project environments (DeFillippi, 2001; Prencipe and Tell, 2001). This is somewhat surprising, given the importance of projects in contemporary organizations (Drucker, 1993; Ekstedt et al., 1999; Hobday, 2000). However, it is less surprising perhaps when one considers that managing knowledge in a project-based setting faces particular challenges. As projects are often 'one-off' and relatively self-contained, discontinuities are created within the organization that make it difficult to develop steady-state routines and maximize the flow of knowledge and learning between projects (DeFillippi and Arthur, 1998). In sectors such as the construction industry, which provides the case material for this chapter, these problems are compounded by the fragmentation of the project team into different professional disciplines (Bresnen, 1990). Each discipline has its own knowledge base and language, which can make the effective codification and diffusion of knowledge even more problematic.

Early debates on knowledge management (KM) centred upon the use of information technology (IT) and communication technology (Cole-Gomolski, 1997; Finerty, 1997). However, it has long been recognized that there are limitations to a purely IT-based view of knowledge codification and capture (Bijker et al., 1987; Tsoukas, 1996; Spender, 1996; Fahey and Prusak, 1998; Swan et al., 1999). Although a good deal of knowledge within organizations may be codified using IT-based tools and techniques, approaches to KM have increasingly explored the ways in which social structures and processes influence the capture and diffusion of knowledge and learning (Blackler, 1995; Brown and Duguid, 2001). The main problem here is that knowledge becomes much more difficult to exploit, even when it can be clearly articulated. This is because it requires appropriate social networks for distributing knowledge and a shared system of meaning for understanding, accepting and using that knowledge (Orr, 1990; Orlikowski, 1996). Consequently, it becomes important to understand the ways in which social structures and processes influence the nature of knowledge and learning, and the impact they have upon attempts to codify knowledge using information and communication technologies.

There is very little detailed research available on the social mechanisms that support knowledge sharing, especially across projects and the different communities of practice that they bring together. Thus, to help to understand further the impact of social processes on KM in project environments, this chapter draws upon research recently conducted in the UK that was designed to explore KM for project-based learning. The research aimed to identify enablers and barriers to the effective capture and transfer of knowledge across projects. Although the study as a whole explored project-based learning across a range of sectors, including pharmaceuticals, telecommunications, construction, health and social services (Edelman et al., 2004), this chapter draws exclusively from the one sector where project working was the norm, namely, construction. The case involved the introduction by a contracting firm of new management processes that were explicitly designed to encourage cross-project learning and knowledge sharing. In effect, the company was attempting to develop a systematic social mechanism for encouraging knowledge sharing and learning across projects, where traditionally this had been done in an ad hoc manner and via the use of IT. The case study therefore provided an opportunity to highlight and examine the role of social factors in enhancing KM capabilities in construction and to draw out more general implications for other project environments.

Managing knowledge in project environments

Project organization ought to be a setting that is highly conducive to innovation. After all, projects typically involve the development of new products and processes, and so provide clear opportunities for new ideas to emerge in a cross-functional, team-working context: conditions that are important in encouraging learning within the organization (Senge, 1990). Indeed, projects are increasingly being seen not only as flexible and adaptable organizational forms in their own right (Drucker, 1993; Hobday, 2000), but also as vehicles of change in traditionally structured organizational settings (Ekstedt et al., 1999; Grabher, 2002). Managing knowledge effectively in project settings therefore has wider implications for understanding organizational learning and change processes.

Recent studies of KM and organizational learning in project environments have tended to emphasize the difficulties faced in capturing project-based learning and diffusing knowledge and learning across projects (DeFillippi, 2001; Prencipe and Tell, 2001). The reasons for this are not difficult to find. Project organizations encounter serious obstacles to the capture and reuse of project-based learning that stem from the 'one-off', relatively self-contained nature of many projects. The finite nature of projects in itself creates discontinuities in the flows of personnel, information and other resources from one project to the next. Capturing and diffusing knowledge and learning across projects (or even between phases within projects) becomes difficult, as does avoiding a tendency to 'reinvent the wheel' when faced with problems and decisions on new projects (Gann and Salter, 2000). In the construction sector, additional problems are created by the complex division of labour between occupational groups involved in the construction management process (Cherns and Bryant, 1984; Bresnen, 1990). Inevitably, such a fragmentation of expertise along organizational lines has adverse effects on attempts to develop shared perspectives on innovation, knowledge and learning (Brown and Duguid, 1991; Lave and Wenger, 1991).

Overcoming barriers to effective KM may involve various types of intervention, which reflect the extent to which knowledge is embedded in organizational systems and processes or embodied in the skill sets of individuals and groups (Blackler, 1995). It is possible, however, to classify existing approaches according to whether they tend towards a 'cognitive' or 'community' model of KM (Swan et al., 1999). The cognitive model stresses the codification of knowledge and is primarily concerned with the application of information and communication technologies to the retention and circulation of knowledge within the organization (Cole-Gomolski, 1997). It is perhaps the most pervasive approach to KM, being driven in large part by the increasing availability of information-based tools such as groupware and intranets. In the construction sector, for instance, much recent work on KM still emphasizes the opportunities created by the application of such technologies (Robinson et al., 2001). However, many of the assumptions underlying this approach have been challenged by studies that question the emphasis placed on explicit knowledge and the stress on knowledge codification through technology (Spender, 1996; Tsoukas, 1996; Swan et al., 1999).

In contrast, the community model emphasizes the tacit dimension of knowledge and the importance of social context (Brown and Duguid, 2001). According to this approach, tacit knowledge is difficult to exploit organizationally because its sharing or appropriation requires a shared mental model or system of meaning that enables individuals and groups to understand and learn from one another (Schwenk, 1988). Shared meanings and understandings that allow one group to understand and apply another's insights to their own context are therefore essential for the diffusion of knowledge (Orr, 1990; Weick, 1995; Orlikowski, 1996). Crucially important are social networks and the development of shared values and norms, such as reciprocity and trust. Such norms are often found in 'communities of practice' (Brown and Duguid, 1991, 2001; Lave and Wenger, 1991; Wenger, 2000), where individuals share ideas and thus construct meaningful knowledge through collaborative mechanisms such as narration and joint work. This process of constructing meaning through joint endeavour provides organizational members with identity and cohesiveness and provides the basis for effective learning. Importantly, the creation, diffusion and application of knowledge are situated in and heavily influenced by the particular context of practice (Lave and Wenger, 1991).

The importance of social processes, however, draws attention precisely to the problems of knowledge diffusion and learning in project settings. Since project teams are temporarily constituted, often geographically dispersed and regularly disbanded and recombined, it becomes difficult to develop well-established communities of practice. In such circumstances, the challenge is not so much to make tacit knowledge explicit (Nonaka, 1994), but to establish how social practices facilitate or inhibit learning and so find ways of reconfiguring them to enable more effective cross-project knowledge diffusion and learning. Precise and immediate project objectives, coupled with a finite lifespan of activity, may act as a practical focus for innovative team efforts. However, because they emphasize the immediate task, they can work against the development of a more widely dispersed organizational community of practice based on shared experiences and understandings. Project organization can thus promote localized learning and encourage the internal 'stickiness' of knowledge that makes its wider organizational diffusion problematic (Szulanski, 1996).

At the same time, it has been noted that knowledge can 'leak' across organizations, in so far as those organizations are enmeshed within multiple, cross-cutting communities of practice (Brown and Duguid, 2001). In certain project environments, such as construction and the media, attempts to develop informal networks for the spread of knowledge and learning inevitably cut across strong institutional, professional and contractual boundaries and demarcations (Windeler and Sydow, 2001). Indeed, it has been argued that such fragmentation has had a detrimental effect on innovation within the construction sector (Winch, 1998; Gann, 2001), through reducing companies' 'absorptive capacity' – their ability to recognize the value of new knowledge, assimilate it with existing knowledge, and apply it to commercial ends (Cohen and Levinthal, 1990). Consequently, the need to fulfil immediate short-term project goals to meet diverse client requirements (which are further filtered through designers' specifications) may have significant negative effects on attempts by individual contracting firms to develop their long-term innovative capabilities (Winch, 1998).

Given this particular type of context, therefore, many important and unanswered questions remain about managing knowledge in project environments and about the factors that influence project-based learning. Principal among these is what part social processes play in the creation and diffusion of knowledge and learning and how these processes relate to the use of technological and other mechanisms specifically intended to capture and transfer knowledge and learning between projects.

Methodology

To address this question, this chapter draws upon research designed to explore KM for project-based learning across various sectors of activity in the UK. The research as a whole took five case studies, one each from the construction, telecommunications, pharmaceuticals, health and social services sectors. Although this chapter only draws upon the construction case study (see also Bresnen et al., 2003), the findings apply to the other cases and material from three other cases is briefly introduced later on to demonstrate key points (Edelman et al., 2004).

All of the projects investigated involved either the development of a new product or service or the introduction of a new management practice. The construction case was one of the latter, with the specific focus of enquiry being a recent reorganization of engineering expertise within the firm. Consequently, the case study was of a change to management processes, rather than the construction of a new project (such as a new road or building). Nevertheless, the initiative did have distinct project characteristics, with specific objectives, a timescale for implementation, a project manager/champion, and systems for monitoring and evaluating the change.

The research relied primarily on semistructured interviews conducted with seven managers involved in the reorganization. These included senior engineering staff and also operations and engineering staff from site and head office level. All interviews were tape-recorded and followed a predesigned interview protocol based on a six-page interview schedule. The schedule covered questions related to the generation and capture of learning within the project and the inward/outward knowledge transfer to and from other groups in the organization. Open-ended questions were specifically asked about: the nature of the project and the role of project team members, mechanisms and practices used for the communication and documentation of knowledge transfer and learning (including the use of information and communication technologies), broader structural/cultural characteristics of the organizations concerned, incentives and motivations for knowledge sharing, and effects on outcomes (knowledge transfer, learning and project performance). Further background information was also obtained from relevant documentation.

Case study: the REM project

This project involved the introduction of a new regional engineering manager (REM) role into a construction company. The aim of the change was to improve company performance by increasing the value engineering of projects, co-ordinating engineering services provision, and providing more effective support, training and career development for engineers. The REM role was to be a conduit for the diffusion of engineering-based knowledge and project-based learning throughout the company. As such, it represented a KM mechanism in its own right.

Project context

The company was a national contractor operating across four regions with an annual turnover of £370 million, consisting mainly of building and civil engineering work (£160 million and £150 million, respectively). The REM role was first proposed five to six years earlier to improve communications within engineering and to assist with the tendering process, particularly with regard to value engineering. At the time of research, ten REMs were employed in the company, including two in each region (one building, one civil engineering). The creation of the role was part of a wider internal transformation process that had started in 1994/95, and which saw an attempt to change from an adversarial style of contracting to greater collaboration. According to the company's technical director: 'a lot of trouble we had got ourselves into, one way or the other [was] due to bad engineering'. A centre of excellence in engineering was established at head office, although engineering in the regions (which were now all established businesses) was not considered to be as strong or as well connected in to the centre.

As the company was receptive to suggestions for change, it did not take much persuasion at board level to introduce the role and REMs were fairly quickly appointed. The REM had three key functions: to contribute towards putting together tenders, to value engineer tenders and existing projects, and to assist with the training and development of site engineers. The position was designed for a midlevel engineer, ideally someone who had been working with the company for a while and who knew what expertise was available. It provided a career route for those who preferred to stay in engineering, rather than take the usual route via site management. The original intention was therefore to recruit entirely from within the company.

As the costs of employing ten REMs in the business amounted to about £0.5 million per annum, the role needed to be cost-effective. Although financial savings targets had originally been set when the role was first established, REMs now performed according to a list of twelve expected 'results', varying from the general (e.g. expecting them to be 'leaders within every business') to the more specific (e.g. establishment of a register of expertise). Many of these centred upon key KM activities, as the REM was expected to be the major link between the sites and regional office and a point of contact for site managers in case of any problems or requests for engineering advice or redesign. Without the REM, there was little possibility of capturing and sharing knowledge and learning between sites and projects. According to one REM, 'Knowledge transfer has been poor. The guys learn it and the only knowledge transfer is [on the] basis of senior engineers working with another engineer on the next job'.

Indeed, REMs themselves were expected to be the embodiment of the collective learning capability of the organization. According to the technical director, 'One of the reasons for the REMs was to have some sort of stability, some focus in the region. A longstayer, if you like, to develop the experience and the expertise in the business so that we are not reinventing the wheel all the time'.

Although it was generally regarded by those interviewed as a successful initiative, the introduction of the role had not been without its problems and early difficulties were experienced in producing a clear job description and selecting qualified staff. According to the technical director, 'The accountabilities were a little vague, and so the REMs weren't sure what they were going to be doing'.

To counter these problems, more specific job descriptions were drawn up and more external appointments were made. However, problems still persisted as different regions emphasized different parts of the job. Overall, there was a tendency for REMs to be more involved in value engineering activity than in the longer term, staff development aspects of the role where outcomes were less immediate and tangible. One REM estimated that the actual time spent on particular tasks (as opposed to that planned) was 70 per cent on tenders (as opposed to 40 per cent), 15 per cent engineering on 'live' contracts (as opposed to 20 per cent), 10 per cent on training and development (as opposed to 30 per cent) and 5 per cent on linking skills on jobs (as opposed to 10 per cent). As the REM did not have any staff of their own or any direct control over site engineers, it meant that they had to matrix manage staff and to rely upon a supportive climate to get their work done. A further consequence was that their success depended significantly upon the skills and aptitudes of the person doing the job (especially communication, persuasion and interpersonal skills).

Networking and modes of communication

REMs relied heavily upon networks of personal contacts inside and outside the firm. E-mail was used extensively as a mode of communication and as a way of eliciting or distributing knowledge. According to one REM, 'If I have a good idea, say, I do that on a report sheet then I will put it on the e-mail to each of the REMs in all regions. They have then got the same information I have got.' However, by adding that 'It's up to the REMs to send that information', he also drew attention to the fact that most communications tended to be query driven. Furthermore, it was very clear from the interviews that, although e-mail was used, so too were other more personal forms of direct contact. For example, although the company had an internal register of expertise, personal knowledge of who to contact was considered much more important.

REMs would meet together every three months at engineering forums to discuss a wide range of issues and to build and reinforce personal contacts and networks. They also arranged biannual forums for site engineers who would meet to discuss project successes and failures, new jobs, current issues, grievances and the like. Apart from this, contact with engineers on site, to provide technical support and career advice, was frequent and informal. However, it was also sporadic and largely in response to queries that were raised. The transfer of technical knowledge between site engineers tended to be largely by word of mouth. More formal processes, such as a system of quality alerts linked to the BS (British Standards) procedures developed by the company's QA (Quality Assurance) manager, did exist. However, this information did not always find its way to REMs or dovetail with other project review procedures.

Although the company had a solid IT infrastructure and used e-mail regularly, the company intranet and associated engineering database were not well used. According to the technical director, 'I find it's easier to dial…one of our regional offices, than it is to get on to the intranet'. Apart from the lack of a standardized system, there were no resources or incentives to keep the database up to date and accurate. As a result, there was still a very strong emphasis placed on direct, face-to-face and telephone contact for communicating and transmitting information across the company. As the technical director put it, 'In these days of electronic wizardry and technology, my opinion is that you can't beat a face-to-face, eyeball-to-eyeball meeting'.

Enablers and barriers to knowledge capture and diffusion

Overall, therefore, there were several important factors that enabled or inhibited the effective capture and diffusion of knowledge via the REM role.

- *Organizational structure effects*: as the drive to establish the REM role came from the centre and as the change project was located within engineering, any problems associated with cross-disciplinary communication were avoided. The size of the company also allowed economies of scale in the use of certain social mechanisms that encouraged cross-regional and cross-project knowledge transfer (e.g. the engineers' forums and training programmes). However, REMs faced a lack of clear definition of roles and responsibilities, especially in the early stages. This role ambiguity could lead to a regression to a more traditional engineering support role and, depending on regional directors' expectations and demands, the tendency for immediate workload pressures to take precedence over longer term developmental needs. Moreover, REMs needed to be proactive and persuasive, as they employed no direct staff (and would be unlikely to be able to justify more help) and had no line authority over engineers.
- *Cultural context and the climate for change*: it was important that the current technical director had been a 'champion' in getting the change introduced in the first place and was able to clarify the role when early problems occurred. Continuing support across the company as a whole was also important. Although REMs were expected to achieve a lot in terms of 'bottom-line' results, it was clear that the climate for change was supportive and that the company was receptive to the idea and convinced by the business case made (and, as a result, had relaxed financial targets).

However, the level of support varied across the regions, especially when the role was first introduced. Moreover, there were still considered to be what one manager described as 'pockets of resistance' and some concerns were expressed that recent restructuring changes would have (unspecified) implications for the role.

- *Skills and capabilities*: the importance of the style of those occupying the role meant that, on the positive side, REMs had considerable discretion in how they performed their role. However, it meant that a lot depended on personal contacts and informal networks (as well as their enthusiasm and personal skills in developing them). The importance of the role occupant also meant that the company had been forced to recruit from outside, thereby reducing the internal career opportunities that the REM position was intended to open up.

- *Communications, networks and information flows*: the network of REMs (each with their own external networks and contacts) provided the information, knowledge and support the REMs needed to help them to diffuse knowledge within their own regions. However, while contact between REMs within the firm (and between REMs and engineers) was frequent, it was rather irregular, informal and ad hoc, and very much in response to specific queries. The geographical spread of sites still had a detrimental effect on the diffusion of knowledge because of the disjunctures created in social networks. There were also other barriers to the free flow of knowledge, information and advice. These stemmed from contractual considerations, the lack of integration of separate information flows (e.g. the distinct 'quality alerts' system), and the lack of mechanisms for capturing project learning (postproject reviews were described by one REM as more like 'post mortems').

- *Technological mechanisms*: e-mail systems were clearly an important enabler of communication, especially between REMs, but also (potentially) among sites and between sites and regional offices. However, several problems were identified with the use of the intranet and company website. These included lack of standardization of the system, practical difficulties in accessing the intranet and website from site offices, a lack of incentive to use and update information on the website and a lack of resources to keep the website up to date and accurate.

- *Objectives and outputs*: although there were some ambiguities, clear objectives for the role nevertheless did provide a framework for monitoring and appraising REM performance. However, while the emphasis on value engineering encouraged the direct application of engineering knowledge to immediate practical business problems, it also led to less emphasis being placed on more developmental aspects that related to the longer term accumulation and development of engineering knowledge.

Discussion

The first point to make about the case concerns the fact that the project involved a management reorganization, rather than the development of a new product or service. Most existing research on project-based learning naturally tends to focus on product innovation (Tidd, 1995). However, this case was primarily concerned with process innovation. The distinction is important, because what emerges from the case is that process innovations such as the REM pose particularly difficult problems for knowledge capture, diffusion and learning. Learning in product innovation projects tends to follow a convergent logic: diverse sources of knowledge are progressively integrated within a single product or service specification. Learning can be captured and more easily transferred in explicit forms, via product design templates, for example. In the case of process innovation, however, what is learned is often tacit, intangible and context dependent, involving changes in work practices, roles and responsibilities, and attitudes and values. Such learning is difficult to capture in explicit forms, in ways that can be easily understood and applied in new contexts (or even applied consistently across different parts of the firm, as demonstrated in the REM case). The resultant knowledge and learning is also easily reinterpretable and subject to complex sense-making processes (Dervin, 1998; Shariq, 1998). Together, these features make such knowledge difficult to embed within organizational systems and standard routines, as well as difficult to enculture within wider collective organizational norms and values (Blackler, 1995).

An implication of this is that process innovations, perhaps more than product innovations, depend crucially upon the context and environment for change, as well as upon the change process itself (Pettigrew and Whipp, 1991). Many studies have highlighted the importance of the wider organizational context for the capture and dissemination of knowledge and learning (e.g. Kogut and Zander, 1992). Clear evidence emerges too from this case study of the importance of a committed project champion (Ginsberg and Abrahamson, 1991) who was able to span internal boundaries and present the case for change to key audiences. It was evident too that a shared ideology and vision of change created the right conditions for the introduction of the new role and that appropriate and adequate resources were made available. However, it is crucially important to acknowledge the inherently political nature of this context. The fact that the initiative fitted in well with an internal discourse that favoured change was not insignificant. Nor was the requirement to present a convincing business case that aligned short-term, tangible outcomes with long-term, developmental aims.

Another implication of the difficulty of embedding such knowledge in practice is that success depends crucially upon interpersonal and social aspects, rather than technological or procedural mechanisms (Hansen et al., 1999). The case illustrated well some of the limitations of using it and other formal systems to diffuse engineering knowledge and learning throughout the network of engineers. Managing knowledge certainly involved the use of documents and electronic communication. However, the case not only demonstrated some of the practical difficulties in using electronic means to link geographically diverse teams (particularly across sites), but also highlighted some of the behavioural factors that influence the use of such technologies (McLoughlin, 1999). Key problems faced were the difficulties in motivating staff to use and refresh the databases available (Scarbrough and Carter, 2000), as well as the strong tendency to revert to interpersonal forms of contact whenever new information or knowledge was needed.

Indeed, what emerges from the case overall is the importance of social and behavioural processes, as opposed to the use of technology aimed at the codification of new knowledge. Given the importance of tacit elements of knowledge combined with the limitations on being able to codify or capture it, knowledge tended to be embodied and 'embrained' (Blackler, 1995) in members of the network of engineers within the firm. REMs were themselves seen as the embodiment of the 'corporate memory' for engineering expertise. The importance attached to personal networks for accessing knowledge, the value attached to regular discussion forums and the significance of the deployment of engineers from one project team to the next as the main means of cross-project learning all signified the importance of the social dimension.

Particularly important, perhaps, were the shared meanings and understandings about engineers' needs within the firm that the role helped to reinforce. Not only did a shared concern with disseminating information, advice and support help to bind together the network of REMs, it also brought together engineers distributed across sites within the organization (site engineers who were interviewed were very positive about the support now available). Reinforcing norms of knowledge sharing was therefore a vital part of the success of the initiative. Achieving this is often difficult in project organization, as many projects are multidisciplinary and face precisely the problem of integrating cross-functional contributions and perspectives (Hansen, 2002). The point here, however, is that success in diffusing knowledge and learning still depended upon developing a shared vision for the role and appropriate norms of knowledge sharing, despite the single disciplinary context. In other words, to leverage the available 'social capital' among engineers within the firm, cognitive and relational aspects were vitally important (Nahapiet and Ghoshal, 1998).

The social networks of individual engineers were also clearly important in providing the basis for support for REMs (Nahapiet and Ghoshal, 1998; Adler and Kwon, 2002). Networks that extended across and beyond the firm gave the REMs access to a wider realm of relevant technical knowledge and expertise, thus potentially providing a way of enhancing the firm's absorptive capacity (Cohen and Levinthal, 1990).

Indeed, it could be argued that such networking across the organization and beyond becomes more crucial in process innovation projects that, by definition, tend to cut across existing processes and routines. Consequently, it was important that REMs were able to act as 'knowledge brokers', bringing together their own personal networks (including information sources from outside the organization) and connecting them to the operational side (through their role in tendering and in supporting site engineers). Wenger (2000) describes 'boundary spanners' and 'roamers', both of which apply well to the REM role. The case study therefore helps to confirm the importance of strong network ties for the sharing of tacit knowledge and of non-redundant weak ties for accessing explicit knowledge from elsewhere (Hansen, 1999).

The case study also illustrates a peculiar dilemma in this respect. The creation of an internal network based on strong, redundant ties may have been perfectly appropriate for accessing knowledge from within the firm that had not yet been articulated or codified in any way. However, it may be much more difficult to tap into new, complex knowledge (e.g. about a new method of construction) if that knowledge is only available elsewhere and largely in tacit form (e.g. from consulting engineers known to the REM). The dilemma here is that the greater the cohesion of the internal network (which is desirable in terms of people 'buying into' the system), the more likely that this may encourage localized search behaviour. Such behaviour, however, may not be as productive a source of new ideas, or as efficient a way of accessing them. In other words, there is a delicate balance between encouraging the development of a network based on strong, redundant ties, while at the same time encouraging the maintenance of other, potentially useful networks that are based on weak, non-redundant ties (Hansen, 1999). There is also the danger of reinforcing an inward-looking perspective, as REMs start to identify themselves as part of a new community of practice. Building up successful internal social relations may well therefore be at the expense of a more outward-looking approach that is able to access and use a variety of sources of knowledge and learning (Uzzi, 1997; Gargiulo and Benassi, 1999).

Furthermore, the reliance on individuals and their tacit knowledge and personal skills has longer term implications for project-based organizational learning in this type of context. First, it is not clear how the organization is able to capture and use learning over the long term, when it is so reliant on the individual and their particular expertise and social contacts. Secondly, what happens when the person leaves and takes their knowledge and contacts with them? It was not clear from the case how the REM network was to be effectively reproduced over the long term. What was clear, however, was that the emphasis on the individual militated against the transfer of such knowledge and learning, except perhaps through the use of various forms of socialization and mentoring (Lave and Wenger, 1991). Whether such support systems were in place and how effective they were, however, was questionable, given the inference from the case that any such additional resources and support needed may have been difficult to come by. The wider implication is that there may be significant human resource constraints on knowledge transfer and learning, and that these are further exacerbated by staffing practices in project organization.

A final point to make is that these findings are not specific to the construction case. The research as a whole found that, despite considerable diversity, the organizations looked at experienced remarkably similar enablers and barriers to managing knowledge for project-based learning. In the health service case, for example, the development of a successful new cataract treatment process crucially depended upon a group of key medical and nursing staff committing themselves to a project initiated by hospital administrators, championed by a consultant and requiring them to accept changes to professional demarcations (Newell et al., 2003). In contrast, the pharmaceutical case showed how the development of a radical new procedure to treat prostate cancer was constrained by the difficulty in getting radiologists and urologists to work together (Edelman et al., 2004). All of the cases contained examples of the limits of technology and the problems caused by internal structural and political factors. In the telecommunications case, for instance, a sophisticated information retrieval system that had been developed to help a group set up to monitor innovation in the sector was not widely used because, according to one project manager, '[people prefer] personal e-mail, the coffee point and meetings' (Bresnen et al., 2004). Space limitations make it impossible to give more detail. However, the overall findings were consistent with the importance placed on the impact of social context and processes on project-based learning (see Edelman et al., 2004, for more information).

Conclusions

This chapter has set out to explore KM processes associated with project-based learning, drawing upon a case study of organizational change in a construction company. The main finding from the case is that processes of knowledge capture, diffusion and learning in project settings rely very heavily upon social practices and processes in ways that emphasize the importance of adopting a community-based approach. These findings have obvious implications for introducing new managerial initiatives in a project environment such as construction, in that they illustrate the difficulties, challenges and limitations of attempting to capture and codify project-based learning principally via the use of technology. Indeed, the study suggests further that developing absorptive capacity for process innovation creates particular problems, since project learning depends as much on replicating elements of the social context and processes involved that have created the learning outcomes, as on transferring the outcomes themselves (Newell et al., 2003). Whereas the development of product innovations can be well recorded through design iterations and artefacts, process innovations are less likely to leave such a trail and more likely to generate tacit or informal procedural knowledge. Learning capture then becomes more dependent on the identification of comparable problems or situations to which the project team's experience can be applied, the representation of those experiences as stories of success or failure, and the incorporation of learning into new routines that are more easily applied elsewhere. The challenge for those concerned with developing practical solutions for managing knowledge is therefore to recognize and allow for the some-what convoluted effects that social processes have upon knowl-edge diffusion and learning in the particular context of project organization.

Acknowledgement

The research was funded by Engineering and Physical Sciences Research Council, grant reference GR/M73286.

References

Adler, P. S. and Kwon, S.-W. (2002) Social capital: prospects for a new concept. *Academy of Management Review* 27(1): 17–40.

Bijker, W. E., Hughes, T. and Pinch, T. J. (eds) (1987) *The Social Construction of Technological Systems*. London: MIT Press.

Blackler, F. (1995) Knowledge, knowledge work and organisations: an overview and interpretation. *Organisation Studies* 16(6): 1021–1046.

Bresnen, M. J. (1990) *Organising Construction: Project Organisation and Matrix Management*. London: Routledge.

Bresnen, M., Edelman, L., Newell, S., Scarbrough, H. and Swan, J. (2003) Social practices and the management of knowledge in proj-ect environments. *International Journal of Project Management* 21(3): 157–166.

Bresnen, M., Edelman, L., Newell, S., Scarbrough, H. and Swan, J. (2004) The impact of social capital on project-based learning. In Huysman, M. and Wulf, V. (eds) *Social Capital and ICT*. Cambridge, MA: MIT Press (in press).

Brown, J. S. and Duguid, P. (1991) Organisational learning and com-munities-of-practice: toward a unified view of working, learning and innovation. *Organization Science* 2(1): 40–57.

Brown, J. S. and Duguid, P. (2001) Knowledge and organisation: a social practice perspective. *Organization Science* 12: 198–213.

Cherns, A. B. and Bryant, D. T. (1984) Studying the client's role in construction management. *Construction Management and Economics* 2: 177–184.

Cohen, W. M. and Levinthal, D. A. (1990) Absorptive capacity: a new perspective on organisational learning and innovation. *Administrative Science Quarterly* 35: 128–152.

Cole-Gomolski, B. (1997) Users loathe to share their know-how. *Computerworld* 31(46): 6.

DeFillippi, R. J. (2001) Project-based learning, reflective practices and learning outcomes. *Management Learning* 32(1): 5–10.

DeFillippi, R. J. and Arthur, M. (1998) Paradox in project-based enterprises: the case of filmmaking. *California Management Review* 40(2): 125–140.

Dervin, B. (1998) Sense making theory and practice: an overview of user interests in knowledge seeking and use. *Journal of Knowledge Management* 2(2): 36–45.

Drucker, P. (1993) *Post-capitalist Society*. Oxford: Butterworth-Heinemann.

Edelman, L., Bresnen, M., Newell, S., Scarbrough, H. and Swan, J. (2004) The paradox of social capital: structural, cognitive and relational dimensions. In Bettis, R. A. (ed.) *Strategy in Transition*. Oxford: Blackwell (in press).

Ekstedt, E., Lundin, R. A., Soderholm, A. and Wirdenius, H. (1999) *Neo-institutional Organising: Renewal by Action and Knowledge in a Project-intensive Economy*. London: Routledge.

Fahey, L. and Prusak, L. (1998) The eleven deadliest sins of knowledge management. *California Management Review* 40(3): 265–276.

Finerty, L. (1997) Information retrieval for intranets: the case for knowledge management. *Document World* 2(5): 32–34.

Gann, D. M. (2001) Putting academic ideas into practice: technological progress and the absorptive capacity of construction organisations. *Construction Management and Economics* 19(3): 321–330.

Gann, D. M. and Salter, A. (2000) Innovation in project-based, service-enhanced firms: the construction of complex products and systems. *Research Policy* 29: 955–972.

Gargiulo, M. and Benassi, M. (2000) Trapped in your own net? Network cohesion, structural holes and the adaptation of social capital. *Organization Science* 11(2): 183–196.

Ginsberg, A. and Abrahamson, E. (1991) Champions of change and strategic shifts: the role of internal and external change advocates. *Journal of Management Studies* 28(2): 173–190.

Grabher, G. (2002) Cool projects, boring institutions: temporary collaboration in social context. *Regional Studies* 36(3): 205–214.

Hansen, M. T. (1999) The search transfer problem: the role of weak ties in sharing knowledge across organisational sub-units. *Administrative Science Quarterly* 44: 82–111.

Hansen, M. T. (2002) Knowledge networks: explaining effective knowledge sharing in multiunit companies. *Organization Science* 13(3): 232–248.

Hansen, M., Nohria, N. and Tierney, T. (1999) What's your strategy for managing knowledge? *Harvard Business Review* 77: 106–117.

Hobday, M. (2000) The project-based organisation: an ideal for managing complex products and systems? *Research Policy* 29: 871–893.

Kogut, B. and Zander, U. (1992) Knowledge of the firm, combinative capabilities and the replication of technology. *Organization Science* 3(3): 383–397.

Lave, J. and Wenger, E. (1991) *Situated Learning: Legitimate Peripheral Participation*. Cambridge: Cambridge University Press.

McLoughlin, I. (1999) *Creative Technological Change*. London: Routledge.

Nahapiet, J. and Ghoshal, S. (1998) Social capital, intellectual capital and the organisational advantage. *Academy of Management Review* 23(2): 242–266.

Newell, S., Edelman, L., Scarbrough, H., Swan, J. and Bresnen, M. (2003) 'Best practice' development and transfer in the NHS: the importance of process as well as product knowledge. *Health Services Management Research* 16: 1–12.

Nonaka, I. (1994) A dynamic theory of organisational knowledge creation. *Organization Science* 5: 14–37.

Orlikowski, W. J. (1996) Improvising organisational transformation over time: a situated change perspective. *Information Systems Research* 7: 63–92.

Orr, J. (1990) Sharing knowledge, celebrating identity: community memory in a serving culture. In Middleton, D. and Edwards, D. (eds) *Collective Remembering*. London: Sage, pp. 168–189.

Pettigrew, A. and Whipp, R. (1991) *Managing Change for Competitive Success*. Oxford: Blackwell.

Prencipe, A. and Tell, F. (2001) Inter-project learning: processes and outcomes of knowledge codification in project-based firms. *Research Policy* 30: 1373–1394.

Robinson, H. S., Carrillo, P. M., Anumba, C. J. and Al-Ghassani, A. M. (2001) Linking knowledge management strategy to business performance in construction organisations. In Akintoye, A. (ed.) *Proceedings of the ARCOM 17th Annual Conference*, University of Salford, UK, 5–7 September, pp. 577–586.

Scarbrough, H. and Carter, C. (2000) *Investigating Knowledge Management*. London: Chartered Institute of Personnel and Development.

Schwenk, C. (1988) The cognitive perspective on strategic decision-making. *Journal of Management Studies* 25: 41–55.

Senge, P. (1990) *The Fifth Discipline: The Art and Practice of the Learning Organisation*. London: Doubleday.

Shariq, S. Z. (1998) Sense making and artefacts: an exploration into the role of tools in knowledge management. *Journal of Knowledge Management* 2(2): 10–19.

Spender, J. C. (1996) Organisational knowledge, learning and memory: three concepts in search of a theory. *Journal of Organisational Change* 9(1): 63–78.

Swan, J. A., Newell, S., Scarbrough, H. and Hislop, D. (1999) Knowledge management and innovation: networks and networking. *Journal of Knowledge Management* 3: 262–275.

Szulanski, G. (1996) Exploring internal stickiness: impediments to the transfer of best practices within the firm. *Strategic Management Journal* 17: 27–43.

Tidd, J. (1995) Development of novel products through interorganisational and interorganisational networks: the case of home
automation. *Journal of Product Innovation Management* 22(11):
307–323.

Tsoukas, H. (1996) The firm as a distributed knowledge system: a
constructivist approach. *Strategic Management Journal* 17: 11–25.

Uzzi, B. (1997) Social structure and competition in interfirm networks: the paradox of embeddedness. *Administrative Science
Quarterly* 42: 35–67.

Weick, K. (1995) *Sensemaking in Organizations*. Thousand Oaks, CA:
Sage.

Wenger, E. (2000) Communities of practice and social learning systems. *Organisation* 7(2): 225–246.

Winch, G. M. (1998) Zephyrs of creative destruction: understanding
the management of innovation in construction. *Building Research
and Information* 26(5): 268–279.

Windeler, A. and Sydow, J. (2001) Project networks and changing
industry practices – collaborative content production in the
German television industry. *Organisation Studies* 22(6): 1035–1060.

Chapter 6

Managing knowledge in project-based professional services firms: an international comparison

Patrick S. W. Fong

Introduction

The aim of this chapter is to create an understanding of how professional services firms serving the construction industry manage knowledge. It takes an exploratory approach to knowledge management (KM) in quantity surveying (QS) practices in both Hong Kong and the UK to compare the similarities and differences between the two locations. The reasons for selecting QS practices as the research focus are four-fold.

First, QS firms are knowledge-intensive organizations or professional services organizations, and quantity surveyors (QSs) are knowledge workers. They possess the means of production (i.e. knowledge), and the product or service that they sell to their clients or customers is knowledge (Drucker, 1993). It is of interest to understand how knowledge is managed in this type of practice in the absence of formal KM policies. The success of this type of firm will ultimately depend on the competence of their professionals, relative to that of their counterparts in rival firms (Sveiby and Lloyd, 1987). Secondly, QS firms function in a project-based industry (Bresnen et al., 2003), where knowledge is regarded as a vital resource for delivering the clients' requirements (Love et al., 2003). In addition, it creates competitive advantage for the firm (Allee, 1997). This provides an incentive to investigate how project knowledge is managed and shared across teams and across time within the company. Thirdly, QS firms are project organizations, in which everyone in the project team is dependent on the others' work, both within the firm and external to the firm, where success is measured by the quality of the joint efforts as well as the degree to which they meet the client's requirements. This makes it difficult to survive unless one co-operates and shares knowledge with colleagues and other professionals on the project. Fourthly, a thorough review of the literature suggests that no previous studies on how knowledge is managed in QS firms have been conducted. In fact, only a limited amount of research has been conducted on KM in the architectural, engineering and construction (AEC) sectors (Egbu et al., 1999), and most of the KM studies in professional services have focused on accounting, legal, management consulting, finance, and information and communication technology consulting. Recently, attention has been directed towards KM in project environments (Winch, 1998; Defillippi, 2001; Prencipe and Tell, 2001; Love et al., 2003; Bresnen et al., 2003). With these four justifications for this research focus, it is anticipated that findings regarding how QS practices manage knowledge could potentially contribute to various fields.

Two fundamental and rather contradictory issues are presented in this research. On the one hand, 'knowledge resides in the minds of individuals, and this personal knowledge needs to be converted into knowledge that can be shared and transformed into innovations' (Choo, 1998, p. 3). On the other hand, new knowledge in organizations is created 'not by individuals, but by teams and groups of people sharing their knowledge and experience throughout the enterprise' (Allee, 1997, p. 10). The challenge faced by most research into KM is to create viable ongoing synergies between what the organization and the individual know.

Quantity surveying is a profession that processes and sells knowledge; therefore, effective knowledge managing skills can help practitioners to increase efficiency, enhance leverage of previous knowledge, make fewer mistakes, add value for clients and increase profits for the company. Knowledge management is a systematic management approach to identifying and capturing the 'knowledge assets' of a firm so that they can be fully exploited and protected as a source of competitive advantage (Scarbrough et al., 1999). It is not just knowledge per se that is important, but rather the integration and sharing of individuals' knowledge that play a vital role (Nonaka and Takeuchi, 1995). As the QS profession is facing a number of challenges, such as clients demanding greater value for money from services offered, an expanding scope to cover wider business interests of clients, and globalization of the world economy and competition, the aim of this chapter is to investigate whether KM can be formally introduced to enhance QS competence in Hong Kong and UK firms.

Managing knowledge in project-based firms

Project team members are different specialists brought together to form the 'project team'. Each specialist has his or her own professional training and knowledge formed from experiences in previous project teams. More often than not, the project team is an interorganizational team consisting of multiple individuals and multiple organizations with different professional cultures. This situation creates more barriers to transmission of knowledge throughout the team, as each participating project organization seeks to protect its own interests. The core project team is likely to be dispersed at, or more likely before, the end of the project. Little time or resources are generally devoted to capturing 'what people know'. Effort is often focused on immediate deliverables (e.g. drawings, reports, calculations, the building or facility itself), with no emphasis on what is being done now to help future projects. Project knowledge resides within the project team and the project itself does not have any organizational memory (Fiol and Lyles, 1985). Compared with non-project organizations that are supported both by the organizational structure and knowledge-absorbing routines, where knowledge becomes routinized and socialized into the organization, project-based organizations generally do not have support mechanisms that enable knowledge transfer to occur.

Project organizations typically involve people with different knowledge, experience and skills who come together to solve a common task; projects can thus be seen as arenas for knowledge creation, integration and sharing, where new and proven ideas and thoughts are combined. A serious drawback in the project-based organization is that learning and projects are not a natural combination (Bartezzaghi et al., 1997) since conflicts of a basic logical character are involved. These conflicts comprise the time aspect, task orientation, team structure and the transitional culture of projects (Lundin and Söderholm, 1995). Even when there is no conflict, continuous changes in technology, market, economy, materials or innovation warrant a need to learn continually from the field what other project teams are doing. One reason for the lack of knowledge transfer between projects is that there is no 'natural' way to incorporate lessons learned from an ongoing or completed project into other projects, since projects do not usually possess their own infrastructure for handling both intraproject and interproject information needs (Lundin, 2000). Moreover, much of the information transfer in projects seems to take place in face-to-face exchanges, via the contact of project team members or team members straddling multiple projects. Thus, finding viable ways in which multiproject organizations can ensure that knowledge is created, expanded and diffused over the lifetime of a single project, across project boundaries and up and down the organizational hierarchy, is a very important issue (Dougan, 2000).

Managing knowledge in project-based organizations means confronting difficulties that are not commonly encountered by non-project organizations. Project-based organizations work on project timescales that are frequently lengthy, non-repetitive, and typically organized around teams assembled specifically for the project and often disbanded upon its completion. In addition, end users' or clients' requirements often evolve and personnel often change during the course of the project. Projects in construction are often unique in their design, location, end user, client and budget: 'one-offs'. The process of planning, design, construction and maintenance is fragmented, constraining the elicitation, creation, flow and capture of knowledge. Feedback from one phase to another rarely happens, so that project team members have little chance to learn from either their good or their poor decisions. Typically, companies, and people and teams, come together for the first time in 'the

Table 6.1   Knowledge types in the architectural, engineering and construction industry

Knowledge type	Meaning	Explicit/tacit knowledge
Sectoral knowledge	Specialist knowledge of various sectors (e.g. commercial buildings, hospitals, schools)	Mostly tacit (e.g. how to design a shopping centre that enhances people flow)
Professional (technical) knowledge	Knowledge and skills related to a particular profession (e.g. architects, structural engineers)	Both explicit (e.g. knowledge kept in books or reports) and tacit (e.g. professional judgement on what is appropriate, rather than just following the rulebook)
Company-specific knowledge	Process and procedural knowledge of a company	Mostly explicit (e.g. company handbook, manuals)

temporary organization' (Kreiner, 1995) (i.e. the project), which is interorganizational. This means there is often difficulty in creating the right KM culture and locating knowledge 'assets', so that accessing and internalizing previous knowledge and learning over the lifetime of a project as well as across project boundaries becomes problematic. The fact that project organizations are by necessity dispersed and fragmented lessens effective knowledge and learning transfer towards their organizations. Table 6.1 shows the various knowledge types in the AEC industry. They span the continuum from explicit to tacit knowledge. Although the distinction between tacit and explicit is important, Tsoukas (1996) suggests that tacit and explicit knowledge are mutually constituted. While it is useful to differentiate and delineate knowledge types, it is recognized that their inseparability has to be acknowledged.

Knowledge worker

A knowledge worker is an employee who possesses valuable experience, knowledge and expertise about the methods, processes and technology used to complete tasks. A manual worker may have lots of valuable experience too, but manual workers do not own the means of production. A knowledge worker, however, owns the means of production, and this knowledge is portable and an enormous capital asset (Drucker, 2000). Therefore, manual workers are usually seen as a 'cost', while knowledge workers are seen as 'capital assets'. Costs need to be controlled and reduced, while assets need to be made to grow (Drucker, 2000).

Businesses need competent people to interpret and utilize information and knowledge effectively to survive and remain competitive within their respective markets. They rely on key individuals to innovate and guide other employees through business processes. They also rely on subject matter experts to provide input into specific applications. Therefore, firms must consider how to attract, develop, track and retain knowledge-able people as part of their KM domain (Tannenbaum and Alliger, 2000). When advocating the usefulness of KM, a rationale often heard is that when a competent or key employee leaves, the firm loses vital knowledge and, in the worst case scenario, an aspect of its competitiveness (Hildreth et al., 2000). With the growing mobility in the labour market, businesses should pay increasing attention to this problem, specifically focusing on improving the conditions for internal knowledge sharing.

Use of knowledge management to enhance quantity surveying professionalism

The economy of the future will be a knowledge economy. Competitiveness is highly related to the level of knowledge and technology (Drucker, 1998). Knowledge is the key resource today, and the companies that can learn to manage it more effectively will win (Clare and DeTore, 2000). To survive and grow in the future, the QS profession must respond quickly and creatively to the challenges of accelerating social, technological, economic and environmental change. An essential element in the future success and expansion of the profession is the skill and knowledge base at the core of professional practice (RICS, 1991). Quantity surveying firms, as project-based professional services organizations that offer client service as their main output, depend on how they manage knowledge. They provide construction cost consultancy services from the inception of planning to the completion of a construction project. They depend on well-educated and skilled personnel, and often concentrate on temporary assignments or projects. They are characterized by knowledge assets that are not central: their critical elements are in the heads of their employees, in networks, customer relations, manuals and service delivery systems. They are strongly dependent on employee loyalty and therefore vulnerable to exits. In this respect, KM helps to speed up the development and competence of staff, prevent 'reinventing the wheel' and the repetition of costly mistakes, improve the quality of services delivered to clients and customers, and avoid knowledge being lost when key personnel leave a company.

Owing to the external and internal competition faced by the QS profession, companies need to improve their competence so as to maintain their competitiveness. There are numerous possible means of enhancing their expertise, such as improving the education of the new generation of QSs or reforming the profession. However, such reforms may take a long time from the point of view of the profession, its society and universities to come to fruition and produce results. Properly managing knowledge may be a relatively quicker and more effective way to enhance QS competence, as it represents a key element of organizational resources.

Methodology

The instrument selected for this research was a questionnaire survey. Interviews were not used as a research method because KM is still in its infancy in the AEC industry as well as the QS profession. Further, the cases where QS firms have deployed KM are limited, so it may be too early and difficult to discuss KM in depth through interviews. Another advantage of using a questionnaire survey compared with interviews is that it is easier to reach a large number of respondents and obtain a generalized view of the situation in the profession. In addition, questionnaires are more anonymous than interviews and can usually be filled in when it is convenient for the respondent. There is also the advantage that no interviewer bias is introduced.

Questionnaires were sent to QSs in QS consultancy firms by mail. These included QSs in Hong Kong and the UK. This study explores how knowledge is managed within the QS profession, which has not been examined previously by other researchers.

Sample

The target population came from random sampling of the Royal Institute of Chartered Surveyors (RICS) and Hong Kong Institute of Surveyors (HKIS) Membership Directories. Two-hundred questionnaires were sent to QS firms in early 2003, half to Hong Kong quantity surveyors (HKQS) and the other half to UK quantity surveyors (UKQS). Out of 100 question-naires sent to QSs in Hong Kong, thirty-eight completed ques-tionnaires were returned (i.e. a 38 per cent response rate), whereas out of 100 questionnaires sent to QSs in the UK, thirty-four completed questionnaires were returned (a 34 per cent response rate). The total response rate was 36 per cent. The following analysis will draw a comparison between responses from HKQS and UKQS.

Findings and analysis

Awareness of knowledge management

The results indicate that more than half of the respondents (58 per cent) did not know about KM, in particular among the HKQS (63 per cent). This reveals that KM has only recently arrived and has not been widely discussed in the QS field. As stated by Davenport (1999) and Hansen et al. (1999), KM as a conscious practice is very young and is not yet tied to enterprise strategy and performance in practice. In general, the findings imply that the QS profession is unaware of the new develop-ment of KM. Fewer than half of the respondents in this study had heard about KM, reflecting that the QS profession is not fully aware of the latest market trends that can bring improve-ments to their organization.

Professional knowledge

Professional knowledge is defined here as the highly specialized knowledge and expertise that is required by QSs to carry
out their professional duties in a competent manner. Ninety-
four per cent of QSs (all of the UKQS surveyed and 89 per cent
of the HKQS) have to apply much of their professional knowledge to their work. This shows that the nature of the QS
profession requires that employees apply much of their professional knowledge to provide professional services to their
clients. Thus, professional knowledge is very crucial to QS
practices.

Surprisingly, 11 per cent of HKQS perceived that they did
not need to apply professional knowledge to their work, and
all of these were at a junior level. There are two possible reasons for this. The first is that the work for Hong Kong junior
QSs is too mechanistic; some of the core skills and knowledge
base reported in the RICS report (1992) are not offered in
Hong Kong. In fact, many QS firms are still offering bills of
quantities production as their 'bread and butter' service. In
addition, junior staff may be responsible for very simple and
routine tasks that may not require the application of their professional knowledge and judgement, so they feel that they do
not need to apply their professional knowledge to their work.
Junior staff sometimes view themselves as going through an
apprenticeship under the supervision of experienced professionals, who in turn repay the hard work and assistance of their
juniors by teaching them their skills (Maister, 1982). Secondly,
every professional has to apply their professional knowledge
to their work, and perhaps from their previous experience
they are unaware that their knowledge has already been
applied.

Knowledge sharing

The findings reveal that knowledge sharing in QS firms is
extremely common. Nearly all QSs (97 per cent) share their
knowledge and experience with others at work, so knowledge
sharing in QS firms is clearly prevalent. The findings also

imply that most QSs are willing to share their knowledge with others at work. It is important that the existing knowledge of the staff, which forms the basis of an organization, will develop continually and be built on. This includes creating and transferring knowledge internally. Knowledge can also be externalized instead of only tacitly held by employees assigned to the project, as project knowledge can be reused in subsequent or concurrent projects. Maister (1982) added that consultants use their knowledge, skills and experience from previous projects with new knowledge and apply it to new situations to meet the needs of their clients as well as society. However, some differences are observed between UKQS and HKQS. All the UKQS surveyed share their knowledge and experience with others at work, but about 5 per cent of the HKQS at junior level do not, indicating that UK junior QSs are more willing to share knowledge with others than are Hong Kong junior QSs. Senior QSs are also more willing to share knowledge with others than junior QSs in Hong Kong. Perhaps there is a perception among Hong Kong's junior QSs that they are not experienced enough to share their insights with others as they are still undergoing apprentice training. In addition, as Fang (1999) explains, traditional Chinese characteristics are unwillingness to take risks or make mistakes, showing indirection, respecting one's superior's decisions and avoiding responsibility. This may explain why a small percentage of junior QSs in Hong Kong think that they do not need to share knowledge in their offices. Further, their ranks within their offices may be viewed as signs of status as well as of function, as workers in the lower ranks of professional service organizations can be viewed as learners rather than contributors.

The mean (M) score of the two QS groups is over 3, revealing that most of them indicated a willingness to share their knowledge or experience with others. In general, HKQS (M = 3.53) are more willing to share their knowledge than UKQS (M = 3.15). These findings imply that unwillingness to share may not be a critical barrier preventing QS firms from developing KM. The results also show that all the UKQS are willing to share knowledge with others, and only about 5 per cent of Hong Kong junior QSs are not willing to do so. As revealed before, some junior QSs may think that their knowledge is not strong enough to contribute, thus they are reluctant to share it with others.

Knowledge transfer and acquisition

Referring to the ranking and mean score in Table 6.2, the pattern of practices (internal/external methods) used by HKQS and UKQS to acquire or transfer knowledge is quite consistent. Their differences are not significant except when using the internet and e-mail systems. UKQS use external methods such as the internet (M = 3.18) and e-mail systems (M = 3.62) to acquire or transfer knowledge much more frequently than do HKQS (M = 2.29 and 2.89, respectively). It is interesting to see that they perceive external sources as useful means of knowledge and information acquisition. One possible reason is that some QS firms in Hong Kong prohibit their employees from using the internet or e-mail systems in their offices to prevent them from using these for leisure or private use. It is

Table 6.2 Summary of ranking and mean score between Hong Kong (HK) and UK quantity surveyors

Practices	Internal/ external methods	Ranking HK	Ranking UK	Mean score HK	Mean score UK	Significant difference (χ^2)
Knowledge-sharing meetings	I	8	9	2.39	2.91	5.37
Internal conference visits	I	11	12	2.24	2.38	3.74
Knowledge-sharing boards	I/E	12	13	2.00	2.29	6.13
Talks and seminars	I/E	6	3	2.79	3.21	7.72
Internal training courses	I	3	6	2.89	3.00	5.97
Peer tutoring	I	7	8	2.42	2.94	5.62
Past project interview sessions for feedback	I	14	11	2.05	2.41	3.65
Lessons learned from previous projects	I	5	3	2.84	3.21	4.14
Reward system	I	15	15	1.63	1.74	1.43
Mentoring system	I	12	14	2.00	2.24	1.82
Company library	E	1	3	3.21	3.21	3.53
E-mail system	E	3	1	2.89	3.62	11.15
Internet	E	10	7	2.29	3.18	12.92
Intranet	I	8	10	2.39	2.79	7.80
Database	I	2	2	3.13	3.24	0.71

$\chi^2 > 7.81$: significantly different.

also true that in some construction-related consulting practices in Hong Kong, the whole company only has one e-mail account, and all e-mail messages received are screened and delivered to the addressees by a 'gatekeeper'. This type of mistrust between employers and employees may prevent the proper acquisition and transfer of knowledge that is required for their work.

Among the practices described by QS firms, the most popular ones used by HKQS to acquire or transfer knowledge, in descending order, are the company library (M = 3.21), databases (M = 3.13), and internal training courses and e-mail system (M = 2.89). The frequency of using these practices ranges from 'seldom' to 'sometimes', which shows that HKQS do not use these practices very frequently. The top two practices can be classified as explicit knowledge as they are codified in physical forms such as books, manuals, trade catalogues, reports and documents. The practice most frequently used by the UKQS to acquire or transfer knowledge is the e-mail system (M = 3.62), the second most popular is the database (M = 3.24) and in joint third place are talks and seminars, lessons learned from previous projects and the company library (M = 3.21). The frequency of using these practices is over 3, i.e. ranging from 'sometimes' to 'often', which is higher than the frequency of their use by HKQS. Indeed, according to the mean score, UKQS use all practices more frequently than HKQS, which reflects the fact that UKQS use company facilities to acquire or transfer knowledge more frequently than HKQS. This also implies that UKQS are more active in seeking and sharing knowledge, while HKQS show less initiative in using company facilities to acquire or share knowledge. Moreover, the findings show that UKQS use lessons learned (M = 3.21) more than HKQS (M = 2.84), which indicates that UKQS are more able than HKQS to capture previous project experience and reuse experience or knowledge.

It is further observed that the practices frequently used by HKQS are relatively personal and do not require any interaction with others, such as using the company library and database; thus, knowledge transfer or sharing by these means will be limited to one person only. In addition, these practices are rather traditional and can be classified merely as information/

document management. These practices can only provide information and data for the user, and can neither provide the user with professional knowledge or experience in helping him or her to make decisions or judgements, nor make a significant contribution to company growth and success. Liebowitz (2000) claims that organizations adopting KM experience business growth and improved decision making. It seems that the practices of QS firms in managing knowledge are not efficient enough. Both HKQS and UKQS use the reward system the least (ranked at 15). This reveals that reward systems are not used as a catalyst to motivate knowledge sharing, and is in contrast to the opinion of Liebowitz (2000), who regards them as very useful in encouraging knowledge sharing. There is therefore a gap between the theory and real-life practice in this area.

Sixty-three per cent of the QSs surveyed (61 per cent of HKQS and 65 per cent of UKQS) cannot acquire all the knowledge they need in their working environment. This reveals deficiencies in QS practice in terms of the means of delivering knowledge: the practices that QS firms provide for transferring knowledge cannot supply sufficient knowledge to their employees; consequently, QS professionals may not be well enough equipped with professional knowledge to provide good service to their clients. Alternatively, they need to seek knowledge elsewhere.

As QS firms cannot provide an environment for their employees to acquire the knowledge they need for their work, this may affect the quality and efficiency of their service. To avoid any lowering of service quality, it is anticipated that work allocation will rely on who has the expertise in particular skills areas, and that companies will put the right person on the right job. As a result, a specific piece of knowledge is owned by a few key personnel only. The company risks losing this particular knowledge if the key person resigns or retires, and the company's competitive advantage will eventually be eroded. In addition, some large QS practices in Hong Kong adopt the 'division of labour' approach, where they divide junior staff members into different specialized job tasks to enhance efficiency. Staff members can become so specialized that they become expert in one trade but not in others. This can create job boredom as they do not perceive any challenge in their work, and also explains why some junior staff find their work monotonous.

However, it is interesting that although HKQS use company facilities to acquire knowledge less frequently than UKQS (referring to the previous section), HKQS (39 per cent) can acquire more knowledge than UKQS (35 per cent) from their work, which implies that the frequency of using company facilities to acquire knowledge may not be directly related to level of acquiring knowledge, and HKQS may use other methods to acquire the knowledge that they need. Those who could not acquire all the knowledge that they needed at work were further asked about the areas of knowledge insufficiency. Table 6.3 shows that some QSs cannot acquire even knowledge of prime QS services such as preliminary cost advice, contracting methods and preparing tender documents from work, which reflects that either the work is too unique or they do not know where to locate such knowledge.

The knowledge that HKQS and UKQS cannot acquire from their work is mainly knowledge of arbitrations and disputes (27 per cent), knowledge of project management (20 per cent) and knowledge in the area of assessing replacement values for insurance (12 per cent). The possible reasons for not having enough expertise in these three areas are: (1) these services are not prime services provided by QSs, thus there is insufficient employee training in this type of knowledge; (2) junior QSs

Table 6.3   Areas of knowledge insufficiency

Area of knowledge	HKQS (%)	UKQS (%)	Total (%)
Preliminary cost advice	8	6	7
Cost planning	2	6	4
Contracting methods	6	6	6
Valuation of construction work	8	6	7
Preparing tender documents and negotiating contract prices	6	8	7
Preparing contract documents and participating in contract administration	6	6	6
Preparing cashflow forecasts and exercising cost control over projects	0	6	3
Project management	24	13	20
Arbitrations and disputes	26	25	27
Assessing replacement values for insurance	14	10	12

HKQS: Hong Kong quantity surveyors; UKQS: UK quantity surveyors.

have less chance to handle these types of work as they require tacit or significant knowledge; and (3) changing demand from clients, which requires new services or expertise that may not have been possessed by QSs in the past.

Regarding the use of personal methods to acquire or transfer knowledge, the patterns of HKQS and UKQS are similar. The most common method used by both of them to acquire knowledge is talking with colleagues (M = 3.48 and 3.82, respectively), and then talking with team members within the same project (M = 3.30 and 3.64, respectively). The third method is reading professional books, journals and magazines (M = 2.74 and 3.36, respectively). All of these practices can facilitate knowledge sharing, enhance knowledge level, and eventually raise employees' expertise and increase the organizational asset. However, apart from these three methods, no other practices are frequently adopted by HKQS to acquire knowledge (M < 3). In particular, professional contact outside the same discipline to acquire knowledge ranked the lowest for HKQS, while UKQS talk with ex-classmates the least.

In general, UKQS use different knowledge acquisition practices more frequently than do HKQS. Even among items given the same rank, such as talking with colleagues and reading professional books, journals and magazines, the frequencies show significant differences, which reflects that UKQS are more active in acquiring the knowledge that they need. The exception is talking with ex-classmates, which HKQS (M = 2.52) do more frequently than UKQS (M = 2.05, ranked the least); this may be due to geographical reasons. Most HKQS work in Hong Kong or on the Chinese mainland after graduation, whereas UK graduates may work in different cities across the country or even overseas; therefore, UKQS have less opportunity to seek knowledge through contact with their ex-classmates. This also suggests that HKQS keep in contact with their former classmates more than UKQS.

Table 6.4 shows a significant difference between UKQS and HKQS in acquiring knowledge through professional contact outside the same discipline (χ^2 = 12.05), with HKQS ranking this method as the one they used the least (M = 2.22). This shows that HKQS seek knowledge only from within their own profession; they seldom seek knowledge from members of

Table 6.4   Summary of ranking and mean score between HKQS and UKQS

Practice	Ranking		Mean score		Significant difference (χ^2)
	HK	UK	HK	UK	
Talking with colleagues	1	1	3.48	3.82	8.61
Talking with ex-colleagues	6	7	2.43	2.73	3.68
Talking with ex-classmates	5	8	2.52	2.05	4.79
Talking with team members within the same discipline	2	2	3.30	3.64	7.44
Professional contact within the same discipline	4	4	2.61	3.23	7.11
Professional contact outside the same discipline	8	5	2.22	3.14	12.05
Taking external seminars/courses	7	6	2.35	2.91	5.31
Reading professional books, journals and magazines	3	3	2.74	3.36	9.25

HKQS: Hong Kong quantity surveyors; UKQS: UK quantity surveyors.
$\chi^2 > 7.81$: significantly different.

other professional disciplines. In other words, communication with external actors such as other professional consultants, suppliers and users is very limited. As they have little specialist knowledge of other disciplines, their professionalism is restricted to QS knowledge only. In addition, the findings reveal that both HKQS and UKQS acquire knowledge through talking with colleagues more frequently than through talking with team members, which implies that project team spirit may not be high enough or other team members are not able to solve the project problems.

Development of knowledge management systems

Over 90 per cent of QSs would like their company to implement KM, which means the QS profession's attitude towards implementing KM in their firms is very positive, and it is anticipated that resistance to implement KM would not be high. The development of better tools or systems for KM facilitates change and the implementation of more structured approaches to managing knowledge. However, such structured approaches should be not only technology centred but also people centred. Most practitioners believe that KM consists of technologies, processes and people. The results show that the distribution between HKQS and UKQS is extremely consistent: 68 per cent of them would like their company to develop KM in the near future, 24 per cent would like their company to develop KM but not now, and only 8 per cent would not like their company to develop KM.

As the findings reveal, the means of the HKQS and UKQS groups are over the central mean of 2.5, which means that most of them would be willing to use a KM system to seek knowledge. Only about 5 per cent of Hong Kong junior QSs would not use the system to seek knowledge. They also show that UKQS would use the KM system to seek knowledge frequently ($M = 3$), whereas HKQS ($M = 2.79$) would use the KM system from 'not frequently' to 'frequently', that is, less frequently than the UKQS. This reveals that UKQS are more open to new practices or initiatives. The conservative approach taken by the HKQS could lead to the loss of their competitive advantage compared with their overseas counterparts.

As shown in the results, the mean of the two groups of QSs is over 2.5, which means most of them would use a KM system to share knowledge. Only about 5 per cent of Hong Kong junior QSs would not use the system to share knowledge. The findings also show that UKQS ($M = 3.03$) would use the system to share knowledge more frequently than HKQS ($M = 2.82$), similar to the findings in the previous question. It is strange that HKQS are more willing to share their knowledge with others than UKQS, but as the two previous questions reveal, relatively less willing to use a KM system to acquire and share knowledge. One possible explanation is that HKQS may prefer to use other personal methods rather than a systematic KM approach to acquire and share knowledge.

Professionals' preference of knowledge management skills

In general, the majority of QSs (43 per cent) would like their company to develop knowledge-sharing skills first, 39 per cent think that their company should develop knowledge-capturing skills first and only 18 per cent think that their company should develop knowledge-creating skills first (Table 6.5). The opinions

Table 6.5   Professionals' preference of knowledge management skills

	HKQS (%)	UKQS (%)	Total (%)
Knowledge-creating skills	19	17	18
Knowledge-capturing skills	35	43	39
Knowledge-sharing skills	46	39	43

HKQS: Hong Kong quantity surveyors; UKQS: UK quantity surveyors.

of the two groups of QSs are quite different, the only fairly consistent one being that the percentage favouring knowledge-creating skills is the lowest in both cases. This implies that QSs regard creating knowledge as no more important than capturing and sharing it. This may reflect the deficiency in project-based organizations where different employees are engaged in different projects: there is little learning or knowledge transfer across project boundaries, so they see sharing unique project knowledge and capturing lessons learned from other projects as more important than creating new knowledge.

There is a difference between HKQS and UKQS: the majority of HKQS (46 per cent) think that their company should develop knowledge-sharing skills first, whereas the majority of UKQS (43 per cent) think that their company should develop knowledge-capturing skills first. This reveals that HKQS think that sharing knowledge is more important than capturing knowledge, whereas UKQS think the opposite. The implication is that KM development in HKQS firms should emphasize sharing knowledge, while KM development in UKQS firms should place an emphasis on capturing knowledge.

Expected benefits

According to Table 6.6, all of the mean scores of the expected benefits are higher than 3.5, which means that QSs' expectations or perceptions of implementing KM are very positive. In general, the mean scores of different benefits in the UKQS group are higher than in the HKQS group, so it seems that the UKQS expectations of KM are higher than those of the HKQS.

As the findings reveal, the ranking and mean scores of different benefits among HKQS and UKQS are similar, and there is no significant difference between the two groups. According to the perceptions of HKQS, the top three expected benefits of

Table 6.6 Summary of ranking and mean scores between HKQS and UKQS

	Ranking		Mean score		Significant
Expected benefit	*HK*	*UK*	*HK*	*UK*	*difference* (χ^2)
Enhanced organizational competitiveness	6	8	4.62	4.65	9.20
Improved service quality	2	1	4.88	5.09	4.89
Higher effectiveness in problem solving	1	5	4.96	4.83	6.27
Improved decision making	4	6	4.69	4.78	2.61
Increased company revenue	14	10	3.77	4.22	8.76
Increased innovation	11	12	4.23	4.17	2.35
Foster business growth	11	10	4.23	4.22	1.81
Practice and process improvement	6	7	4.62	4.74	1.32
Increased client satisfaction	9	4	4.50	4.91	7.30
Higher levels of expertise and knowledge	2	1	4.88	5.09	3.90
Enhanced employee capability and organizational learning	4	3	4.69	5.00	2.36
Increased employee morale, creativity and ingenuity	13	13	4.08	4.13	5.56
Employee stimulation and motivation	10	14	4.42	3.91	9.92
Raised company professional image	6	9	4.62	4.48	3.35

HKQS: Hong Kong quantity surveyors; UKQS: UK quantity surveyors.
$\chi^2 > 11.07$: significantly different.

KM, in descending order, are higher effectiveness in problem solving (M = 4.96), improved service quality (M = 4.88), and higher levels of expertise and knowledge (M = 4.88). By contrast, UKQS think that the top three benefits are improved service quality (M = 5.09), higher levels of expertise and knowledge (M = 5.09), and enhanced employee capability and organizational learning (M = 5.00).

It was found that the benefits desired by QSs were for their personal benefit (e.g. higher levels of expertise and knowledge, higher effectiveness in problem solving and enhanced employee capability) rather than for that of the company (e.g. enhanced organizational competitiveness, fostering business growth, and practice and process improvement), which indicates that QSs may be looking for KM to help them on a personal level more than on the company level. Although increased company revenue (M = 3.77) and employee stimulation and motivation (M = 3.91) were ranked lowest by all the QSs surveyed, the mean score was still over 3.5, which means that it is still regarded as an expected benefit, since improvement in personal professional competence means that they can provide better service to their clients. The reason for the perception of less like-lihood of increasing company revenue and improving employee motivation is that as knowledge level is not directly related to company profit, its benefit to company profit is not easily recog-nized. In addition, according to the Motivation– Hygiene theory put forward by Robbins (1994), the key personal motivators are achievement, recognition, advancement and responsibility. Knowledge management does not emphasize improving these motivators, thus it is less likely to improve motivation.

Critical issues for knowledge management

Factors with a mean score higher than 2.5 are seen as signifi-cantly critical to KM success. In the opinion of the HKQS, all of the factors are critical to KM success except for the reward sys-tem (M = 2.35). For the UKQS, neither the reward system nor investment capital is a critical element (M = 1.74 and 2.17, respectively). Although there is a significant difference between HKQS and UKQS in their view of reward systems, they both ranked it as the least important success factor (Table 6.7). Liebowitz (2000) claims that reward systems are powerful in encouraging employees to acquire and share knowledge through a KM system; however, most QSs think otherwise. Investment capital is ranked as the second least important factor by both groups, implying that QSs believe that KM does not need much investment to develop. Perhaps they are orientated more towards the personalization approach than the codifica-tion approach.

Both HKQS and UKQS think that top management support is the most critical factor in KM success (M = 3.73 and 3.52, respectively), and employee participation the second most critical factor (M = 3.65 and 3.35, respectively). This agrees with Liebowitz (2000), who states that without senior manage-ment commitment and involvement, KM cannot be carried out successfully. In addition, HKQS think that creating sharing space is the third most important factor (M = 3.15), while

Table 6.7   Summary of ranking and mean scores of HKQS and UKQS

Factor	Ranking		Mean score		Significant difference (χ^2)
	HK	UK	HK	UK	
Top management support	1	1	3.73	3.52	2.27
Creating learning atmosphere	4	5	3.08	2.91	2.56
Creating sharing space	3	6	3.15	2.61	5.72
Employee participation	2	2	3.65	3.35	3.51
Creating trust between employees/employer	6	3	2.77	3.09	2.86
Reward system	8	8	2.35	1.74	7.94
Investment capital	7	7	2.62	2.17	3.67
Application of IT system	4	4	3.08	3.04	2.15

HKQS: Hong Kong quantity surveyors; UKQS: UK quantity surveyors.
$\chi^2 > 7.81$: significantly different.

Table 6.8   Reasons for disagreeing with their company in implementing knowledge management (KM)

Factor	HKQS (%)	UKQS (%)	Total (%)	Ranking
KM is not practical	4	3	4	10
Our practice is already good enough	2	3	3	11
KM system development is not mature yet	15	7	12	3
Lack of time	11	17	13	2
Lack of resources or funding	13	10	12	3
Lack of management support	11	10	10	5
Lack of understanding of KM	15	23	18	1
Lack of successful models within the profession as a guide	9	7	8	7
Knowledge is difficult to locate, capture, generalize and store	9	10	9	6
Individuals are unwilling to share their own knowledge	6	3	5	9
Wait and see how other companies apply KM	6	7	6	8

UKQS think that creating trust between employee and employer is the third most important factor (M = 3.09). These findings tie in with those of Hibbard and Carrillo (1998), who suggest that trust between employees and employers and creating a knowledge-sharing environment are crucial to KM.

As Table 6.8 reveals, the three major barriers to QS firms in developing KM systems, in descending order, are lack of understanding, time and maturity. These factors may lead to a

QS firm not developing KM at all or in the near future. The prime reason for the two groups of respondents disagreeing with their firms in implementing KM is their lack of understanding of KM, which reflects the fact that KM is very new to them. HKQS regard the immaturity of KM system development as the second barrier (15 per cent), while UKQS regard lack of time (17 per cent) as the second barrier.

Future directions for quantity surveying firms

Adopt knowledge management skills

It was found that QS firms have good systems for storing data and information, but do not have a systematic method of managing their knowledge. Although databases and company libraries are commonly used, these can only provide information for the user, and may not help the employee in making decisions or judgements. Some useful KM skills are not applied frequently, such as lessons learned, project review interviews and knowledge-sharing space, so that most knowledge cannot be captured and reused effectively.

It is suggested that QS firms adopt KM skills instead of just managing information only. Lessons learned, project review sessions, knowledge-sharing space and peer tutoring are effective means to capture and transfer knowledge. As the organizational and human capital increase, the company's competitiveness can be sustained and further increased. An organizational learning atmosphere should also be created: as employees actively acquire and share knowledge, their expertise will be enhanced and service quality will improve. In addition, QS firms should emphasize both technology-centred and people-centred KM approaches, as an imbalance can send the wrong message to their employees.

Strengthen employees' professional knowledge

The survey found that most QSs cannot acquire all the knowledge they need from their work, even within their own expertise. It is suggested that QS firms conduct an internal survey to identify the needs of their employees, and strengthen the training for employees to enrich their professional knowledge, especially that which is unique to particular employees. It is also suggested that QSs try to seek knowledge from external sources, instead of limiting it to within their firms or profession only. Mentoring systems and knowledge-sharing spaces can also be effective methods for junior staff to acquire the knowledge they need. In addition, there should be a common approach by universities and the industry to future knowledge requirements, as the former are at the frontier of developing the new breed of professionals for the industry.

Cultivate positive attitude and culture

The survey reveals that the Hong Kong QS profession is more stagnant than its British counterpart. The HKQS are relatively less aware of market changes, and are less open to new management concepts. The Hong Kong QS profession's conservative approach could result in it losing its competitive advantage compared with other professions in Hong Kong and with overseas QS professions.

In addition, a comparison of senior and junior QSs reveals that the latter group is not active enough. Some of them do not like to share knowledge with others or seek knowledge from others. One possible reason may be that their work is too mechanical and does not require them to share or acquire any professional knowledge. However, this working attitude does not contribute to the company's growth and success. In today's knowledge economy, competition is rigorous. Hong Kong QS firms must be aware of market changes and adopt forward-thinking policies to maintain and increase their competitive advantage. They should also cultivate positive and aggressive working attitudes among their employees, and provide more challenging work for junior QSs to enhance their knowledge level and increase employees' job satisfaction.

Develop knowledge management in quantity surveying firms

The survey reveals that most QSs welcome their firms' development of KM systems and anticipate that KM will bring many benefits to QS firms. However, as the biggest barriers to them in implementing KM are a lack of understanding of KM and the fact that the KM system is not mature enough, it is suggested that top management study more about KM and formulate particular KM strategies that are custom-made for their firms. If they decide to develop KM but do not have the know-how, they can either employ KM personnel or recruit external consultants who will be responsible for the KM initiatives by identifying, analysing, managing, maintaining and disseminating knowledge to appropriate individuals within the organization and externally to other stakeholders.

Conclusions

Knowledge sharing in QS firms is extremely common. Almost all QSs share their knowledge with others at work, and the methods used by the HKQS and UKQS groups to acquire or transfer knowledge are very similar. In terms of practices provided by their companies, the most common practices that they use to acquire or transfer knowledge are, in descending order, use of database, company library, e-mail system, internal training course, talks and seminars, and lessons learned from previous projects. In terms of personal methods to acquire or transfer knowledge, the most common practices they use are, in descending order, talking with colleagues, talking with team members on the same project, and reading professional books, journals and magazines. In general, the extent to which the QSs surveyed use those prevalent methods ranges from 'sometimes' to 'often', which means that they use those practices frequently. However, for other practices such as knowledge-sharing meetings, or peer tutoring and mentoring systems, the frequency ranges from 'seldom' to 'sometimes', which means that these QSs use other practices rarely.

These findings reflect that the practices commonly used by QSs are rather traditional, such as the company library, e-mail system and database, whereas more innovative methods, such as knowledge-sharing boards and interviews to capture or transfer knowledge, are relatively seldom used. As company libraries, e-mail systems and databases merely transfer information or codified knowledge to the user, which may not help them in making decisions, the efficiency of these practices in transferring knowledge is limited. In addition, the practices they commonly use mainly facilitate internal knowledge transfer: they seldom seek knowledge externally, such as through talking with other professionals not from the same discipline and attending external seminars or courses. As little new knowledge or other specialist knowledge is gained, their professionalism is restricted to traditional QS services only.

It was revealed that information/document management in QS firms is well developed but that relatively few systematic knowledge-managing methods are used in these firms to manage professional knowledge; hence, knowledge and experience cannot be captured and reused effectively. Although QSs share knowledge with others at work and use company facilities to acquire knowledge, more than half of the respondents claim that they cannot acquire all the knowledge they need from their work. This is the case even in their prime services, such as preliminary cost advice, contracting methods and preparing tender documents: some QSs still cannot acquire this knowledge from their work. This indicates that their professional standards are in doubt. There are three main areas in which QSs commonly lack knowledge: arbitrations and disputes, project management, and assessing replacement values for insurance. These require experience and tacit knowledge, as there are no hard and fast rules. As QSs cannot acquire these three types of knowledge from their work, their competitive advantage in those areas is also affected; consequently, other competing professionals who do not mainly serve the construction industry, such as solicitors, accountants, management consultants and project managers, can easily become involved in this work and compete directly with QSs. The RICS (1991) report, *Quantity Surveying 2000*, described entry from other professionals as a major challenge to the QS profession. If QS professionals want to maintain their competitiveness, they must better equip themselves with such knowledge and improve their organizational learning environment.

The professionals' attitude towards implementing KM in their firms is very positive. Over 90 per cent of the QSs surveyed are willing to share their knowledge with others and would like their company to introduce KM. In addition, most of them are willing to use a KM system to seek or share knowledge frequently if KM is developed in their firms. Only a small proportion of them are unwilling to use KM to acquire or share knowledge, so it is anticipated that human resistance would not be a prime barrier for QS firms implementing KM.

However, the findings indicate that HKQS are less motivated to use the KM system to seek or share knowledge, although they are willing to share their knowledge with others. This suggests that there are some differences between HKQS and UKQS. HKQS prefer to use other methods to acquire and share knowledge, rather than systematic KM tools. The research finds that HKQS are more passive than UKQS, and that they are less open to change. So implementing KM in UKQS firms may be easier than in HKQS firms. It was found that if KM is to be implemented in QS firms, HKQS would prefer to develop knowledge-sharing skills rather than knowledge-capturing and knowledge-creating skills. This means that they consider sharing knowledge to be more important or useful than capturing and creating knowledge. UKQS would prefer to develop knowledge-capturing skills rather than knowledge-sharing and knowledge-creating skills. Therefore, QS firms from different countries should adopt different strategies in managing knowledge to meet their employers' and employees' needs. Both groups of QSs think that knowledge-creating skills are less important than knowledge-capturing and knowledge-sharing skills. When creating knowledge is not emphasized, innovation and creativity within the profession may be limited.

Most of the QSs agree that KM would bring many benefits to the company and themselves, so their perception of KM is very positive. The most significant benefits they expect are, in descending order, improved service quality, raised levels of expertise, enhanced employee capability and organizational learning, and higher effectiveness in problem solving. However, they anticipate that increased innovation, increased company revenue and increased employee morale, creativity and ingenuity may be less likely to occur as they do not place emphasis on creating knowledge. These results reveal that QSs expect KM to bring more personal benefits than benefits to the company. One possible reason for this perception is that, in knowledge sharing, the knowledge and experience gained are mainly personal and not attributed to their companies.

Most respondents believe that the most critical factors to KM success are, in descending order, top management support, active employee participation, having knowledge-sharing space, and creating trust between employees and employers. Indeed, these factors are considered very important: without top management support, KM cannot be implemented successfully; without employee active participation, even if an excellent KM system is provided, no results can be achieved; without knowledge-sharing space, knowledge cannot be shared effectively; without trust between employees and employers, nobody would share their personal knowledge assets with their companies. Most QSs perceive that the potential barriers faced by QS firms in developing KM are underdeveloped systems, lack of time, lack of understanding of KM and lack of management support.

To conclude, the common current practices that QSs use to acquire or share knowledge are not enough to enhance employees' knowledge levels. Over half of the QSs sampled still cannot acquire all the knowledge they need from their work, so improvement in KM methods must be made to enhance their knowledge levels. As QSs overwhelmingly welcome KM and it is expected that KM can bring a lot of benefits to employees' and companies' performance, KM may represent a means of enhancing QS professionalism. However, even if KM is implemented, there are some hidden limitations to the positive effects that it can have on firms. First, as QSs seek knowledge mainly within their firm and seldom from external sources, the range of knowledge that they acquire is limited to within the profession; new knowledge or other specialist knowledge may be less likely to be acquired, so the effect of KM in enhancing their professionalism will be limited to their own field only. Secondly, knowledge creation is less emphasized in the QS profession, so even if QS firms deploy KM, no new knowledge will be created and hence the profession will be less likely to expand.

References

Allee, V. (1997) *The Knowledge Evolution: Expanding Organizational Intelligence*. Boston, MA: Butterworth-Heinemann.

Bartezzaghi, E., Corso, M. and Verganti, R. (1997) Continuous improvement and inter-project learning in new product development. *International Journal of Technology Management* 14(1): 116–138.

Bresnen, M., Edelman, L., Newell, S., Scarbrough, H. and Swan, J. (2003) Social practices and the management of knowledge in project environments. *International Journal of Project Management* 21(3): 157–166.

Choo, C. W. (1998) *The Knowing Organisation*. Oxford: Oxford University Press.

Clare, M. and DeTore, A. W. (2000) *Knowledge Assets: Professional's Guide to Valuation and Financial Management*. San Diego, CA: Harcourt.

Davenport, T. H. (1999) Knowledge management and the broader firm: strategy, advantage, and performance. In Liebowitz, J. (ed.) *Knowledge Management Handbook*. Boca Raton, FL: CRC Press.

DeFillippi, R. J. (2001) Project-based learning, reflective practices and learning outcomes. *Management Learning* 32(1): 5–10.

Dougan, N. (2000) Project organisations that learn: understanding the barriers to organizational learning in project environment – a case study. In *Paradoxes of Project Collaboration in the Global Economy: Interdependence, Complexity and Ambiguity*. Proceedings from IRNOP IV (Fourth International Conference of the International Research Network on Organizing by Projects), University of Technology, Sydney, pp. 380–390.

Drucker, P. F. (1993) *Post-capitalist Society*. New York: Harper Collins.

Drucker, P. F. (1998) The coming of the new organization. *Harvard Business Review on Knowledge Management*. Boston, MA: Harvard Business School Press, pp. 1–20.

Drucker, P. F. (2000) Knowledge–worker productivity: the biggest challenge. In Cortada, J. W. and Woods, J. A. (eds) *The Knowledge Management Yearbook 2000–2001*. Woburn, MA: Butterworth-Heinemann.

Egbu, C., Sturges, J. and Bates, M. (1999) Learning from knowledge management and trans-organisational innovations in diverse project management environments. *Proceedings of the Fifteenth Annual Conference of the Association of Researchers in Construction (ARCOM)*, Liverpool John Moores University, Liverpool, UK, 11–13 September.

Fang, T. (1999) *Chinese Business Negotiating Style*. Thousand Oaks, CA: Sage.

Fiol, C. and Lyles, M. (1985) Organizational learning. *Academy of Management Review* 10(4): 803–813.

Hansen, M. T., Nohria, N. and Tierney, T. (1999) What's your strategy for managing knowledge? *Harvard Business Review* 77(2): 106–116.

Hibbard, J. and Carrillo, K. M. (1998) Knowledge revolution. *InformationWeek* 663: 49–54.

Hildreth, P., Kimble, C. and Wright, P. (2000) Communities of practice in the distributed international environment. *Journal of Knowledge Management* 4(1): 27–38.

Kreiner, K. (1995) In search of relevance – project management in drifting environment. *Scandinavian Journal of Management* 11(4): 335–346.

Liebowitz, J. (2000) *Building Organizational Intelligence: A Knowledge Management Primer*. Boca Raton, FL: CRC Press.

Love, P. E. D., Edum-Fotwe, F. and Irani, Z. (2003) Management of knowledge in project environments. *International Journal of Project Management* 21(3): 155–156.

Lundin, R. A. (2000) Business in the world of projects. In *Project Management Research at the Turn of the Millennium*. Proceedings of PMI Research Conference PMI, USA, pp. 73–78.

Lundin, R. A. and Söderholm, A. (1995) A theory of the temporary organization. *Scandinavian Journal of Management* 11(4): 437–455.

Maister, D. (1982) Balancing the professional service firm. *Sloan Management Review* 24(1): 15–30.

Nonaka, I. and Takeuchi, H. (1995) *The Knowledge-creating Company*. New York: Oxford University Press.

Prencipe, A. and Tell, F. (2001) Inter-project learning: processes and outcomes of knowledge codification in project-based firms. *Research Policy* 30(9): 1373–1394.

RICS (1991) *Quantity Surveying 2000: The Future Role of the Chartered Quantity Surveyor*. London: Royal Institution of Chartered Surveyors.

RICS (1992) *The Core Skills and Knowledge Base of the Quantity Surveyor*. London: Royal Institution of Chartered Surveyors.

Robbins, S. P. (1994) *Management*. Englewood Cliffs, NJ: Prentice-Hall International.

Scarbrough, H., Swan, J. and Preston, J. (1999) *Knowledge Management: A Literature Review*. London: Institute of Personnel and Development.

Sveiby, K. E. and Lloyd, T. (1987) *Managing Knowhow: Add Value by Valuing Creativity*. London: Bloomsbury.

Tannenbaum, S. I. and Allifer, G. M. (2000) *Knowledge Management: Clarifying the Key Issues*. Austin, TX: Rector Duncan & Associates.

Tsoukas, H. (1996) The firm as a distributed knowledge system: a constructionist approach. *Strategic Management Journal* 17: 11–25.

Winch, G. (1998) Zephyrs of creative destruction: understanding the management of innovation in construction. *Building Research and Information* 26(5): 268–279.

Chapter 7

Building a learning organization in a project-based environment

Peter E. D. Love, Jimmy Huang, David J. Edwards and Zahir Irani

Introduction

The culmination of research by Senge (1990) has popularized the now widespread concept of the learning organization, which has evolved to meet new corporate challenges. These challenges rest upon the need to survive in a competitive and turbulent environment, while simultaneously generating sufficient profits. Senge (1990, p. 4) proposed that the 'most successful corporations of the 1990s will be something called the learning organization. The ability to learn faster than your competitors may be the only sustainable competitive advantage'. The need to transform an organization into an active learning entity is reinforced by other conceptual and empirical accounts that aim to convert organizational learning (as a passive action performed by an organization) into a driving force that invigorates an organization. Accounts provided by theorists, such as Kim (1990), Garvin (1993), Thurbin (1994), Pearn et al. (1995) and Rowley (2000), support such a notion.

Three commonly shared presuppositions found in the current learning organization debates are outlined as follows. First, in a learning organization, continuous learning at individual, group and organizational levels is embedded within the company's culture (Brown and Duguid, 1991). Secondly, a learning organization engenders an environment where synergy is created, developed and nurtured based on collective actions and shared understanding (Hutchins, 1991; Weick and Roberts, 1993). Thirdly, the argument that one type of learning is superior to another (e.g. double-loop learning is more desirable than single-loop) can no longer be sustained (Argyris and Schön, 1978). As argued by Miner and Mezias (1996), the type of learning required is dependent on the individual task as well as environmental demands. In other words, organizational learning requirements, together with the development and implementation of these, require a comprehensive understanding of the organization's unique characteristics and the environment within which it operates. In summary, the learning organization must be dynamic and thus evolve to suit individual organizations and bespoke market environments.

From the evaluation of current theoretical debates about learning in traditional project-based industries, such as construction, it is evident that the creation of a learning organization has received scant academic attention. The studies of Gherardi et al. (1998) and Gherardi (2000) represent two exceptions that have provided useful insights into how safety knowledge can be embedded into work practice through 'situated learning'. Despite their contributions, our understanding of the unique processes of construction businesses, which are by their very nature project focused, and how learning organizations can be created to align with their uniqueness remains underexploited. In particular, the growing awareness of providing service quality has highlighted the need for a construction learning organization to create and manage a learning mechanism through which continuous quality improvement can be enhanced (Kululanga et al. 2001; Love and Irani, 2002). According to Nesan and Holt (1999), total quality management (TQM) should be embedded within a construction organization so that new knowledge can be generated through the continuous refinement of quality. Even though the need to build a learning organization founded upon quality is clear, it is unfortunately evident that numerous construction organizations are reluctant to embrace TQM as part of their learning to reduce quality failures in their projects (Love et al., 2003). As a result, this has contributed to continual quality-related problems in projects. Thus, this chapter aims to provide a blueprint that managers and key decision makers can use to understand better how a learning organization can be nurtured and how their respective organization can contribute to improving the overall performance of projects in which they are involved.

Elements of a learning organization

Drawing upon the current debates and perspectives related to the learning organization, three distinctive yet interrelated elements are presented, namely actions, mindset and learning environment. Although these three elements do not exhaust all discussions, this chapter seeks to provide a conceptualization for other research to build upon. Before elucidating further on the three elements of a learning organization, two key debates observed in the organizational learning literature are worth noting and briefly discussing. First, can an organization be perceived as an independent learning entity? Hedberg (1982) and Dodgson (1993) argue that organizations as such cannot learn, as they do not exist outside the cognitive reasoning of individuals. In other words, learning is an activity performed by individuals who facilitate organizational learning.

Secondly, is learning an experience of cognitive refinement (Argyris and Schön, 1978; Kolb, 1984) or a continuous exercise of behavioural adjustment (Cyert and March, 1963)? According to Miner and Mezias (1996), both schools of thoughts are equally crucial and complementary to each other. Thus, the study of organizational learning cannot isolate the cognitive aspect from the behavioural aspect because of the mutual reinforcement between the two (Fiol and Lyles, 1985). An integrative aspect is needed because it is argued that organizational learning is a multifaceted phenomenon, collectively shaped by a community of learners (Brown and Duguid, 1991; Lave and Wenger, 1991) and influenced by the social context where learning takes place (Nicolini and Meznar, 1995; Wenger, 2000).

From the two debates, it is clear that to understand the elements of a learning organization, knowledge of the learning process (both at the individual and the collective level) and how it is promoted (or opposed by the contextual factors) must be acquired (Robey and Bourdeau, 1999). Based on the notion that individuals are the organization's principal learners, it is apparent that individual actions are vital during the conception of a learning organization. In terms of the actions, reference should be made to those that are routinized and non-routinized (Adler et al., 1999). While routinized actions can generate incremental learning, non-routinized actions are a critical source of radical learning (Miner and Mezias, 1996). So, learning can be accumulated through repeated actions, as reflected in the traditional concept of a learning curve (Epple et al., 1991). In addition, learning can be triggered by the growing demand for new knowledge, interpretation and action so as to make sense of unfamiliar and non-repeated activities (March et al., 1991; Nonaka, 1994; Adler et al., 1999).

In addition to the actions performed, the understanding of the mindset possessed and shared within a learning organization is equally vital. As indicated earlier, organizational learning is essentially a social and cognitive process. The way in which a collective mind is developed and modified determines how actions are executed (Weick and Roberts, 1993). Hence, building a learning organization largely depends on how an appropriate mindset can be nurtured and developed. According to Pavitt (1991), a correct learning organization mindset is not merely about the individuals' awareness of the importance and need for learning. Rather, the learning mindset must embrace the development of a shared belief. Shared belief is essential because cross-functional collaboration can only stimulate mutual learning when mental barriers are overcome (Boland and Tenkasi, 1995). In addition, according to Argyris and Schön (1978), the mental defence of individuals curtails double-loop learning.

Within the learning organization one must also consider the learning environment. The term social context is referred to when learning occurs as well as factors that affect the social context. Based on theorists such as Senge (1990) and Garvin (1993), a learning organization requires an environment where experimenting with new approaches is encouraged and errors are not perceived as failures. In addition, a successful learning environment is able to disseminate learning effectively from one part of the organization to others within it (Starbuck, 1992). Hence, a learning environment is closely related to how people perform their actions and perceive the need to take and change their actions. More importantly, a learning environment is associated with the organization's structure. For instance, it is argued by Pavitt (1991) that a high degree of centralization can result in overambitious, radical and ill-conceived learning, while a lack of centralization can blind an organization to foresee the need to learn.

In summary, the process of organizational learning mediates between the experiences that its members share and the culture that is established (Kolb, 1984). If people experience new challenges, but continue to interpret these challenges in the old way, the organizations culture will not evolve (Argyris, 1993). It is important to note that the processes involved in organizational learning are substantially different to those used in individual learning. Organizational learning is reflected in the organization's culture, which consists of the structure, values and outcomes of the overall organization. Individual learning does not necessarily lead to organizational learning, but it is not possible to have organizational learning without individual learning.

To create a learning organization, it is critical that employees are motivated to learn to use and disseminate their newly acquired knowledge. However, one problem that organizations typically face is transferring the new knowledge from the learning situation (and the individual) to the actual work situation and throughout the organization (Rifkin and Fulop, 1997). Therefore, the challenge is to transfer specific knowledge into general knowledge. One of the positive outcomes of a learning organization is the synergy resulting from multidimensional communication (Pedler et al., 1991). To create such synergy, learning must be automatically embedded in employees' mindsets and the epistemological artefacts of the organization's environment (Watkins and Golembiewski, 1995). If this encoding or transfer does not occur, it may only be the individuals who learn and not the organization as a whole.

Project environment of construction organizations

The construction industry in countries such as Australia and the UK has been absorbed in an intense period of introspection as a result of a several government-initiated studies, which have been critical of its performance and work practices (e.g. Gyles, 1992; Latham 1994; Egan, 1998; DIST, 1998). The Australian Procurement and Construction Committee has been particularly critical of the industry and has suggested that initiatives such as partnering have focused on addressing the symptoms rather than the causes of its poor performance (APCC, 1997). This is because construction organizations are unable to respond to almost exponential technological and social changes that have occurred throughout the marketplace (Nesan and Holt, 1999). Consequently, many organizations have been simply outperformed by international competitors and unable to deliver high-quality products or services on time.

Traditionally, contractors have relied heavily upon the goodwill of professional firms for gaining contracts and have, therefore, been reluctant to seek direct contact with clients (Nesan and Holt, 1999); however, this appears to be changing as relationship marketing is beginning to take centre stage within some organizations. Research undertaken by Tucker et al. (1996) revealed that contractors' marketing efforts tend to focus on being placed on the tender lists of federal, state and local government and private-sector clients, rather than contacting them directly. Indeed, this attitude prevents some construction organizations from fully appreciating their clients' expectations and requirements. A lack of understanding concerning client demands may result in the redesign or correction of work (i.e. rework) if certain aspects of the service or product fail to conform to client expectations. Such works invariably erode contractor profits and reduce productivity, and may engender an adversarial relationship with the client.

The absence of quality management and mechanisms has resulted in many construction organizations becoming reactive to customer demands being imposed upon them throughout the project supply chain. Moreover, an immediate focus on the project and its economy encourages a rather short-term perspective, which places emphasis on competitive bidding as the main tool for supplier evaluation (Holt et al., 2000). Such a strategy has resulted in 'distant' customer–supplier relationships in construction rather than 'close-working' partnerships (Cox and Thompson, 1997). Consequently, construction organizations have tended to differentiate themselves on price rather than the level of service quality and value that they can provide (Dubois and Gadde, 2000). This form of market differentiation may lead to a higher incidence of quality failures being incurred in projects, as firms try to maximize their profit by using only minimal resources.

Time and cost constraints of the project environment juxtaposed with the non-implementation of quality and learning practices can further vex quality failures, which in turn manifest themselves as rework and, therefore, cause customer dissatisfaction. Many construction organizations have not proactively embraced TQM because it is often mistakenly considered to be synonymous with quality assurance (Love and Li, 2000). Many businesses in Australia and New Zealand, for example, that have implemented quality management have found it to be ineffective in providing the benefits that they initially expected (Terziovski et al., 1997). Research undertaken by Love et al. (2003) for construction organizations concurs with the following finding; considering this evidence, it would appear that the Australian construction industry has generally become parsimonious to investing in quality. According to Love et al. (2000a,b), quality has failed to receive the recognition it deserves because it has often been treated as separate to a programme of change. Demonstrable evidence is provided by those construction organizations that have set out with the best intentions of becoming quality focused but have only managed to become certified to a recognized standard (Love et al., 2003).

Building a learning construction organization

If construction organizations are to improve their performance and sustain a competitive advantage, a conscious endeavour should be made to improve their organizational 'learning capability' by embracing innovative mechanisms that stimulate organizational learning and continuous innovation (Kululanga et al., 2001; Love et al., 2003). Few construction organizations have systems to acquire, capture, convert and connect their lessons learned systematically or demonstrate any interest in doing so (Love et al., 2003).

The lack of mechanisms to learn effectively does not necessarily mean that most construction organizations are not learning. Rather, it is the actions performed, mindset possessed and learning environment developed by construction organizations that cannot create the synergy proposed by the theorists (e.g. Senge, 1990; Pavitt, 1991). This is because learning in construction organizations focuses primarily on detecting errors and correcting them, while at the same time maintaining existing organizational norms (Love and Smith, 2003). If, for example, rework is to be reduced, then design consultants, contractors and other construction professionals need to change their existing business strategy so that the implicit organizational norms and objectives can be modified in order to prevent errors rather than detect them. To become prevention focused, construction organizations should aspire to develop generative learning in order to maximize synergy (Senge, 1990). Moreover, in doing so, the organization will be able to 'create systems which put in place long term capacities that are able to capture knowledge, to support creation and empower continuous transformation' (Watkins and Golembiewski, 1995, p. 88). The organization will be able to learn from experience and, therefore, detect and correct errors (e.g. rework) and with experience eradicate such completely.

A shift in strategy

In addition to the need to evaluate an organization's current reality, a comprehensive understanding of the change in the dynamics operating within the construction industry (e.g. changes in client values and new competitors) is crucial. In particular, the shift towards a customer value strategy will require construction organizations to rethink their approach to quality, so that the organization and individuals can learn in a mutually reinforcing manner (March, 1991; Boland and Tenkasi, 1995). Improving a construction organization's performance, particularly by reducing the incidence of rework, requires a change in the current method of doing business by recording, learning and acting upon past experiences. Furthermore, individuals must change their cognitive approaches and emotional responses about the organization's image and their beliefs about how things should work within it (Ledford et al., 1989).

Individuals effectively learn to improve their future actions through challenging their past assumptions, usually via open dialogue with other organizational members (Argyris and Schön, 1978; Fiol and Lyles, 1985). In doing so, they change their individual perspective on the organization and how they give meaning to events that take place. As new meanings are disseminated among other individuals and, thus, embedded within the organizational norm, the new-shared meaning serves to reshape the organizational culture (Nevis et al., 1995). Thus, to build a learning organization largely depends on the collective reflection and reaction of individuals to immediate difficulties, imbalances and problems rather than on deliberate planning (Argyris and Schön, 1978). Outcomes emanating from these actions will become fused within an organizational memory that stores, retrieves and communicates ways of knowing and acting (Walsh and Ungson, 1991). In this sense, an organization's culture is a product of collective learning (Cook and Yanow, 1996), while the collective action and shared mindset are the building blocks of a learning organization. Without the building blocks in place, a culture that is adaptive to change will be unable to foster continuous improvement and support a customer-orientated and value-added strategy (Garvin, 1993; Buckler, 1996; Garvan, 1997).

Organizational transformation

To embed and actualize the customer-orientated and value-added strategy into a construction organization, business process re-engineering (BPR) has been advocated by the Australian government as a key change mechanism for construction (DIST, 1998). Although the Australian government has set out with the right intentions, it has not acknowledged that improving quality to satisfy customers should be ingrained within an organization's internal business activities before such a radical approach to process improvement can be effectively embraced and successfully implemented. If construction organizations embrace BPR without having the appropriate enablers for change in place, then the desired performance improvements may not be achieved (Love and Li, 1998). Consequently, it is suggested that construction organizations need to rethink their approach to quality and move themselves forward through an ongoing process of organizational learning, which is especially critical for preventing quality failures. Given sufficient time and commitment, this approach may lead to the creation of an appropriate learning environment where an adaptive and generative stance to change can be encouraged and an organization's capability to improve customer value can be actualized (Dubios and Gadde, 2000). In pursuing this goal, a construction organization should seek to address the following areas:

- *organization*: its existing systems, managerial practices, methods and technologies
- *external environment*: strategies and practices of competitors, opportunities to adopt new technologies and operational methods
- *customers*: their needs and their use of products and services.

To address these areas effectively, it is suggested that construction organizations should embrace a degree of transformational change and implement a strategy that focuses on customer value (Cox and Thompson, 1997). Such change should be driven by shifts in business strategy; whereby an organization's mission, action, shared mindset and core values are redefined. Cultural change is also needed, but this is difficult to instigate without initial changes to norms, values and beliefs, which typically manifest themselves in the modes of behaviour and physical settings of the organization. Managers should not be immediately concerned with creating a 'new culture' per se, as this approach is an ineffective way of changing an organization (Beer, 1988). Rather, the change strategy should be linked to the organization's core strategic issues and the demand of its environment (Nadler, 1988).

In particular, managers who have an understanding of their organization's culture should champion the change process, since their leadership will ensure the workforce's commitment to this process (Nesan and Holt, 1999). According to Beer et al. (1990), the critical path to organizational transformation begins by redefining the roles, responsibilities and relationships of the organization and its employees. In particular, Beer et al. (1990) state that this approach addresses informal behaviour at the organizational level, which then filters down towards the coaching, training, team-building and process interventions at the individual and group levels. As argued by Senge (1990), building a learning organization is essentially a learning process that must encompass the participation of everyone.

Successful organizational transformation tends to begin at the individual units and then moves from remote and relatively isolated units into the corporate core (Beer et al., 1990). The value of placing an initial focus on roles and evolving an ad hoc approach to change is that this approach can minimize the threat often associated with formal structural change. Furthermore, it permits learning to flourish before demanding that people adopt a new, fixed organizational structure. Bounds et al. (1994) suggest that the use of leverage points may support a strategy for achieving customer value. These include:

- the criteria used for staffing decisions
- education, training and development efforts targeted towards members of the organization
- reward systems reworked and linked to strategy
- the leadership and behaviour modelling provided by key executives and managers
- employee involvement processes
- the operative goals of the organization.

Providing customer value should be the focus of the entire change and perceived as the vision to build a learning organization. Without such a focus in place, unfreezing the existing system could increase unnecessary variation in the organization's performance. Managers should encourage staff to challenge their assumptions and actions from 'disconfirming experiences' that arise from the 'old culture' (Adams, 1992). Through such a constructive and questioning approach, a new understanding towards the customer value strategy can be generated and appreciated. For example, staff working for a design consulting firm may question their management's decision to ignore particular information technology applications that communicate with and transfer drawings to other project design team members' applications, which may in turn eliminate errors due to co-ordination and integration difficulties. Moreover, staff who are equipped with past experience of client-instigated rework may suggest that the firm should embrace visualization technologies and involve clients interactively during product development and physical construction.

Over time, a new culture that institutionalizes a strategy of customer value will emerge. The emergence of the new culture will reshape the shared mindset that is required for building an effective learning organization (Pavitt, 1991). With this in mind, management should nurture the workforce's willingness by critically appraising their individual contribution to the organization. In particular, they need to examine how their behaviour manifests itself in the new dynamic learning environment and the subconscious signals that their behaviour sends to others within the organization.

Customer-orientated and quality-centred learning organizations

Hammer's (1990) article on BPR has spurred evangelists of change to espouse the use of a dogmatic, decimated and re-created approach to process improvement. However, such evangelists do not consider the fact that for process improvement to occur, the process of learning should take place sequentially with quality acting as an enabler for change (Buckler, 1996). Moreover, the prescriptive approach offers little practical advice about what and how processes are to be re-engineered and how previous knowledge is to be utilized in the new process. Thus, it is suggested that before construction organizations consider implementing BPR initiatives they should address the principles, tools and techniques embedded within TQM. This will enable knowledge to be acquired about their internal and external environments and engender a culture founded on adaptation.

An important objective for any construction organization is to integrate learning with day-to-day work processes so that lessons learned are distributed throughout the workforce in such a way that the business continues to operate efficiently and effectively as it responds to a changing environment. In other words, organizations must strive to create a learning environment where instances of 'reinventing the wheel' are minimized (von Hippel et al., 1999). Fundamentally, without putting lessons learnt into action, there is no learning. Thus, construction organizations need guiding principles to ensure that the emphasis of learning on quality improvement and perfecting customer service is effectively channelled towards improving business activities so that they can learn about their relationship with their respective environments.

Knowledge and learning are fundamental factors that need to be addressed if organizational performance is to be improved. By having the foundations for learning in place, concepts such as construction process re-engineering (CPR) and supply-chain management (SCM) can be effectively implemented. Yet, some researchers in construction have advocated these techniques as being panaceas, without acknowledging the fact that these constructs rely heavily on a quality foundation being in place before their implementation (e.g. Koskela, 1992; Mohamed and Tucker, 1996; London et al., 1998; Howell and Ballard, 1998). Figure 7.1 depicts the enabling role of TQM for initiating change and learning in construction. Here TQM assumes a fundamental role as an enabler for creating a learning environment (Kim, 1990; Barrow, 1993; Cicmil, 2000), as well as that of BPR, CPR and SCM (Love and Li, 1998).

In the manufacturing industry where TQM has matured, it is argued that organizations cannot rely solely on quality for their survival (Harrison and Storey, 1996). While Luthans et al. (1995) recognize the importance of TQM in the change process, they suggest that organizations need to move beyond TQM

Figure 7.1 *Role of total quality management in the change process.*

and embrace the concept of organizational learning if they are to adapt to their environment and improve their future performance. If construction organizations are to become adaptive and responsive to the environment then they must rethink their approaches to quality so that learning can become an organizational norm and the vision of building a learning organization can be actualized. This may require construction organizations to revisit their approaches to organizational survival, strategy development and organizational change.

To sum up the above discussion, Figure 7.2 presents a blueprint of a learning construction organization, which considers the relationship between TQM and customer value strategy as well as the inherent nature of the industry's project environment. Management in construction organizations needs to recognize that if TQM is practised as a philosophy (i.e. continuous improvement) as well as a set of learning techniques (i.e. plan–do–act–check cycle) it can be used to cultivate continuous change, learning and knowledge. Organizations operating in the industry must recognize the need to learn and to reduce the incidence of those activities that do not add value to

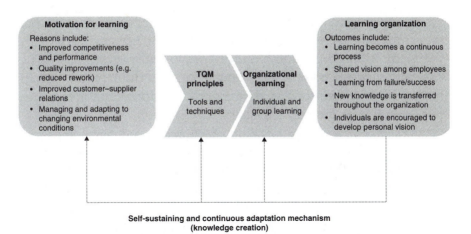

Figure 7.2 *A blueprint for a learning organization in the project-based environment of construction. TQM: total quality management (adapted from Love et al., 2000b).*

operations and customers. A TQM philosophy can be used as a framework for organizations to develop a fully shared, even synergistic understanding of information, experiences and goals of all individuals within the organization so that change can be consciously and proactively managed.

The above conceptualization has provided a blueprint for organizations that need to respond to change, which is being imposed on their external and internal environments. As elaborated earlier, the learning organization is designed for continuous responsiveness, ongoing learning, as it utilizes feedback loops to inform future decisions. It is suggested that a learning organization in construction has to be more than simply the detection of error and endless reworking. Rather, it is to promote and create an adaptive and responsive organization that is able to foster continuous improvement and provide customer value throughout its supply chain. Within this framework, there needs to be a deep understanding of the prerequisites for an organization to be essentially adaptive rather than focusing on the effectiveness of one of a series of organizational adaptations. For example, the organization cannot solely focus on preventing quality failures, as other facets of the business may be neglected. It must examine how it can provide a better overall service as well as gain a strategic competitive advantage in its particular marketplace. So, there is a need for parallel changes in how an organization is interpreted and to identify those factors considered important for survival and growth (Huber, 1991; Garvin, 1993). This could have direct implications on how managers in construction organizations think and what they think about, specifically in the context of integrating information technology within daily work activities.

If learning becomes a driving force in construction organizations it may replace the functional control of management (Thompson and Wallace, 1996; Clarke and Clegg, 1999). Thus, managers may need to learn how to account for and evaluate the intellectual capital of their organization. The key success factor for each individual organization may no longer be a matter of size or the number of assets, but the amount and quality of experience that it can apply and manage (Nonaka and Takeuchi, 1995; Kotnour, 2000).

Simply repeating strategies that have failed can lead to a reduction in profits and poor performance. Sadly, organizations in project-based environments such as construction often tend to follow such an approach (Kotnour, 2000). Construction organizations will need to promote continuous learning so as to challenge the underlying concepts, paradigms and the Weltanschauung that have determined their way of thinking in the past, in examining models of action. Such approaches also have implications for thinking about the organizational change process. It is suggested that both the nature of the change needed and how the change should be effected depend on understanding the context and the pattern of interrelationships that surround the organization and how it has been formed. This approach may produce profound change and learning over time, in contrast to many ephemeral *en vogue* change initiatives that seem to start from a different base point on each occasion.

Conclusions

The development and subsequent implementation of a learning environment within an organization is widely cited as representing a viable means through which to gain further understanding of a business venture and how it interacts with its external market environment. In turn, an opportunity for the organization to capitalize upon changes in the market environment is created and the likelihood of generating higher profit margins is increased considerably. Yet, despite the aforementioned palpable benefits associated with developing the learning organization, the construction sector has thus far largely failed to embrace the concept either in academic research work or in practice. Various industry barriers to adoption exist, for example, the unwillingness of contractors to employ TQM and an inherent inability to grasp fully the complexities of the learning philosophy.

In an attempt to readdress these observed adoption problems, a blueprint for building a learning organization in a project-based environment was presented. This blueprint allows key decision makers involved with the construction process to understand better how the learning organization can be nurtured and how overall project performance output can simultaneously be improved. The work commenced with a detailed description of the three distinctive yet interrelated elements of the learning environment (actions, mindset and learning environment) and used these as a platform upon which to build the blueprint. Concepts considered thereafter included shared belief, the learning environment, knowledge transfer, change dynamics within the industry and customer needs.

Following various damning governmental reports in countries such as Australia and the UK, it is all too evident that construction organizations need pragmatic guidance as well as criticism if desired improvements in work practices and performance are to be realized. This chapter does not provide a panacea to all construction-sector problems, but it has been successful in providing clear and lucid guidance with which decision makers can begin to learn from historical errors and move industry forward in a positive manner.

Note

An earlier version of this chapter was published in *Construction Innovation: Information, Process and Management*, 2004, Volume 4, Issue 2, pp. 113–126.

References

Adams, M. (1992) TQM: OD's role in implementing value-based strategies. In Jackson, C. N. and Manning, M. R. (eds) *Intervening in Client Organizations. Organizational Development Annual*, Vol. IV. Alexandria, VA: American Society for Training and Development.

Adler, P., Goldoftas, B. and Levine, D. (1999) Flexibility versus efficiency? A case study of model changeovers in the Toyota production system. *Organization Science* 10(1): 43–68.

Argyris, C. (1993) *Knowledge for Action: A Guide to Overcoming Barriers to Organizational Change*. San Francisco, CA: Jossey-Bass.

Argyris, C. and Schön, D. (1978) *Organizational Learning: A Theory of Action Perspective*. Reading, MA: Addison-Wesley.

Australian Procurement and Construction Council (APCC) (1997) *Construct Australia: Building a Better Construction Industry in Australia*. Deakin West, ACT: Australian Procurement and Construction Council.

Barrow, J. W. (1993) Does total quality management equal organisational learning? *Quality Progress* (July): 39–43.

Beer, M. (1988) The critical path for change: key to success and failure in six companies. In Kilmann, R. H., Covin, T. J. et al. (eds) *Corporate Transformation: Revitalizing Organizations for Competitive World*. San Francisco, CA: Jossey-Bass, pp. 17–45.

Beer, M., Eisenstat, R. A. and Spector, B. (1990) *The Critical Path to Corporate Renewal*. Boston, MA: Harvard Business School.

Boland, R. and Tenkasi, R. (1995) Perspective making and perspective taking in communities of knowing. *Organization Science* 6(4): 350–372.

Bounds, G., Yorks, L., Adams, M. and Ranney, G. (1994) *Beyond Total Quality Management: Toward the Emerging Paradigm*. New York: McGraw-Hill.

Brown, J. and Duguid, P. (1991) Organisational learning and toward a unified view of working, learning and innovation. *Organization Science* 2(1): 40–56.

Buckler, B. (1996) A learning process model to achieve continuous improvement and innovation. *Learning Organisation* 3(3): 31–39.

Cicmil, S. (2000) Quality in project environments: a non-conventional method. *International Journal of Quality and Reliability Management* 17(4/5): 554–571.

Clarke, T. and Clegg, S. (1999) *Changing Paradigms: The Transformation of Management Knowledge for the 21st Century*. London: Harper Collins Business.

Cook, S. and Yanow, D. (1996) Culture and organisational learning. In Cohen, M. and Sproull, L. (eds) *Organisational Learning*. London: Sage.

Cox, A. and Thompson, I. (1997) Fit for purpose contractual relations: determining a theoretical framework for construction projects. *European Journal of Purchasing and Supply Management* 3(3): 127–135.

Cyert, R. M. and March, J. (1963) *A Behavioral Theory of the Firm.* Cambridge, MA: Blackwell.

Department of Industry Science and Tourism (DIST) (1998) *Building for Growth: A Draft Strategy for the Building and Construction Industry.* Canberra: Department of Industry, Science and Tourism, Commonwealth of Australia Publication (February).

Dodgson, M. (1993) Organisational learning: a review of some literatures. *Organisation Studies* 14(3): 375–394.

Dubois, A. and Gadde, L.-E. (2000) Supply strategy and network effects – purchasing behavior in the construction industry. *European Journal of Purchasing and Supply Management* 6(3/4): 207–217.

Egan, J. (1998) *Rethinking Construction, Construction Task Force Report.* London: Department of the Environment, Transport and the Regions.

Epple, D., Argote, L. and Devadas, R. (1991) Organisational learning curves: a method for investigation intra-plant transfer of knowledge acquired through learning by doing. *Organization Science* 2(1): 58–70.

Fiol, C. M. and Lyles, M. A. (1985) Organisational learning. *Academy of Management Review* 10(4): 803–813.

Garvan, T. (1997) The learning organisation: a review and evaluation. *Learning Organisation* 4(1): 18–29.

Garvin, D. (1993) Building a learning organization. *Harvard Business Review* (July– August): 78–91.

Gherardi, S. (2000) The organizational learning of safety in communities of practice. *Journal of Management Inquiry* 9(1): 7–18.

Gherardi, S., Nicolini, D. and Odella, F. (1998) Toward a social understanding of how people learn in organisations. *Management Learning* 29(3): 273–297.

Gyles, R. (1992) *Royal Commission into Productivity in the Building Industry in New South Wales*, Vols 1–10. Sydney: Report by the NSW State Government.

Hammer, M. (1990) Re-engineering work – don't automate, obliterate. *Harvard Business Review* (July–August): 104–112.

Harrison, A. and Storey, J. (1996) New wave manufacturing strategies: operational, organisational and human dimensions. *International Journal of Operations and Production Management* 16(2): 63–76.

Hedberg, B. (1982) How organisations learn and unlearn. In Nystrom, P. and Starbuck, W. (eds) *Handbook of Organisation Behaviour.* Oxford: Oxford University Press.

von Hippel, E., Thomke, S. and Sonnack, M. (1999) Creating break-throughs at 3M. *Harvard Business Review* 77(5): 47–57.

Holt, G. D., Proverbs, D. and Love, P. E. D. (2000) Survey findings on UK construction procurement: is it achieving lowest cost, or value? *Asia Pacific Building and Construction Management Journal* 5(2): 13–20.

Howell, G. and Ballard, G. (1998) Implementing lean construction: understanding and action. *Proceedings of the Sixth Annual Conference of the International Conference for Lean Construction (IGLC-6)*, Guarujá, Brazil, 13–15 August.

Huber, G. P. (1991) Organisational learning: the contributing processes and the literatures. *Organization Science* 2(1): 88–115.

Hutchins, E. (1991) Organizing work by adaptation. *Organization Science* 2(1): 14–39.

Kim, D. (1990) *Toward Learning Organizations: Integrating Total Quality Control and Systems Thinking*. System Dynamics Group. Cambridge, MA: Sloan School of Management, MIT.

Kolb, D. A. (1984) *Experiential Learning*. Englewood Cliffs, NJ: . Prentice-Hall.

Koskela, L. (1992) *Application of the New Production Philosophy to Construction*. Technical Report No. 72. Stanford, CT: Center for Integrated Facility Engineering, Department of Civil Engineering, Stanford University.

Kotnour, T. (2000) Organisational learning practices in the project management environment. *International Journal of Quality and Reliability Management* 17(4/5): 393–406.

Kululanga, G. K., Edum-Fotwe, F. and McCaffer, R. (2001) Measuring construction contractors' organisational learning. *Building Research and Information* 29(1): 21–29.

Latham, M. (1994) *Constructing the Team: Joint Review of Procurement and Contractual Arrangements in the UK Construction Industry*. London: Department of the Environment.

Lave, J. and Wenger, E. (1991) *Situated Learning: Legitimate Peripheral Participation*. Cambridge: Cambridge University Press.

Ledford, G. E., Jr, Mohrman, S. A., Mohrman, M. A., Jr and Lawler, E. E. III (1989) The phenomenon of large scale organizational change. In Mohrman, M. A., Mohrman, M. A., Jr, Ledford, G. E., Cummings, T. G., Lawler, E. E. III et al. (eds) *Large Scale Organizational Change*. San Francisco, CA: Jossey-Bass.

London, K., Kenley, R. and Agapiou, A. (1998) Theoretical supply chain network modeling in the building industry. *Proceedings of the 14th Annual Conference of the Association of Researchers in Construction Management (ARCOM)*, University of Reading, UK, 9–11 September, pp. 369–379.

Love, P. E. D. and Li, H. (1998) From BPR to CPR – conceptualising re-engineering in construction. *Business Process Management Journal* 4(4): 291–306.

Love, P. E. D. and Li, H. (2000) Overcoming the problems associated with quality certification. *Construction Management and Economics* 18(2): 139–149.

Love, P. E. D. and Smith, J. (2003) Bench-marking, bench-action and bench-learning: rework mitigation in projects. *ASCE Journal of Management in Engineering* 19(4): 147–159.

Love, P. E. D., Li, H., Irani, Z and Faniran, O. (2000a) Total quality management and the learning organisation – a dialogue for change in construction. *Construction Management and Economics* 18(3): 321–332.

Love, P. E. D., Li, H., Irani, Z. and Holt, G. D. (2000b) Total quality management: a framework for facilitating organisational learning and change in construction. *International Bi-Monthly for Total Quality Management: TQM Magazine* 12(2): 107–117.

Love, P. E. D., Irani, Z. and Edwards, D. (2003) Learning to reduce rework in projects: analysis of firms' learning and quality practices. *Project Management Journal* 34(3): 13–25.

Luthans, F., Rubach, M. and Marsnik, P. (1995) Going beyond total quality: the characteristics, techniques, and measures of learning organisations. *International Journal of Organisational Analysis* 3(1): 24–44.

March, J. (1991) Exploration and exploitation in organisational learning. *Organization Science* 2(1): 71–86.

March, J., Sproull, L. and Tamuz M. (1991) Learning from samples of one or fewer. *Organization Science* 2(1): 1–13.

Miner, A. and Mezias, S. (1996) Ugly duckling no more: pasts and futures of organisational learning research. *Organization Science* 7(1): 88–99.

Mohamed, S. and Tucker, S. N. (1996) Options for applying BPR in the Australian construction industry. *International Journal of Project Management* 14(6): 379–385.

Nadler, D. A. (1988) Organizational frame bending: types of change in the complex organization. In Kilmann, R. H., Covin, T. J. and Associates. (eds) *Corporate Transformation: Revitalizing Organizations for Competitive World*. San Francisco, CA: Jossey-Bass, pp. 66–83.

Nesan, J.-L. and Holt, G. D. (1999) *Empowerment in Construction: The Way Forward for Performance Improvement*. Hertfordshire: Somerset Research Studies Press.

Nevis, E., DiBella, A. and Gould, J. (1995) Understanding organisations as learning systems. *Sloan Management Review* (Winter): 73–85.

Nicolini, D. and Meznar, M. (1995) The social construction of organisational learning: conceptual and practical issues in the field. *Human Relations* 48(7): 727–746.

Nonaka, I. (1994) A dynamic theory of organisational knowledge creation. *Organization Science* 5(1): 14–37.

Nonaka, I. and Takeuchi, H. (1995) *The Knowledge Creating Company*. New York: Oxford University Press.

Pavitt, K. (1991) Key characteristics of the large innovating firm. *British Journal of Management* 2(1): 41–50.

Pearn, M., Roderick, C. and Mulrooney, C. (1995) *Learning Organisations in Practice*. London: McGraw-Hill.

Pedler, M., Burgoyne, J. and Boydell, T. (1991) *The Learning Company*. Maidenhead: McGraw-Hill.

Rifkin, W. and Fulop, L. (1997) A review and case study on learning organisations. *Learning Organisation* 4(4): 135–148.

Robey, D. and Bourdeau, M.-C. (1999) Accounting for the contradictory organisational consequences of information technology: theoretical directions and methodological implication. *Information Systems Research* 10(2): 167–185.

Rowley, J. (2000) From learning organisation to knowledge entrepreneur. *Journal of Knowledge Management* 4(1): 7–15.

Senge, P. M. (1990) *The Fifth Discipline: The Art and Practice of the Learning Organisation*. London: Century.

Smith, J. and Jackson, N. (2000) Strategic needs analysis: its role in brief development. *Facilities* 18(13/14): 502–512.

Starbuck, W. (1992) Learning by knowledge intensive firms. *Journal of Management Studies* 29(6): 713–740.

Terziovski, M., Samson, D. and Dow, D. (1997) The business value of quality management systems certification: evidence from Australia and New Zealand. *Journal of Operations Management* 15(1): 1–18.

Thompson, P. and Wallace, T. (1996) Redesigning production through team working: case studies from the Volvo Truck corporation. *International Journal of Operations and Production Management* 16(2): 103–112.

Thurbin, P. J. (1994) *Implementing the Learning Organisation. The 17-day Programme*. London: Pitman.

Tucker, S. N., Love, P. E. D., Tilley, P. A., Salomonsson, G. S., MacSporran, C. and Mohamed, S. (1996) *Perspectives of Construction Contractors Communication and Performance Practices: Pilot Survey Report*. DBCE DOC 96/29 (M) (May). Melbourne, Australia: CSIRO.

Walsh, J. and Ungson, G. (1991) Organisational memory. *Academy of Management Review* 16(1): 57–91.

Watkins, K. E. and Golembiewski, R. (1995) Re-thinking organisation development for learning organisations. *International Journal of Organisational Analysis* 3(1): 86–101.

Weick, K. and Roberts, K. (1993) Collective mind in organisations: heedful interrelating on flight decks. *Administrative Science Quarterly* 38(3): 357–381.

Wenger, E. (2000) Communities of practice and social learning systems. *Organisation* 7(2): 225–246.

Chapter 8

Reflection, participation and learning in project environments: a multiple perspective agenda

Svetlana Cicmil

Introduction

This chapter offers insights into the nature of knowledge and learning in project environments as experienced by practitioners. Drawing on a large-scale study reported in Cicmil (2003), it aspires to make a contribution towards developing a framework within which these experiences could be contained and which could guide the process of creation and evaluation of knowledge relevant to a successful accomplishment of project objectives and realization of expected benefits. The chapter does not specifically address knowledge management (KM) principles and practices, as these have been addressed earlier in this book. Moreover, the enquiry, argument and discussion presented in this chapter do not provide closure on unsolved issues in the field, nor do they aspire to suggest better prescriptions on how to manage knowledge for successful project performance. Rather, the intention is to understand and make sense of how project practitioners view the issues of knowledge and learning in project work, and what type of knowledge, according to their experience, is considered useful and relevant to successful accomplishment of the goals of a project. Through the practical considerations of the concepts of holistic, unbounded systems thinking, a multiple perspective-based participative enquiry and public reflection, the chapter offers an alternative way of thinking about the processes in which project practitioners create and share useful knowledge.

The chapter unfolds in the following way. First, the assumptions about the nature of knowledge that are of interest to projects are outlined within the field of project management. Based on an overview of the selected relevant literature and research, the key issues and challenges related to knowledge dissemination and learning in project-based environments are discussed. Then, an empirical study on which this chapter is based, its conceptual underpinning and key outcomes are presented. The results are used to develop a practical project management multiple perspective (PM-MP) framework that can be used to stimulate learning and the sharing of knowledge between project team members.

Understanding project environments: projects, knowledge and learning

We live and work in the world of projects. The term 'projecticized society' captures well the expansion of project-based organizing and management in contemporary organizations and industries beyond the traditional project environments of construction, aerospace and defence. Projects are now widely used as a structural device for integrating diverse functions of organizations for the performance of uncertain and complex tasks (Packendorff, 1995). The impact of contemporary projects on society is immense. Their outcomes qualitatively change the way in which people live by creating independence from space and elimination of distance, thus framing a frictionless society (Flyvbjerg et al., 2003). Although the principles of project work and project-based management have been promoted as a blueprint for successful performance in the contemporary business world, and despite the effort to raise the profile of contemporary large-scale complex projects and their benefits across the globe, the rate of project ventures qualified as failures is not decreasing. Several studies emphasize the need to improve performance of projects in terms of environmental concerns, safety, economy and sustainable future opportunities (Atkinson, 1999; Maylor, 2000; Saad et al., 2002; Flyvbjerg et al., 2003). The frequently quoted reasons for continuous problems with project performance are the uniqueness and temporality of project arrangements, and uncertainty in the execution of project work (Young, 1998; Meredith and Mantel, 2000; Maylor, 2001). The constraints under which individual project team members perform their work include a high degree of complexity and interconnectedness of tasks where the formal structures needed to facilitate co-ordination and control of work are lacking, and high dependence on diverse skills and collective knowledge in the arrangement where individuals have little time to find out who knows precisely what. Further complexity is added through the intertwining of political, technological, cultural, social and organizational factors (Meredith and Mantel, 1995; Cicmil, 2000). Yet, this engenders a paradoxical situation. The very characteristics of a project that promote it as an ideal template for work design – a unique temporary unit, multifunctional multidisciplinary teams, customer focus, strategic orientation, disciplined approach to management of time, cost and quality – simultaneously present the major obstacles to information exchange and collaborative accomplishment of tasks within agreed constraints of time, cost and quality, by various parties involved in a project (Greiner and Schein, 1981; Packendorff, 1995; Kreiner, 1995; Das and Teng, 1998; Marshall, 2001; Sydow and Staber, 2002).

Concurrently, knowledge as a form of social capital has been identified as one of the major competitive requirements in the emerging information age, in which projects are playing an increasingly important role. Love et al. (2003, p. 155) for example, state: 'If managed effectively, knowledge can be used to reduce project time, improve quality and customer satisfaction as well as minimize "reinventing the wheel". ... [knowledge management] is a necessary prerequisite for project success in today's dynamic and changing environment'.

There is a concern that the rate of projects qualified as 'failures' is a consequence of little learning taking place in relation to the main methodology of decision making behind contemporary projects. For example, Flyvbjerg et al. (2003) claim that 'the reason for the lack of learning is that projects and their ... impacts are rarely audited ex post, and without post-auditing learning is impossible' (p. 49). Postproject reviews are effective in disseminating knowledge about good practices, correcting errors in individuals' knowledge, especially their knowledge about other functions within the organization, or about other parties within the project coalition or specific groups of project stakeholders, and predicting how alternative practices would have turned out (Busby, 1999). Project evaluation practices which encourage knowledge sharing and communication are promoted as important learning mechanisms and have value in disseminating insights about a completed project throughout the organization and society (Meredith and Mantel, 2000). Successful project outcomes are often related to the ability and willingness of project parties to learn from each other within a single project and across projects over time and space (DeFillippi, 2001; Flyvbjerg et al., 2003; Bresnen et al., 2003).

However, the strategies, including regular project evaluations, that should facilitate communicative understanding and learning among project participants, are not common practice in project environments, nor are they always effective in achieving improved mutual understanding, knowledge sharing and dissemination, even if practised. The next section of this chapter will shed some light on the key problematic and 'unsolved' issues identified in the efforts to capture, share and disseminate relevant knowledge from a specific project. These challenges are:

- dealing with complex problems that practitioners face in contemporary organizational environments and society
- the problematic nature and definition of knowledge
- the issues of participation, intersubjective understanding and reflection in complex and dynamic organizational arrangements.

Creating knowledge and learning about complex problems

Mitroff and Linstone (1993) and Stacey (2001, 2003), among others, have urged academics and practitioners to adopt new methodologies of enquiry in studying complex issues in contemporary businesses. They argue that traditional analytical approaches and methods prescribed in the mainstream business and management literature poorly equip individuals and communities of practice with thinking skills and competences necessary for creating knowledge about, and acting on, complex issues that they face in their practice in local environments in the living present. One of the underlying arguments is that all complex problems involve a multiplicity of actors (groups and individuals) and various scientific and technical disciplines. In principle, each sees a problem differently and thus generates a distinct perspective on it. The integration of these, often conflicting, views makes intersubjective understanding, learning and knowledge sharing challenging to achieve or manage.

In project environments, the temporary nature of organizational arrangements implies an intensive interdisciplinary and, frequently, interorganizational social interaction. By implication, knowing and learning in such environments involve a degree of interpretation (Fernie et al., 2003) as different groups and individuals focus on different aspects of project reality or create the meaning according to their own experience and understanding of the gains, purpose, expectations and the operation of power in the specific context. A significant body of literature and research has identified a range of complex issues to do with the influences and assumptions of multiple stakeholders affected by or connected with a project (Cleland, 1995; Williams, 1999; Bresnen and Marshall, 2000; Newcombe, 2000; Sydow and Staber, 2002).

The nature of knowledge

Another important consideration in developing the enquiry relevant to the theme of this chapter and the edition as a whole is our understanding of the nature of knowledge. Blackler (1995) has argued that the concept of knowledge is complex and its relevance to organizational theory has been insufficiently developed. Knowledge is often assumed to exist independently of the context, and the possibility of its capturing and codification is taken for granted. Blackler (1995) considers such approaches to knowledge as problematic. He argues for replacing the traditional speculations about knowledge with the notion of knowing as an active process, where the central focus of enquiry embraces the systems through which people achieve their knowing, the changes within such systems and the creation of new knowledge. There has been a recent development in the literature critically orientated towards mainstream assumptions (e.g. Brown and Duguid, 1998; Krogh et al., 2000), arguing that it is not only that the individual's absorptive capacity is required, but rather that knowledge is produced and held collectively (Brown and Duguid, 1998). This is argued by acknowledging that the power to create knowledge is not just with the person but in the interaction with others and the environment. Knowledge and learning are context dependent and are 'performed', actualized in conversations and other types of communication that involve individual and group relations in the media of symbols, artefacts and power relations (Stacey, 2001).

In their study of knowledge and best practice transfer from one industrial context to another, Fernie et al. (2003) also demonstrate the critical role of recontextualization, social interaction and dialectic debate in understanding the process of knowledge sharing. They take the stance that 'any knowledge sharing method must hold at its core the notion of the interaction of individuals' (p. 179). The proposition emerging from this stream of debate about knowledge creation, sharing and learning in organizational arrangements focuses on the importance of communicative intersubjective understanding in a specific context.

Reflection and participation

Drawing on the preceding discussion, this section considers the processes of reflection and participation in the context of sustained learning and knowledge sharing in project environments. Raelin (2001) introduced the notion of public reflection as a possibility through which 'we may create a collective identity as a community of inquiry' (p. 11). Reflection as the practice of 'periodically stepping back to ponder the meaning to self and to others in one's immediate environment about what has recently transpired' (Raelin, 2001, p. 11) illuminates actions, beliefs and feelings that have been experienced by both self and others, thus providing a basis for future action. This is possible, according to Raelin (2001, p. 11), if reflection takes a public form; that is, if it is practised in the company of others who are also 'committed to the experience in question'.

Reporting on his observation of project review meetings, designed to facilitate cross-project learning, Busby (1999) illustrates this point by stating: 'Some of the knowledge that was learned was not so much task knowledge as knowledge that helped social relationships. For example, people would find out how hard others' jobs were, understand how severe were the constraints others operated under, and how hard it could be for others to be helpful' (p. 26).

The recommended action is the joint exploration of, and reflection on, patterns of participation in the ongoing flow of communicative interaction in which knowledge emerges. Busby further identifies that knowing other people's points of view is an important kind of knowledge for effective members of organizations. Such knowledge is not easily created during the course of accomplishing given activities, but requires willingness among the collaborators to reflect together on the quality of their participation (Stacey, 2003). Raelin, Busby and Stacey emphasize collective reflection as an important quality of learning and knowledge sharing among project participants. In practice, it requires the ability of individuals to embrace holistically and simultaneously multiple perspectives of an issue of concern, and to develop a strong sense of accountability, transparency and self-reflection.

The project management–multiple perspective framework: participation, learning and reflection

A framework based on practitioners' experiences with complex projects with regard to project performance is now presented. Over 150 practitioners participated in the study, which captured their experiences in relation to over 100 different projects. The respondents' backgrounds were diverse and their roles in projects varied, including senior decision makers, project managers and project team members. The empirical research was longitudinal, designed as an integral part of management development and training programmes from which the interview respondents were selected.

Participative enquiry

The empirical part of the study was designed as a participative co-operative enquiry to generate insights into project-related experiences of practitioners on the basis of their accounts, reflections and thoughts, obtained mainly through the method known as active interviewing (Reason, 1988; Holstein and Gubrium, 1995; Silverman, 2001). In this type of empirical study, the respondents are simultaneously participants (the researcher's partners) in the process of the enquiry, rather than merely the sources of relevant information or answers (Johnson and Duberley, 2000). Participative enquiry, generally, departs from a positivist principle of objectivity and focuses on the experiences and explanations of the individuals concerned, allowing them to participate in deciding what questions and issues are worth researching in the first place (Reason, 1988; Easterby-Smith et al., 1991). They become fully engaged with their reflections and experiences and frequently see them in a new way (Johnson and Duberley, 2000). Fundamental to any form of participative research is that 'it makes a difference to individual's experience and that those who are being researched play an active role in the process, rather than being passive subjects' (Johnson and Duberley, 2000, p. 139). The author's approach was to encourage participation from those whose experiences are being researched and to legitimize knowledge of those engaged in project work at a variety of hierarchical and professional levels in practice. Construction of meaning within the active interview is a dynamic process where the research topic frames the initial questions, but the meaning of what emerges is actually constructed within the interview interaction between the interviewer and the respondent (Holstein and Gubrium, 1995, p. 52).

The following was of interest in the enquiry: to gain insights into what the various project actors and decision makers see as most important to know, be aware of or understand in order to cope with, and act (get the job done) in, project-based arrangements, taking into account the interests and benefits of all collaborating parties and affected social groups, as well as the possibility and need for future collaborative ventures. This participative enquiry was based on open questions and qualitative methods. The participants were asked to reflect on their experience with projects, give examples, and comment on those aspects of knowledge, individual awareness and learning processes that they could identify as relevant to effective decision making, problem solving and management in project environments. The interviews were recorded and codified by presenting insights in a tabular and graphical format.

The interpretation of practitioners' accounts generated through the active interviewing process indicated the existence of a range of positions and perspectives from which the participants view the nature of knowledge and learning in project environments, and their relevance to the successful accomplishment of project tasks. Through the participative (co-operative) interpretation of the insights and accounts between the researcher and respondents, five perspectives were identified, representing distinct domains of awareness, learning, information and knowledge, which broadly define the complexity of issues that affect the performance and outcome of projects under the conditions of uncertainty and relational and technological complexity (Table 8.1). These domains frame the experiences of different types of project actors in a variety of project situations (including traditional engineering, organizational change, innovation and information technology projects). Codification of the project perspectives, for the ease of recording and communication in the subsequent stages of the enquiry, took place simultaneously with their definition (CX: context; CN: content; OB: organizational behaviour; Comm: communication processes; P: project congruence). It is interesting to note the qualitatively different properties of these domains/perspectives (Table 8.1). The important observation that emerged from this participative enquiry was the interconnectedness of the perspectives, not their hierarchical presupposing. The section below illuminates this issue.

Interpreting the interconnectedness of the perspectives

Although it was possible to identify and explain each perspective in its own right (Table 8.1), the interpretation of the participants' accounts and interview material show that, in

Table 8.1   Domains of knowledge, learning and collaborative interaction in project environments

Perspectives/domains of knowledge and learning	Themes, concerns and interventions
Context The origins of the idea, strategic decisions, historical attributes, projected benefits; holistic understanding of performance objectives, risks, end-users' context, impact on society over time and space	– The reason for project initiation; the projected ultimate benefit – Performance objectives and their relationship with policy objectives/strategy/ethical norms – Criteria for project approval; sources of finance and funding – Type of contractual arrangement and procurement method – What are the potential sources of risk? – Who are the project stakeholders/customers/the client/the end-users? – What are their expectations related to the project deliverable? – To what extent have the success criteria for the project been identified, defined and agreed within the project coalition? – Industrial and social context of the project: environmental, legal and political influences, regulations and level of hostility towards project
Content Technical, scientific and technological traits of the scope of work and nature of the projected deliverable/outcome	– Nature/type of expected end-product; technical solution proposed – Nature and scope of work involved – Requirements for professional expertise and technical know-how – Degree of innovation in project product/process/development/work/methods – Level of expected change in project product definition or work method throughout project life due to technological uncertainty
Organizational behaviour Organizational and individual implications and individual and group behaviour in a multiparty coalition; social characteristics of project arrangements	– Structural and relational traits of the project coalition: the attitude among project parties; power asymmetries; historical background – Possible impediments to cross-functional/multiprofessional collaboration on project; conflicts, confidence and trust – Selection of project manager; project manager skills and competences

(Continued)

Table 8.1   *(Continued)*

Perspectives/domains of knowledge and learning	*Themes, concerns and interventions*
Organizational behaviour (Continued)	– Emotions: moods and feelings; motivation; personal growth; learning – Availability of professional expertise and technical know-how needed; specific training needs – Reward and recognition issues – Wider organizational involvement and influences; sources and degree of resistance towards project; micropolitics – Issues of ethics, aesthetics, culture and accountability related to the implementation, operations and economic impact of the project
Communication	– Communication and social interaction of individuals and groups in project-related decision making, working and management – Monitoring and responding to risks; evaluation of options – Dealing with conflict – Processes of generating useful knowledge in the ongoing accomplishment of project work, and learning for future projects, for personal growth of individual project actors – Use of information and communication technology in designing and maintaining a project-spanning web of communication channels
Project congruence	– Accomplishment of project objectives (time, cost, quality) in congruence with the overall performance criteria (economic, environmental/ health and safety, and efficiency) agreed within the project coalition and accepted by a wider range of affected stakeholders – Project management procedures for planning, quality, budget and scope control; configuration management and control to attain the congruence between the project criteria, the method of work and the outcomes/ deliverables over time

practice, it is difficult to focus on a particular perspective and knowledge domain without acknowledging the influence of the others. Everything seems to be connected with everything, and each individual perspective is inseparable from any other perspective. The P perspective (project congruence), in its own

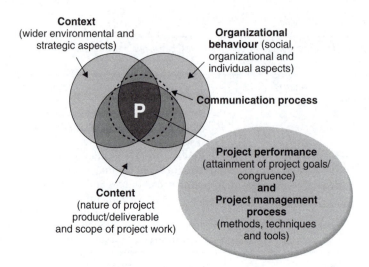

Figure 8.1   *The project management multiple perspective framework.*

right, represents the accomplishment of a sophisticated, co-operative project activity (encompassing organizational, individual and technical aspects) in congruence with the overall performance criteria agreed within the project coalition and accepted by a wider range of affected stakeholders. It is captured in a Venn diagram (Figure 8.1) as an intersection of all other domains, interpreted and understood as simultaneously being created by the other four perspectives and integrating them to create the project itself. The CX, CN and OB perspectives encourage the considerations of a dynamic and extended project life cycle, which means taking into account different 'raters' (Atkinson, 1999) and differing views on project performance assessment and criteria for evaluation, the technical nature of project work, behavioural and political issues, project risk, complexity and paradox inherent in the phenomenon of the project.

In an attempt to capture and maintain the richness, dynamics and interconnectedness of the themes and concerns experienced by the practitioners, a Venn diagram (Figure 8.1) was used to visualize the proposed construct, the PM-MP framework. The accounts quoted below are taken from the empirical material to illustrate this interconnectedness among the domains of knowledge or perspectives.

A construction project professional, a participating respondent in this enquiry, explained:

> It is notoriously difficult to perform a genuine, purposeful evaluation of project performance (P) at any stage of its life cycle while struggling to figure out and clarify what the real project goals are (CX) and what factors need to be addressed to achieve these. The more usually accepted and tangible objectives of time, cost and quality are often focused on (CN), but it soon becomes clear that their attainment or otherwise (P) is critically linked to the attitude and commitment of the project team (OB) across a much wider range of issues.

Similarly, another respondent, a production manager, experienced in capital investment and organizational change projects in the food processing industry, identified the following:

> ... although structured and planned for in advance, the project work (CN) and project management procedures (P) always get distorted by unexpected unforeseen problems during the course of project implementation: resistance to change, lack of support (OB), inadequate budget (CX, CN) and poorly monitored costs (CX, OB, Comm) ....

A change manager in a large service organization with experience in a wide range of both in-house and contracted projects commented on critical issues as interconnected, simultaneous and inseparable:

> Getting a joint understanding (Comm, OB) of what the project objective is (CX, CN) – surfacing individual agendas (OB); understanding how loyalty to other communities (OB) can distort the project progress (P); understanding how to achieve win–win outcomes (P, CX) ... Beware egos, politics (OB) ..., close the communication loop (Comm); you rarely achieve what you had set out to, you need to be aware of your minimum requirement (CX, P, CN).

A hospital laboratory manager, commenting on his experience with knowledge domains and concerns affecting project performance, said:

> ... adherence to regulations; coping with 'red tape'; working with a team – knowing how and when to compromise (OB,

P, CX); co-ordination – communication – need to chase (Comm); flexibility – modify requirements to meet stakeholders' criteria (CX, CN); endurance – meetings to discuss all process elements (Comm, OB)'.

Communication: an overarching domain

On the basis of the empirical material containing interpretations of rich expressions and experiences of participating project actors, the processes of project planning, evaluation and control can be interpreted as processes of communication, knowledge creation and learning. Referring to the problems with a lack of communication, understanding and knowledge in the context of a construction project in the situations when one needs to deal with changes due to uncertainty and imperfection of plans, a participant stated:

> ... each element of the project is represented by an individual with differing views, knowledge and goals ... mutual understanding of risks and learning to cope with the paradox is part of our daily practice. From my experience it is all down to communication, information sharing and agreement on realistic achievable objectives. You have to simultaneously handle different sources of information and make decisions ....

Projects seem to be experienced as dynamic social arrangements where communication and conflicts emerge as integral to learning and knowledge sharing. In the interviews, accounts and reflections, insights were generated that indicate that technical complexity of projects, knowledge creation, sharing and learning can almost always be qualitatively understood as a form of conversation or communication in the medium of symbols and defined by power relations that create, and are created by, the project coalition. Participants see knowledge not as cumulative, but as complex, dialectic and reflexive in nature. They talk about their experience from previous projects, where learning from history takes place through intersubjective communicative understanding in the specific context and by making reference to concrete examples or project artefacts to explain what worked and what did not work. Reference is frequently made to the conditions of radical unpredictability of project work execution, polyphony of voices, negotiation and improvisation relevant to all five domains (Table 8.1).

Applications of the project management multiple perspective framework in practice

Given the nature of the process in which it has been developed, the PM-MP framework offers a platform for critical engagement with knowledge, learning, and decision making in project practice, from a variety of perspectives defined by the five domains (Table 8.1, Figure 8.1). Inevitably, these perspectives exist simultaneously in the environments of temporary multiparty coalitions such as projects and should be recognized in any discussion of KM in project environments. In the years since the framework described in this chapter was first developed, the author and her colleagues have had opportunities to apply it to a number of organizations, both public and private (Saad et al., 2002), and to integrate it on a continuous basis in their educational programmes, including both academic courses and in-house training. A number of the research participants incorporated the issues raised during the interviews and development of the framework into their own in-company projects or consultancy activities in their local environment (e.g. Naybour, 1999; Rae, 2000). Ideally, the framework can be used in practice in engaging with practitioners and organizations, to facilitate, through a dialogue, mutual understanding of their everyday experiences with the project and knowledge sharing. In addition to it, and in more normative terms, it can be used as an evaluation framework, a diagnostic instrument and a risk assessment tool in the process of co-operative analysis of a given project situation throughout its life cycle.

Achieving a balanced consideration of all possible perspectives or domains of knowledge in the decision-making process, being aware of limitations of letting one take over all the others, and understanding the consequences of such an approach, would be a significant step forward in knowledge creation, dissemination, sharing and learning in project environments. There is always some tension between the perspectives from which a project situation can be viewed and assessed. The author has noticed that certain individuals or groups favour or identify their interests with a particular perspective, almost to the exclusion of others. In practice, the CN and P perspectives are frequently seen as most important by project managers and senior decision makers, OB and Comm by team members, and CX by external stakeholders. (The study presented here was not designed to measure this difference in priorities.)

Skill and ability are required to cope with such tensions and simultaneously hold conflicting views, and to arrive, through communicative intersubjective relating, at a decision that enables joint action towards the accomplishment of the project goals. Flyvbjerg et al. (2003) also claim that 'assessments of projects are often restricted to check listing procedures that stress well-established knowledge on local impacts, while ignoring interregional, global, systemic or long-term effects' (pp. 49–50). Certain issues (mostly technical specification and financial performance criteria) are frequently prioritized over other possible aspects of the given project, which present valuable areas of knowledge and learning. Busby, for example, observed empirically and phenomenologically how people, collectively, went about learning from project reviews. He identified a phenomenon which he termed 'dialectic argument': 'One person would voice an explanation of something, another would come back with a contradictory explanation, and someone would find a third explanation that incorporated both the previous ones ...' (Busby, 1999, p. 24). In other words, a multiple perspective understanding of a project situation can be created only through intersubjective communicative relating as no one person alone has enough information to consider all sides of the argument.

The author's experience to date in applying the PM-MP framework in educational and organizational settings shows that it encourages a constructive and reflexive dialogue between those who play an active role in making decisions with respect to environmental, safety, economic and other aspects of a project. The proposed qualities of the framework resonate well with Busby's key recommendations for managing learning and knowledge sharing in project environments, including the capacity to:

- encourage the examination of the bigger system beyond the immediate confines of the project
- 'discourage glib categorization' (1999, p. 29); in a large body of literature dealing with knowledge sharing and learning in project environments, communication among participants is identified as a critical factor (Clarke, 1999; Das and Teng, 1998)
- approach communication problems in complex projects, only as 'a starting point to the diagnosis, not a finishing point' (Busby, 1999, p. 29); a proper diagnosis would examine how different assumptions arise and why they persist even when they lead to errors.

Following from Busby's findings on the basis of his observations of project review meetings, the PM-MP framework can be used in similar situations to encourage groups, organizations and individuals to play a constructive role in determining how to meet the objectives and benefits that they would like to see met with a project. As discussed in the earlier sections of this chapter, three considerations have been identified as being important to facilitate the process of learning and communicative intersubjective understanding among individuals and groups in complex social situations, such as project arrangements. It is useful to revisit these prerequisites and discuss how the utilization of benefits from the PM-MP framework in practice can be strengthened.

Unbounded systems thinking and the project management multiple perspective framework

Mitroff and Linstone (1993) have suggested a concept known as unbounded systems thinking (UST) rooted in the multiple perspectives (MP) method of enquiry, as a suitable approach to creating knowledge about complex business phenomena in the 'information age' and 'knowledge economy', where everything interacts with everything. They argue that in today's world, economic success demands that one must be able to examine problems from multiple perspectives, to formulate multiple, often conflicting definitions of critical problems, to examine how the problem will affect and be affected by different people scattered throughout every level of society, and to consider the most critical aspects of all problems: their aesthetic and ethical dimensions. The UST and MP methods promote a simultaneous, holistic understanding of an organizational phenomenon and its complexity, capturing the system's instability over time, the technical aspects, the dynamic inter-subjective communicative relating, and organizational and structural implications and political traits of the temporary coalition that is the project.

In contrast to analytical thinking, systems thinking assumes that the entity in question can only be understood in the context of its wider environment. The qualities of that entity, which we are seeking to discover and make sense of, are the property not only of the entity itself, but also of the relation-ships between the entity under investigation and the other entities that compose its environment. Furthermore, the phe-nomenon is simultaneously seen as both a system composed of smaller elements and a subsystem of a larger system. If the dimensions of time and space are brought into consideration, an application of systems thinking implies that to understand any component of the universe we must understand its rela-tionships with other entities and the dynamics of those rela-tionships over time.

In principle, UST assumes a transdisciplinary epistemol-ogy; that is, it problematizes the possibility of solving import-ant problems by respecting the current structure of the disciplines, knowledge fields and professions (Mitroff and Linstone, 1993), and it recognizes that every:

- science is to be found within every other
- model presupposes (implies, includes) every other model
- problem is to be found within every other problem.

Participation, public reflection and the project management multiple perspective framework

Reflective practice considers data beyond our personal, interpersonal and organizational taken-for-granted assumptions to explore historical and social processes (cultural background) behind individual knowing, and in that process of learning to include those groups that may be marginalized, or previously left behind, in specific project settings. Such practices involve accountability and transparency, and are not easy to instil in project environments where continuous conflict, asymmetries of power and political agendas too frequently dictate what counts as 'relevant' knowledge and what 'learning', and by whom, is considered useful and beneficial. Learning practices through a dialogue and public reflection can be threatening unless accompanied by an environment that intellectually and emotionally supports individuals and their learning and development (Raelin, 2001).

When underpinned by unbounded systems thinking and dialectic argument incorporating public reflection and participation, as discussed in the preceding sections, the PM-MP framework engages the practitioners as active, thinking participants in the process of knowing, learning and decision making, emphasizing ethical aspects of knowledge creation and the role of power in acknowledging what counts as knowledge in a specific project environment. This calls for a participative involvement of extended peer communities (Funtowicz and Ravetz, in Flyvbjerg et al., 2003, p. 112) that are 'competent but representing interests outside the social paradigm of the official expertise' related to the project initiation and governance. Thus, wider groups of project stakeholders are no longer merely 'impacted', but they are 'knowledge generators' enhancing the knowledge base for the project. The nature of the original research design placed the researcher and the practitioners in a communicative situation that contributed to enhanced intersubjective understanding between participants and their associated paradigms, which are not mutually exclusive. This resonates with the insights from the literature discussed above, identifying the following characteristics of the process of learning from a dialogue-based project review or evaluation which need to be understood and facilitated:

- Participation induces multiple definitions of the problem.
- It surfaces different scientific, professional and philosophical positions of participating project actors in their decision-making processes.
- It requires an ability for simultaneous and holistic coping with the multiple perspectives involved in analysing, interpreting and creating knowledge about a given project issue.

As mentioned earlier, certain professions, management functions and project stakeholders tend to prioritize or recognize only one or very few domains of knowledge and learning identified within the PM-MP framework, and to treat them as critical to their involvement in a given project. There is always a tension between the perspectives held by different parties to the same project that influence the view of what is and what is not considered as relevant to the project. Unbounded systems thinking, as a philosophical system, acknowledges and endorses multiple epistemological positions in creating knowledge about the phenomenon of interest. The participants in project evaluation exercises based on the propositions behind the PM-MP framework are encouraged to reflect on what they learn and on what is presented to them as knowledge, and to explore the adequacy of such knowledge in their particular organizational and project contexts. They are encouraged to take the role of practitioner/researcher and conduct constructive enquiries of their specific practices as part of their everyday professional activity, and to do it from the perspective of participative enquiry. The quality of learning proposed by the PM-MP framework can be seen as resembling dialectical knowing, which calls for recasting and reframing conventional ways of understanding and for paying attention to features of the project-related issue that were previously ignored or taken for granted. The proposition is that participative reflection facilitated by the PM-MP framework can increase learning at all levels of experience, even at the societal level, by allowing the participants to search collectively for opportunities for co-operative action on the project, by considering present conditions and deliberating about the future.

Potential problems and limitations

One of the acknowledged limitations of frameworks incorporating systemic, processual or participative approaches to management knowledge and, for that matter, to management of knowledge lies in their limited explicit usefulness to practitioners and immediate practical application (Huczynski and Buchanan, 2001). As stated earlier in the chapter, the aim has not been to provide another prescriptive authoritative model of knowledge sharing, codification and management in project environments, but to focus on more subtle issues related to the meaning of these phenomena and how they can be theorized from the position of UST and the MP method. The evaluation and refinement of the ways in which the PM-MP framework can be used have been a continuing and ongoing research task. If used as part of the routine project management process and procedures, it encourages project practitioners to appreciate a 'big picture' of their project, and to make decisions about emerging issues and problems relevant to project planning, risk assessment, execution and performance evaluation, by considering the five perspectives simultaneously and holistically. This frequently includes deliberation about multilevel, multiple aspects and interests within a specific project organization, and ethical and moral consideration of the future possibility for joint action and involvement.

Conclusions

The study presented in this chapter aspires to make a contribution towards developing a framework within which experiences from projects could be located, and which could guide an evaluation of knowledge for improved understanding and accomplishment of project objectives and benefits. The participative research design on which the study was based has captured the voices and experiences of a wide range of project actors and organizational members, covering a range of project types and industrial sectors. The resulting framework captures the interrelated domains of learning, knowledge and awareness relevant to decision making and action for improved project performance. The discussion of the proposed framework, and its application in practice as a learning platform in project environments, is positioned within three broad concepts, which have been argued for throughout the chapter: (1) the propositions of intersubjective understanding as a driver for social action, (2) the notion of reflective practice, and (3) the multiple perspective enquiry method founded in unbounded systems thinking.

It is useful to conclude the chapter by reiterating the view of knowledge as a fundamental production factor loaded with immense economic, ecological and cultural values. It has been suggested here that not only knowledge (the content), but also the methods of creating knowledge and methods of learning (the form) are important. Thus, our understanding of the process of knowing and learning should be presupposed by our reflection on what the knowledge that is created or acquired in project environments, including its ultimate presumptions, really is knowledge about. The proposed PM-MP framework encompasses five interrelated domains of knowledge and information that practitioners experience as relevant to, and useful for managing and co-operatively accomplishing, the given project tasks. These domains can also be interpreted as the ontological perspectives in which the learning process within a multiparty coalition such as the project is embedded. As such, the framework can serve as a generic platform for thinking about KM in project environments in terms of what the learning or knowledge that is to be managed in project environments is learning or knowledge about. It can be used as an awareness map for better understanding of the multiple issues affecting project performance, as a self-assessment tool and a diagnostic instrument related to the design and implementation of a holistic system for project performance evaluation and risk assessment, as a guide to the structuring of educational strategies related to the role of projects in contemporary business and management, and for an enhancement of the conventional project management courses by offering a multiple perspective-based meta-framework embedded in the approach of UST.

References

Atkinson, R. (1999) Project management: cost, time and quality, two best guesses and a phenomenon; it's time to accept other success criteria. *International Journal of Project Management* 17(6): 337–342.

Blackler, F. (1995) Knowledge, knowledge work and organizations: an overview and interpretation. *Organization Studies* 16(6): 1021–1046.

Bresnen, M. and Marshall, N. (2000) Motivation, commitment and the use of incentives in partnerships and alliances. *Construction Management and Economics* 18: 587–598.

Bresnen, M., Edelman, L., Newell, S., Scarbrough, H. and Swan, J. (2003) Social practices and the management of knowledge in project environments. *International Journal of Project Management* 21: 157–166.

Brown, J. S. and Duguid, P. (1998) Organizing knowledge. *California Management Review* 40(3): 90–111.

Busby, J. S. (1999) An assessment of post-project reviews. *Project Management Journal* 30(3): 23–29.

Cicmil, S. (2000) Quality in project environments: a non-conventional agenda. *International Journal of Quality and Reliability Management* 17(4/5): 554–570.

Cicmil, S. (2003) Knowledge, interaction, and project work: from instrumental rationality to practical wisdom. PhD Thesis. Leicester: De Montfort University.

Clarke, A. (1999) A practical use of key success factors to improve the effectiveness of project management. *International Journal of Project Management* 17(3): 139–145.

Cleland, D. I. (1995) *Project Management – Strategic Design and Implementation*. New York: McGraw-Hill.

Das, T. K. and Teng, B.-S. (1998) Between trust and control: developing confidence in partner cooperation in alliances. *Academy of Management Review* 23(3): 491–512.

DeFillipi, R. (2001) Project based learning, reflective practices and learning outcomes. *Management Learning* 32(1): 5–10.

Easterby-Smith, M., Thorpe, R. and Lowe, A. (1991) *Management Research – An Introduction*. London: Sage (reprint 1999).

Fernie, S., Green, S., Weller, S. and Newcombe, R. (2003) Knowledge sharing: context, confusion and controversy. *International Journal of Project Management* 21: 177–187.

Flyvbjerg, B., Bruzelius, N. and Rothengatter, W. (2003) *Megaprojects and Risk: An Anatomy of Ambition*. Cambridge: Cambridge University Press.

Greiner, L. E. and Schein, V. E. (1981) The paradox of managing a project-oriented matrix: establishing coherence within chaos. *Sloan Management Review* (Winter): 17–22.

Holstein, J. A. and Gubrium, J. F. (1995) *The Active Interview.* Thousand Oaks, CA: Sage.

Huczynski, A. and Buchanan, D. (2001) *Organizational Behaviour; An Introductory Text*, 4th edn. Harlow: FT–Prentice-Hall, Pearson Education.

Johnson, P. and Duberley, J. (2000) *Understanding Management Research – An Introduction to Epistemology.* London: Sage.

Kreiner, K. (1995) In search of relevance: project management in drifting environments. *Scandinavian Journal of Management* 11(4): 335–346.

Krogh, G. V., Ichijo, K. and Nonaka, I. (2000) *Enabling Knowledge Creation.* New York: Oxford University Press.

Love, P. E. D., Edum-Fotwe, F. and Irani, Z. (2003) Editorial: Management of knowledge in project environments. *International Journal of Project Management* 21: 155–156.

Marshall, N. (2001) Knowledge, identity, and difference in project organization. Paper presented at the 17th EGOS Colloquium, The Odyssey of Organising, Lyon, France, 5–7 July 2001.

Maylor, H. (2001) Beyond the Gantt chart – project management moving on. *European Management Journal* 19(1): 92–100.

Meredith, J. R. and Mantel, S. L. (1995) *Project Management – A Managerial Approach*, 4th edn. New York: John Wiley & Sons.

Meredith, J. R. and Mantel, S. L. (2000) *Project Management – A Managerial Approach*, 5th edn. New York: John Wiley & Sons.

Mitroff, I. I. and Linstone, H. A. (1993) *The Unbounded Mind: Breaking the Chains of Traditional Business Thinking.* New York: Oxford University Press.

Naybour, P. (1999) Cause and effect relationship between critical success factors in new product development. Unpublished MBA dissertation. Bristol: University of the West of England.

Newcombe, R. (2000) The anatomy of two projects: a comparative analysis approach. *International Journal of Project Management* 18: 189–199.

Packendorff, J. (1995) Inquiring into the temporary organization: new directions for project management research. *Scandinavian Journal of Management* 11(4): 319–333.

Rae, D. (2000) Achieving competitive advantage through project management: an investigation into the project management system employed by F H Limited. MBA dissertation. Bristol: University of the West of England.

Raelin, J. A. (2001) Public reflection as the basis of learning. *Management Learning* 32(1): 11–30.

Reason, P. (1988) *Human Inquiry in Action.* London: Sage.

Saad, M., Cicmil, S. and Greenwood, M. (2002) Technology transfer projects in developing countries – furthering the project management perspectives. *International Journal of Project Management* 20: 617–625.

Silverman, D. (2001) *Interpreting Qualitative Data: Methods for Analysing Talk, Text and Interaction*, 2nd edn. London: Sage.

Stacey, R. (2001) *Complex Responsive Processes in Organizations: Learning and Knowledge Creation.* London: Routledge.

Stacey, R. (2003) *Strategic Management and Organizational Dynamics – The Challenge of Complexity*, 4th edn. Harlow: FT–Prentice-Hall, Pearson.

Sydow, J. and Staber, U. (2002) The institutional embeddedness of project networks: the case of content production in German television. *Regional Studies* 36(3): 215–227.

Williams, T. M. (1999) The need for new paradigm for complex projects. *International Journal of Project Management* 17(5): 269–273.

Young, T. (1998) *The Handbook of Project Management – A Practical Guide of Effective Policies and Procedures.* London: Institute of Directors–Kogan Page.

Chapter 9

Managing projects through reflection

Magnus Gustafsson and Kim Wikström

Introduction

Processes and directives form a central part in the company as they guide the operations and activities of people and machines. By means of intricate specifications of input, processing and output, the division of labour is enacted both within and between companies, along the lines of Fredrick Winslow Taylor and Henry Ford. The modern corporation and present-day Western society would not exist were it not for a strict division of labour, with input, processing and output well specified. However, for each properly functioning, time- and resource-saving process there is often another process that is at best irrelevant, at worst counterproductive and inhibiting the personnel in their daily work. These are processes that may seem rational, but which often do not reflect the process in practice and which personnel ignore if possible or otherwise half-heartedly live up to. Other processes take on a life of their own, producing entire organizations dedicated not to production but to maintaining the internal process from which they arose in the first place.

In this chapter the authors argue that processes can be divided into two separate types: rational and intuitive processes. Furthermore, it is argued that these processes differ from each other on a fundamental level, with the former applying to stable processes that have been isolated from the outside world. The latter in turn applies to processes that are not closed to the outside world and where the question of information and its processing is almost by definition impossible to codify and standardize. These two kinds of process coexist in the organization, but it may be argued that the latter have been paid little attention. This negligence is considered to be dangerous, as the two kinds of process cannot be approached in the same way. Forced into the logical frame-work of rational processes, it is suggested that the practical intuitive process becomes dysfunctional and inevitably leads to suboptimization (the same applies vice versa).

It is suggested that, by taking into account the human ele-ment included in intuitive processes, companies can better utilize the reflecting capabilities of their personnel. This is most crucial in project-based companies. Whereas the process industry has largely managed to isolate its daily operations so that the relationship with the unstable environment is addressed mostly by the upper echelons of management, the project industry is characterized by a high degree of instabil-ity also on the operational level, with employees forced to make judgement decisions on a more or less daily basis. It is therefore important for project-based companies to organize themselves in a manner that supports reflective action rather than mechanical rule-following.

This chapter is based on ten years of studies of industrial project deliveries, consisting of over 3000 interviews with cus-tomers, suppliers, authorities and other third parties from eighty countries, a participant observation study of twenty building sites resulting in 2000 pages of field diaries and pho-tographs, and general studies of the project-based company. In addition, the authors have participated in a number of evaluations of reporting processes as well as organization restructuring projects.

Two different worlds

In an attempt to draw attention to the fundamental character-istics differentiating project from process industries, Wikström and Gustafsson (1999) compare the modern paper mill with the shipyard. The paper mill is clean; it is cleaner than most people's homes, its floors are polished and everything is in place. It is also fairly quiet. The only sound emanating is a hum from the machines as they continue to spew out paper at breakneck speeds close to a mile per minute. The only person seen in the large production hall is gliding along on a bicycle dressed in clean overalls, and he only does so every once in a while. The only people seen around are the people up in the control room, who sit watching the production hall and the screens monitoring the production. This is also the only place of untidiness to be found: the spent coffee mugs. All in all it gives a very orderly picture, a value creation process that has been well thought through and implemented according to plan.

The shipyard is the direct opposite. There are people everywhere: welding, walking, climbing, cycling, smoking, and carrying things here and there. A shipyard is full of sounds and smells emanating from the myriad of cranes, forklifts, welding and other work processes going on. The place is cluttered with equipment in different quantities and sizes being moved around or just lying there. All in all it gives a chaotic picture, as if no one had bothered to make up a clear and distinct plan as to what should be done at which point in time by whom.

The two environments could not be more different. In the paper mill most of the activities taking place have been planned long beforehand, some of them many years ago as the mill was designed, others months ago. There are very few deviations from the process; the rules guiding the process are more than clear and well founded. The chains of events are clearly known and accounted for, and the consequences taken into account long ago. The input and output requirements for each subprocess are clearly defined. Even in those cases where the input may vary to some degree, the alternatives have been narrowed down and clearly defined and the sensors adjusted accordingly. Seen as an information process, the working paper mill consists of nothing but clear, objective and indisputable information starting from the state of the pulp being fed in, to the quality and amount of paper on the big roll at the other end. One may feel tempted to see it as value creation at its finest: rational, well planned, with little or no waste.

At the shipyard very few events have been planned very long beforehand. It is hard to find events that have been planned a year beforehand. Most of the events have been planned a few months earlier, others a few weeks or days before, some that very morning, and others are being decided and acted upon right on the spot. As Lindahl (2003) shows, managing a project is very much a question of constantly weighing up the information to hand and therefore making decisions. Only by constantly making small adjustments and sometimes forgoing the plan completely is the project manager able to guide the project to the goal that was planned for. There are very few rules that would apply to the project. The ones that do exist are mostly general and need to be applied specifically with judgement. Most of the rules and actions being implemented are decided on by the project or site manager during the project according to the situation at hand and according to his or her judgement. Which information the manager takes into account and which is disregarded can often seem unclear or at least surprising to the untrained eye. Lindahl (2003) argues what we are dealing with here are decisions based not on common, well-known, objective or rational rules, but on something much more elusive but nevertheless quite real. These decisions are based on judgement and intuition.

Reflection, improvisation, intuition and judgement are all important aspects of managing a company, a project and especially a project-based company. As noted above, Lindahl (2003) shows eloquently how the project, by forgoing the formal plan and improvising, is able to achieve the goal of the plan. The same is shown by Forsberg (2002a) in the way that ship-owners go about their business, both when it comes to the investment decision of a ship and in the daily business of locating cargoes. In a study on sea pilots, Forsberg (2002b) also shows how judgement forms an essential, lifesaving aspect of the work, and how formalized pilot education threatens the work of pilots by missing that specific dimension. Guve (2003) shows how the decisions to invest or not to invest are taken in a venture capital organization. These decisions are taken not according to some formal rules or weighing of objective data, but rather on the basis of conviction.

Two processes

How should this be approached? How and when should judgement, intuition, improvisation and reflection be included in the processes of a company? Jaafari (2003), among others, argues for separating projects into the kind characterized by a high degree of uncertainty and creativity and those demanding less. However, it may be argued that we are dealing with basically two completely different kinds of process, rational and intuitive processes, which exist simultaneously in the project and in the organization as such. However, before further describing the role that these processes play in the organization, it is necessary to elaborate on what characterizes these processes and differentiates them from each other.

Rational processes are the kinds of process that usually come to mind when speaking of processes in organizations. They include the assembly line along which people are standing assembling cars, each person performing an assigned task consisting of more or less predetermined moves; the computer processing data and ending up with another piece of data; and the straightforward set of rules telling the project manager how to go from start to finish. These are straightforward processes that can be clearly described and understood by most people. Technical rationality, notes Schön (1987, pp. 3–4), 'holds that practitioners are instrumental problem solvers who select technical means best suited to particular purposes. Rigorous professional practitioners solve well-formed instrumental problems by applying theory and technique derived from systematic, preferably scientific knowledge'.

Intuitive processes differ from the above. An intuitive process is the process that the artist goes through when creating a piece of art; the process of forging a piece of iron into the preferred shape, heating, striking and cooling it over and over again; and how an investor picks between stocks and bonds or decides to fund a risky venture (Guve, 2003). An intuitive process is the project manager deciding to discard the project plan to achieve the target (Lindahl, 2003). Intuitive processes are less clear than and not as easily described as rational processes.

Rational and intuitive processes differ from each other in two aspects: the view of knowledge and meaningful information and the view of the actor. The difference between these two aspects is fundamental and should not be seen as a mere difference in degree. The authors argue that this difference lies on both an epistemological and ontological level, and that the rational and intuitive processes are therefore profoundly different from each other.

The view of knowledge and meaningful information

Rational

A rational process is isolated from the surrounding world. From an objective point of view the sources of information are well defined, structured and stable, as is the content of the information. In a rational process the causal chain is clear and predetermined. Depending on the input, different predetermined outcomes will take effect. The actor, be it a computer processor or a human in Taylor's or Ford's division of labour, does not make any decision, but merely performs according to set rules. Rational processes are therefore rule orientated. Observed within its well-defined borders, a rational process makes a first class example of a positivistic environment where there exists a single, objective truth with clear causalities. This is also stressed by Schön (1987, p. 3): 'technical rationality is an epistemology of practice derived from positivist philosophy, built into the very foundations of the modern research university'. As noted above, examples of rational processes are computer programs and mechanical work that is strictly divided in the classic Taylorian sense.

Intuitive

Intuitive processes are not isolated from the environment; they are considered to be a fundamental part of it. From an objective point of view the sources of information are therefore unstructured, varying and undefined. Because of this the content of the information is also unclear, as is the causal chain. The only thing that is more or less objectively agreed upon is the goal. Intuitive processes are therefore goal orientated and the processing of the information is reflective.

This does not mean that these processes cannot be performed or that the information does not exist. Intuitive processes reflect a more relativistic worldview where there is no single truth, but rather an unspecified number of different, sometimes competing truths. In this perspective, information is not informative by itself. The same information used in a rational process could also be used in an intuitive one; what matters is the context, the frame of reference in which the information is seen. Information becomes informative or relevant knowledge only when the actor perceives it to be so (Nonaka and Nishiguchi, 2001). This can be described as a reflective process where the actor combines different pieces of information that he perceives as relevant based on his experience. The source, structure, content and relevance of information are decided by the individual actor. Whether the information used and the way in which it was used are relevant and accurate cannot be judged by objective means, but rather by the outcome: if the actor was successful then he must have done the right thing, and vice versa. This is in line with both James (1907/1995) and Wittgenstein (1953/1996), who note that the correct interpretation is the one that works. In that sense, the end justifies the means to the degree that they were used in order to achieve that end. Examples of intuitive processes are the making of budgets and plans and their respective implementation.

The view of the actor

Rational

In a rational process the actor, the performing part, has no direct responsibility for the outcome or its quality. Whether the actor is a computer or a person in Taylor's or Ford's factory, the responsibility for the process and the outcome lies with those who have designed the program or the process of movements, together with the division of labour. The programmer or the manager is responsible for making sure that the input format is well structured, that the content of the information is clear and unambiguous, and that the causal chain is clear and efficient. The actor performing the task is not responsible for its success and receives little or no incentive from its success, but is often penalized for not following the set directives. The purpose here is not to equate people with machines, but to point out that many people are treated more or less as machines in their work.

Intuitive

In an intuitive process the responsibility for choosing and judging the source and character of information and its consequences, and thereby the outcome, lies with the actor, because there is no clear understanding of what information is relevant when it is the project manager or the manager in general who has to decide on what should be done, or what the outlook is at the given point in time. As noted above, the accuracy of that judgement is measured by the degree of success. Making the correct judgement on a multitude of different signals is no easy feat and there are therefore large differences in the success of different actors when it comes to, for example, picking stock or making a project plan. Considering the differences in outcome, some people are better than others at judging the signals. To give an example: Warren Buffet is (as of this day) much better at picking stocks than either of the authors: when it comes to stocks his success and the authors' lack of it is proof thereof. Similarly, most managers (general, investment, project, etc.) are better at managing than the average person in the street, or at least they should be. After all, that is what they are paid for; it is their job, it is a key dimension in being a manager. The company trusts them to make the right judgement in some future situation precisely because that situation cannot be solved by means of some objective rule or theory, as is done in a rational process. The steering process also differs from a rational process. Since the sources of information and their causalities are unclear, deviation from a predetermined process cannot be sanctioned (it does not exist). Instead, it is the achieving of the goal that is used as a measure for incentives.

The knowledge implied in the ability to make judgement calls is often not articulated and it may be tempting to apply

Table 9.1 Technically rational and intuitive processes

	Technically rational processes	*Intuitive processes*
Context	Closed system	Open system
Character of information	Objective	Relative
Way of gathering information	Rational	Intuitive
Way of processing information	Rule-orientated	Reflective/goal-orientated

the concept of tacit knowledge to describe it. That may, however, not be completely appropriate. Clearly, the actors (managers, skilled people in general) know how to act in different situations; the success of their actions speaks for itself. The fact that the actor cannot exactly explain the reason for his or her decision does not diminish the value of their act. The focus could also be on the listener rather than on the one explaining. The explanation is not necessarily insufficient just because the listener does not understand. A skilled blacksmith probably understands the explanation given by another skilled blacksmith. Calling this knowledge tacit would be directly patronizing. In most cases it is the act that is important. It is many times more important to make a decision than to explain the reasons for it if one were to make that decision. Thus, knowledge is expressed in action, not in words. The differences between the two processes are summarized in Table 9.1.

A mixture of processes

Rational and intuitive processes coexist in every company as a mixture. Almost every job contains both rational (repetitive, predetermined) action patterns and judgement calls. The judgement calls can be included in a larger, repetitive pattern. For example, at the beginning of every project a project manager makes a plan. In addition, most companies do some form of budgeting every quarter (or at least annually). Thus, the daily processes of a company are a mixture of rational and intuitive decisions.

This should also be recognized when designing organizational structures and steering and reporting processes. Whereas numerous processes within companies can be handled rationally, and ought to be handled so, those that cannot be handled rationally should not be approached in the same way. For example, when it comes to making calculations, or turning out paper at one mile per minute, there is no reason to involve people in the process. They are slow and inefficient and require periods of rest. In the Western world this type of tedious, repetitive, mechanical assembly-line work has been largely taken over by machines or outsourced to countries where the labour is still cheap enough for the process to make economic sense. However, there is a number of processes where attempts to automate have so far been fruitless and, it may be argued, will continue to be so. Because of the constantly changing environment and the absence of objective, clearly relevant information, intuitive processes cannot be put into a closed rationally logical system. (A classic example of this is air-traffic control. Although air-traffic control processes are systematized to a very high degree, it is well known that controllers often flaunt the regulations to get the job done. The formal processes are so stifling that there is no reason for controllers to go on strike if they want to bring operations to a halt; it is enough just to work according to the rules and regulations. This sort of strike is called work-to-rule. Thus, when it comes to intuitive processes the rational approach is by no means helpful, but acts more like a straightjacket, keeping the actor in place but making movement almost impossible.) Examples of intuitive processes are numerous and can be found at all levels in an organization. The proportion of intuitive processes in an organization varies partly with the activities, but even more so depending on the industry. Whereas the process industry is characterized by a stable operative environment with uncertainty mostly confined to the strategic level, the project industry is characterized by a high degree of uncertainty both at the higher managerial levels and at the operative level.

Some processes that have been handled by people can be formalized and taken care of by machines. This is quite natural and the paper mill is once again a prime example. However, two kinds of process cannot be specified. First, there are processes that are highly context specific, such as customer relationship management (CRM) and, to a large degree, project management. The requirements of the customers and their way of reacting to different events are specific to the individual customer. Although it may be theoretically possible to design an objective process that successfully adapted to the individual customer in an individual project, practically speaking it would not be possible to develop such a process. When it comes to customer relations the human interface is unparalleled, especially when dealing with complex products in dynamic environments. This has to do with the nature of formal rules, which by definition are always general and cannot be applied directly to an individual case in an open system. This leads to the rule being bent or interpreted so that the actor can reach a functioning solution. By not specifying the workflow in detail, a higher precision in the decision making is achieved as the actor applies the rules demanded by the specific situation. (Fuzzy logic is of no help in a situation like this. What is needed is not an approximation but a precise decision for the specific situation.)

Secondly, some decision-making and management processes are characterized by the fact that their logic is not well known. An example of this is the processes used for picking stock or choosing investments. The individual investor's superiority lies specifically in the fact that he or she views information in a different manner. Were the logic of, say, Warren Buffet's highly successful way of picking investment objects to become common knowledge, then it would lose its relevance immediately. Thus, the strength of the logic lies specifically in its singularity, in the fact that it is not common knowledge.

The need for recognizing intuitive processes

Although the role of intuition, judgement, improvisation and reflection has received a lot of attention in research, it still does not show in organizations. This is not to say that practitioners do not think, use intuition and judgement, improvise and reflect on the situation at hand. However, these practices form an essential part of management; they are not included in the organizational design and the flowcharts describing the value-creation process. One could argue that although practitioners are aware of the need for reflection and judgement in day-to-day operations, these are often disregarded when working procedures are set up.

It is important to recognize the intuitive dimensions in a company's processes, not just because of the added value that they can provide, but because it can prove directly counter-productive to force them into a technically rational mode. Because it is impossible to catch all the relevant dimensions in a rational process, there is a danger that critical information is overlooked. Compensating this by increasing the number of parameters or sources of information is no cure, since that only increases the tidal wave of information from which most companies, thanks to information technology (IT), are already suffering. Since switching to a technically rational mode means switching to a top-heavy, rule-orientated way of work-ing, there is also a clear risk that people will be less motivated by their work. Simply put, an overemphasis on the technically rational dimension risks turning the company into a bureau-cracy, which unfortunately is far from unusual.

This problem is highlighted in applications such as CRM and enterprise resource planning (ERP), and other IT systems. Systems of this kind are built according to a rational ideal. After all, the strength of the computer is its ability to compute, which easily surpasses that of humans. However, its ability to draw conclusions is strictly limited to the rules given to it by its programmer. As noted above, knowledge is most often expressed in action, not in words. Articulating the informa-tion is probably many times more complicated, especially if one is asked to articulate it in a way that the uninitiated would understand. The reporting categories found in CRM systems therefore often turn out to be too limited or com-pletely misdirected, forcing personnel to report completely meaningless information. Alternatively, the system is opened up to any kind of information, which admittedly permits the actor to note, report and find the information (if it is noted in the first place). However, this can easily lead to a tidal wave of information where it is almost impossible to find any relevant information because the relevance of the information is so sit-uation specific. Because of this, most CRM systems tend to contain very superficial information that is of no or little rele-vance to the decision maker.

An even bigger problem lies in ERP systems, which force the actor into the rational straightjacket described above. It is for good reason that many ERP systems have been compared to pouring cement on a company's operations: it brings stability but also takes away whatever flexibility there was. This should not be seen as a Luddite tirade against technology. The problem is not computers, but primitive assumptions that are reflected in the structure of CRM and ERP systems.

Conclusions: a time for reflective management

As noted above, intuitive processes are goal orientated, which in practice translates into a process based on reflection. Rather than defining the process as a set of rules to be followed, the actual implementation is largely left up to the actor. Instead, the goals of that specific process are defined. Thus, the actor is given the freedom to choose their own favoured approach, while at the same time taking responsibility for achieving the goal. The process builds on the idea that the actor, rather than blindly following a given set of rules, elaborates and reflects on the goal that he or she is supposed to achieve, and on that basis decides the course of action.

Incorporating reflective management into companies changes the structure of the process descriptions and rules guiding the workflow. Reflective management is, on the one hand, far less detailed, as entire work sequences or processes are blackboxed to be decided by the person responsible. On the other hand, the goals and the output of the process are well defined, giving an overall structure to the company's processes. Thus, reflective management should not be seen as an argument against good organization and being systematic. It is an argument for focusing on the essential value creation process and avoiding the temptation to micromanage.

Since reflective management leads to a loosening of the formal process in favour of a more action-orientated approach, the requirements for formal reporting are also reduced significantly. In many cases formal reporting can be dismissed altogether and be replaced by a reporting procedure based on the project management tools, something that is quite simple with today's information and communication technology. However, reflective management demands a great deal of trust. When responsibility is turned over to operative staff such as project managers, they are given the freedom to act according to their own judgement. The means used may, at times, seem unorthodox to higher management (to the degree they ever see what goes on at the operational level). However, those are the means chosen by the project manager. In a reflective organization, what counts is the end result, not the means used to achieve it. For reflective management to function and to utilize fully the skills of its personnel, management must be ready, indeed have the courage, to let go of certain tasks and leave the definition of how they are to be executed to those whose job it is to perform them. Just because all the parameters and variables of a task cannot be specified or scientifically proven does not mean it cannot be done. The proof lies in the fact that the task is successfully executed. In that sense success is an argument by itself. The successful completion of a task is also proof enough that the person responsible knows how to do it, which warrants giving them the responsibility for it; after all, that is their job.

This does not mean that the project manager, or any other person with responsibility, cannot be criticized or evaluated. Nor does the end automatically justify the means. Quite the contrary: since reflective management is goal orientated it is of utmost importance that the goals are well defined and comprehensive. The goals set the target that should be achieved and form the basis against which the evaluation and follow-up of the project and the project manager take place. Together, the goals of each process show part of the company's strategy, and just as the strategy is regularly evaluated so too should be the goals for the different processes.

Reflective management is especially suitable in the project-based industry, which is characterized by a high degree of uncertainty. The project industry can be described as a long series of deviations and exceptions, to the degree that there really is no 'normal' project. It is therefore a highly labour-intensive industry. Reflective management provides a way of utilizing the project-based company's greatest asset: the ability of its personnel to finish the project under any circumstances.

Acknowledgement

The authors would like to thank Marcus Lindahl for all his insightful comments during discussions on intuition and improvisation.

References

Forsberg, P. (2002a) Piloting as a profession. In *Proceedings of the Third Nordic Seminar on Project Studies*, Nagu, Finland, 15–16 June.

Forsberg, P. (2002b) Judging and storytelling in the everyday life of a ship-owner. Doctoral dissertation. Göteborg: Göteborg University. (In Swedish.)

Guve, B. (2003) Att Bestämma Sig Utan Grund – Om Omdöme Ochövertygelse i Riskkapitalinvesteringar. Doctoral dissertation. Stockholm: Royal Institute of Technology. (In Swedish.)

Jaafari, A. (2003) Project management in the age of chaos – a study of professionalism in the 21st century. In *Proceedings of the IPMA Congress*, Moscow, Russia.

James, W. (1907/1995) *Pragmatism*. New York: Dover Publications.

Lindahl, M. (2003) Produktion Till Varje Pris – Om Planering och Improvisation i Anläggningsprojekt. Doctoral dissertation. Stockholm: Royal Institute of Technology. (In Swedish.)

Nonaka, I. and Nishiguchi, T. (2001) *Knowledge Emergence – Social, Technical, and Evolutionary Dimensions of Knowledge Creation*. Oxford: Oxford University Press.

Schön, D. (1987) *Educating the Reflective Practitioner*. London: Jossey-Bass.

Wikström, K. and Gustafsson, C. (1999) Ett Skapande Kaos. *Projektitoiminta* 1(99): 24–25.

Wittgenstein, L. (1997) *Philosophical Investigations* (transl. Anscombe, G. E. M.). Oxford: Blackwell.

Chapter 10

Making sense of learning landscapes in project-based organizations

Andrea Prencipe, Tim Brady, Nick Marshall and Fredrik Tell

Introduction

Recent years have seen an increasing 'projectification' of organizations (Söderlund, 2000). There are several reasons for this trend. With increasing complexity of products and underlying knowledge bases, interdisciplinary projects form an important organizational device for accessing and integrating the breadth and depth of knowledge pertinent to products (Grant, 1996). Moreover, as lead times and time to market shrink, project-based forms of organizing allow for focusing on specific tasks within certain time limits and therefore contribute to customer focus and quality orientation in organizations. In this chapter the authors explore some implications of project-based organizing for organizational learning.

The chapter reports on findings from a three-year study investigating interproject learning in the production of complex product systems (CoPS). CoPS have been defined as capital, engineering and information technology (IT)-intensive, business-to-business products, networks, constructs and systems (Hobday, 1998). They tend to be high in value and produced on a project basis, often in multifirm alliances, as one-offs or in small and customized batches for specific customers and markets (Hobday, 1998). Examples of these types of products and systems are flight simulators, global business telecommunications networks, aircraft and avionics systems, power stations, offshore oil and gas platforms, process plants, mobile telephone systems, intelligent buildings and large civil engineering projects. These products provide particularly interesting insights because of the severe challenges that they present for effective learning between projects, especially compared with more routine organizational activities. The customized nature of CoPS, the discontinuous nature of, and the level of complexity, interdependence and uncertainty inherent in CoPS projects reduce both the repeatability of projects and the potential for project-to-project learning.

Approaches to knowledge management (KM) in both theory and practice have suffered from a tendency to focus narrowly on certain dimensions of knowledge practices in organizations at the expense of others. For many, KM has become almost synonymous with the use of information and communication technologies (ICTs). More than that, it has become associated more with the capacity of ICTs to capture and store information than with their role in mediating communications. A sole focus on the information-capturing capabilities of ICTs often leads to a static view of knowledge in organizations and it is easy to forget important considerations such as how information is used and to what ends.

The authors' approach was to search for not only ICT-based solutions to KM, but also for social solutions. This search enabled the documentation of a variety of mechanisms and practices developed and adopted by project-based firms. This empirical diversity presented (and still presents) a major challenge for interpreting interproject learning approaches, since the different practices tend to come together in a variety of ways. Following Prencipe and Tell (2001), the authors argue that the practices associated with interproject learning are widely arrayed across a learning landscape characterized by variations in knowledge processes, levels of formality, use of technologies, social relations and communicative interactions. The authors also argue that the emergence of learning landscapes is dependent upon a number of contingency factors, such as technical complexity, project style and organizational size.

Obstacles on the road to interproject learning

There is a commonsense association between repetition and learning. This is exemplified by the long-established way of thinking about organizational learning through the notion of the learning curve. Research carried out by the Rand Corporation in the 1960s on maintenance activities in the US Airforce observed that the number of hours it took to perform a given activity declined by a constant percentage each time total repetitions of that activity doubled (Ascher, 1965). In this view, learning and repetition are intimately related. The experience of doing something makes future attempts at doing the same thing easier.

For Nelson and Winter (1982), the idea of repetition is implicit to their understanding of organizational routines as the building blocks of firm-level capabilities. They also recognized that routinization is more likely to be appropriate for organizations 'engaged in the provision of goods and services that are visibly "the same" over extended periods', while 'organizations that are involved in the production or management of change as their principal function – organizations such as R&D laboratories and consulting firms – do not fit neatly into the routine operation mould' (Nelson and Winter, 1982, p. 97).

The production of CoPS is equally problematic for the generation of routines. The strong focus on projects displayed by firms developing CoPS suggests that there might be problems associated with organization-wide learning (Lindkvist et al., 1998). While in a functionally based firm, departments act as knowledge silos, the pure project-based firms lack the organizational mechanisms for the knowledge acquired in one project to be transferred and used by other projects. Two further issues impair organization-wide learning in project-based firms: the unique and the temporary nature of projects (Prencipe and Tell, 2001). With regard to the former, projects differ from each other in several, critical aspects. They entail heterogeneous activities that may well not be repeated in successive projects. If projects exhibit one-off characteristics, the project-based firm confronts the difficult task of 'learning from samples of one or fewer' (March et al., 1991). In addition, projects may be characterized by relatively long life cycles, requiring similar project activities to be retrieved and repeated after long time intervals. With regard to the temporary nature of projects, projects can be characterized by the temporary constellation of people they entail (DeFillippi and Arthur, 1998; Tell and Söderlund, 2001). This feature implies that new human encounters and relationships take place whenever a new project is started, which may increase the barriers to learning from the previous experience of others.

Methodology

This chapter draws on qualitative data collected during a three-year research project designed to explore the management of interproject learning in a convenient sample of fifty project-based firms developing CoPS. A major component of the study involved an interview-based survey of interproject learning practices among firms in Europe, North America and Japan. The survey was based on face-to-face, in-depth and semistructured interviews, with at least one informant drawn from three organizational levels, namely senior management, project management and project practitioner. The aim was to gain some insight into the perceptions of project learning practices at different points of the organization. This method was adopted given the intricacy of knowledge practices and the importance of understanding at least something of the context within which they are enacted. Also, where possible, opportunities to conduct more interviews were taken. Each interview lasted for approximately ninety minutes. Relevant company documentation was also collected and those interviewed were subsequently asked to complete a short questionnaire. Depending on the practicality of making a return visit, the results of the interviews and questionnaires were reported back to the companies, providing an opportunity for the findings to be validated. Although the companies that took part in the survey all shared common features in terms of being involved in large, complex projects, there were nevertheless important variations according to size, turnover and industrial sector.

Interproject learning and learning landscapes

The survey indicated that firms adopt various mechanisms to learn from one project to another. This result indicates something of the diversity of practices and mechanisms that have a bearing on interproject learning. These practices vary according to the project phases within which they typically occur, as well as according to the types of knowledge process that they represent. This empirical diversity presents a major challenge for interpreting interproject learning approaches since the different practices tend to come together in a variety of ways.

Based on a subsample of six of the studied firms, the notion of learning landscapes was introduced in an earlier paper (Prencipe and Tell, 2001). This was originally an attempt to discern alternative patterns of interproject learning according to their location within a matrix of learning processes and organizational levels (Table 10.1), resulting in three main ideal types. The analysis of the horizontal and vertical dimensions enabled the identification of what was termed a firm's learning landscape in relation to project-to-project learning (Prencipe and Tell, 2001). A firm's learning landscape was defined as the mix of project-to-project learning mechanisms adopted and implemented. Learning mechanisms are empirical instances such as 'lessons learned' meetings, databases or informal encounters. The learning landscape then refers to the collection, or portfolio, of such mechanisms, here clustered into three distinct patterns. This concept of learning landscape reflects the multidimensional nature of a firm's approach to project-to-project learning.

Learning landscapes just as maps come in a variety of projections and focus on certain features at the expense of others. Not only are the landscapes of interproject learning differentiated, but also the possibilities of representing them are varied. In this spirit, the concept of learning landscapes provides a useful metaphor through which to think about different knowledge practices, rather than thinking of them as a fixed representation. Although the authors offer one reading of the landscape, they recognize its limitations and would welcome other maps of the territory.

The initial notion of learning landscapes generated three ideal types (Tables 10.2–10.4). It is based on Zollo and Winter's (2002) typology of experience accumulation, articulation and codification processes, augmented to consider their operation at individual, group and organizational levels. The L-shaped

Table 10.1   Interproject learning mechanisms (adapted from Prencipe and Tell, 2001)

Level of analysis	Learning processes		
	Experience accumulation	Knowledge articulation	Knowledge codification
Individual	• On-the-job training • Job rotation • Specialization • Reuse of experts	• Figurative thinking • Thinking aloud • Scribbling notes	• Diary • Reporting system • Individual systems design
Group/ project	• Developed groupthink • Person-to-person communication • Informal encounters • Imitation	• Brainstorming sessions • Formal project reviews • Debriefing meetings • Ad hoc meetings • Lessons learned and/or post-mortem meetings • Intraproject correspondence	• Project plan/ audit • Milestones/ deadlines • Meeting minutes • Case writing • Project history files • Intraproject lessons learned database
Organiza-tional	• Informal organizational routines, rules and selection processes • Departmentalization and specialization • Communities of practice	• Project manager camps • Knowledge retreats • Professional networks • Knowledge facilitators and managers • Interproject correspondence • Interproject meetings	• Drawings • Process maps • Project management process • Lessons learned database

landscape (Table 10.2), which may also be characterized as a socially driven approach, comprises firms that rely to a great extent on people-embedded knowledge. Here, the emphasis is on creating and sharing implicit and experience-based knowledge through joint participation in work activities. Face-to-face communication and interactions across social networks tend to be important. Interproject learning has a more informal character and involves the sedimentation of new practices in the form of routines.

Table 10.2 The L-shaped learning landscape (adapted from Prencipe and Tell, 2001)

Level of analysis	Learning processes		
	Experience accumulation	Knowledge articulation	Knowledge codification
Individual	• On-the-job training • Job rotation • Specialization • Reuse of experts	• Figurative thinking • Thinking aloud • Scribbling notes	• Diary • Reporting system • Individual systems design
Group/project	• Developed groupthink • Person-to-person communication • Informal encounters • Imitation	• Brainstorming sessions • Formal project reviews • Debriefing meetings • Ad hoc meetings • Lessons learned and/or post-mortem meetings • Intraproject correspondence	• Project plan/audit • Milestones/deadlines • Meeting minutes • Case writing • Project history files • Intraproject lessons learned database
Organizational	• Informal organizational routines, rules and selection processes • Departmentalization and specialization • Communities of practice	• Project manager camps • Knowledge retreats • Professional networks • Knowledge facilitators and managers • Interproject correspondence • Interproject meetings	• Drawings • Process maps • Project management process • Lessons learned database

The T-shaped landscape (Table 10.3) characterizes firms with a broadly sociotechnical approach, although with a greater emphasis on articulation processes at all organizational levels. Meetings and other arenas for enhanced communication are pursued as means for transferring knowledge gained in one project to another. The staircase learning landscape (Table 10.4) includes firms involved in the advanced development of ICT-based tools to support interproject learning. Their emphasis is on deliberate attempts to codify and

Table 10.3   The T-shaped learning landscape (adapted from Prencipe and Tell, 2001)

Level of analysis	Learning processes		
	Experience accumulation	Knowledge articulation	Knowledge codification
Individual	• On-the-job training • Job rotation • Specialization • Reuse of experts	• Figurative thinking • Thinking aloud • Scribbling notes	• Diary • Reporting system • Individual systems design
Group/ project	• Developed groupthink • Person-to-person communication • Informal encounters • Imitation	• Brainstorming sessions • Formal project reviews • Debriefing meetings • Ad hoc meetings • Lessons learned and/or post-mortem meetings • Intraproject correspondence	• Project plan/ audit • Milestones/ deadlines • Meeting minutes • Case writing • Project history files • Intraproject lessons learned database
Organizational	• Informal organizational routines, rules and selection processes • Departmentalization and specialization • Communities of practice	• Project manager camps • Knowledge retreats • Professional networks • Knowledge facilitators and managers • Interproject correspondence • Interproject meetings	• Drawings • Process maps • Project management process • Lessons learned database

store knowledge developed during the execution of a project, and document it so that it can be disseminated and reused by other projects. These are technically driven approaches where learning is primarily directed at creating and updating formal procedures.

The practices within this matrix of learning approaches can also be considered along other complementary dimensions, such as the degree of formality/informality of interproject learning processes, the degree to which IT is used to support

Table 10.4 The staircase learning landscape (adapted from Prencipe and Tell, 2001)

Level of analysis	Learning processes		
	Experience accumulation	Knowledge articulation	Knowledge codification
Individual	• On-the-job training • Job rotation • Specialization • Reuse of experts	• Figurative thinking • Thinking aloud • Scribbling notes	• Diary • Reporting system • Individual systems design
Group/project	• Developed groupthink • Person-to-person communication • Informal encounters • Imitation	• Brainstorming sessions • Formal project reviews • Debriefing meetings • Ad hoc meetings • Lessons learned and/or post-mortem meetings • Intraproject correspondence	• Project plan/audit • Milestones/deadlines • Meeting minutes • Case writing • Project history files • Intraproject lessons learned database
Organizational	• Informal organizational routines, rules and selection processes • Departmentalization and specialization • Communities of practice	• Project manager camps • Knowledge retreats • Professional networks • Knowledge facilitators and managers • Interproject correspondence • Interproject meetings	• Drawings • Process maps • Project management process • Lessons learned database

interproject learning, and how far communication takes place through face-to-face interaction compared with more distanced styles of communication.

The concept of learning landscapes provides an interesting starting point for attempting to unravel the similarities and differences in learning styles between these organizations. A few caveats and words of warning are in order, however. First, these ideal types tend to downplay internal variations within the survey organizations. Different divisions, departments and projects may exhibit different learning approaches. Moreover, at the level of detailed project activities, it is typically the case that different knowledge practices come to the fore during particular types of activity. For example, the emphasis on intense, face-to-face interaction is generally higher during creative, problem-solving activities, such as those that can be found at the beginning and often the end of projects. More distanced, process-based practices and routines tend to be more in evidence during the middle phases of the project, once requirements and project plans have been established.

Secondly, as Engeström (2000) argued, there are problems in attempting to represent dynamic processes in the form of a static matrix. Not only are organizations likely to shift between different approaches over time, there is also a sense in which, as already suggested, it is difficult to understand such processes as experience accumulation, articulation and codification in isolation.

Understanding the diversity of learning landscapes

As discussed earlier, approaches associated with interproject learning are widely arrayed across a landscape characterized by variations in knowledge activities, levels of formality, technologies, social relations and communicative interactions. It is appealing, but almost certainly misleading, to offer a standard contingency explanation that sets out to relate the nature of learning practices to key differences in project and organizational characteristics. The all too familiar danger here is of positing a one-to-one correspondence between organizational contingencies and learning practices which suggests a transparent and unidirectional causality where organizational actors design rational strategies in response to clearly recognized internal and external environmental stimuli. Having said that, it is equally tempting to throw one's hands up in despair at the complexity of it all and refuse to explore any of the interrelationships among different organizational phenomena.

In this section the authors aim to offer nothing more than a few initial pointers regarding relationships between organizational contingencies and learning approaches. The survey indicated that several conditions broadly help to define the zones of manoeuvre within which the evolution of inter-project learning practices takes place. There is not enough space to consider all of these in detail, but a few of the more relevant are outlined briefly under the following headings: technical complexity, technical novelty, project timing, organizational size, style of project organization and project staffing.

Technical complexity

Variation in the degree of technical complexity of projects is largely related to the different sectors in which the survey companies operate. Companies in the aerospace and defence sectors are typically involved in highly complex, technologically intensive projects. Projects in telecommunications, information systems and rail systems are also technically complex, although marginally less so. The remaining companies, which largely fall within the building and engineering sectors, tend to be involved in projects that have a rather lower technical content. As complexity increases it is more likely that knock-on effects and feedback loops will generate unanticipated outcomes. With high complexity arises the problem of transferring knowledge. Interviewees in a company operating in the defence industry acknowledged that informal mechanisms, such as face-to-face meetings and gatherings of project managers were indispensable for interproject learning in complex environments. Even given the generally lower technical content of building and civil engineering projects, however, there is still sufficient variety in components and technological interfaces to make many outcomes difficult to predict.

Technical novelty

The technical novelty of projects refers to the extent to which each project requires a customized technical solution different from previous solutions. One indication of this is the design effort that is needed. Again, there appears to be a tentative relationship between the industry sector and technical novelty.

This belies, however, important differences in project activities often carried out within the same company. A firm operating in the aerospace sector is simultaneously involved in aircraft development projects incorporating radical technological innovations, as well as projects where incremental changes are made to established technologies. Similarly, an airport operator is involved in a wide range of building, infrastructure and civil engineering projects, some of which are relatively straightforward and recur regularly in a similar form (e.g. runway repairs and resurfacing), while others are highly customized and complex packages of work (e.g. baggage handling facilities and terminal buildings). Not surprisingly, the potential for continuous improvements is generally higher for the more repetitive projects than for those that involve higher levels of customization.

Project timing

The duration of projects and the degree to which they overlap with other similar projects also have a crucial effect on how far interproject learning is possible and relevant. Not only do development projects in aerospace and defence tend to be of several years' duration, but there are also usually major gaps between them. Notwithstanding the dramatic technological changes that can occur during and between such projects, it is difficult to maintain continuity in experience and expertise over such extended timescales. Even where the turnover of projects is more rapid, there may be considerable timelags between projects of a similar scope. A surveyed company was involved in two industrial plant projects for the same client, separated by a gap of several years. Many of the same mistakes made on the first project were repeated on the second. While people who participated in the original project were still employed by the company, they were not available for the later project. The project team assembled for the second project had no previous experience of this type of industrial plant and were unaware of what had happened on the preceding project. At the opposite extreme, there are projects that are very similar but which occur in parallel or with significant overlaps. These can be just as challenging for interproject learning because an intense focus on internal project activities often means that potentially useful lessons are not communicated to other projects.

Organizational size

The companies involved in the survey vary widely in size. At one extreme there are companies with only fifty to sixty employees, while at the other there are huge multinational conglomerates employing several thousand people. The smaller companies in the survey are more likely to be based at a single location and tend to be less differentiated in terms of the number and diversity of functions and activities. The larger organizations are almost invariably multilocational and made up of highly variegated functions. These characteristics have an important influence on knowledge practices and learning styles. A manufacturer of high-quality communications systems and a supplier of defence electronics products are at the smaller end of the scale. All staff are based at the same location and the company is small enough that most people know each other on a first name basis. The majority of interactions occur face-to-face and the style of management is fairly informal. Formal procedures for carrying out projects do exist, but they are not slavishly adhered to and, indeed, there appear to be rather low levels of awareness about what they actually are. This is not considered too much of a handicap because a large proportion of staff are long-serving employees who have effectively internalized the way things are done at the company. Given these characteristics, the style of interproject learning is strongly personalized, reliant on individually accumulated experience, and spread through well-established social networks.

A diversified industrial conglomerate represents the opposite extreme. It is involved in a wide range of business activities including information and communication systems, transport systems, and control and manufacturing systems. Even within business divisions, activities tend to be spread globally over several sites. In contrast to smaller organizations, there is a much greater emphasis on formal processes to ensure harmonization between the geographically and functionally dispersed parts of the organization. There is also a greater reliance on the use of ICTs, both for capturing and archiving information and for supporting interactions between distantly located groups where face-to-face communication is not always possible. However, even with formal processes it is difficult within an organization of this size to enforce totally centralized control. In line with other similarly massive organizations, this firm devolves considerable autonomy to its individual operating units. This is reflected in its approach to KM, which is based on a number of parallel initiatives developed within the different divisions. There is a small corporate-level group responsible for tracking these different KM programmes and attempting to transfer good practices between divisions.

Style of project organization

One of the key influences on interproject learning is the style of project organization and the way in which projects relate to each other and to the wider organization. They vary between those that involve a greater functional orientation and those based on dedicated and integrated project teams, with some companies exhibiting a mixture of approaches in between. Whether activities are orientated around functions or products/projects is a long-standing organizational dilemma and one for which there is no definitive solution because both orientations have something to recommend them. The benefits of a strong project orientation are related to the potential for greater integration and co-ordination of project functions. Given the complexity and open-ended nature of the types of project carried out by the survey companies, such co-ordination is by no means straightforward. Design and implementation activities tend to unfold in an emergent fashion and it is important for there to be intense dialogue between different functions to ensure that the various system elements are not incompatible.

The same characteristics of a strong project orientation that are its strengths are also a source of weakness. Heavyweight project organizations tend to be strongly focused on internal project activities. The density of interactions within the project is much greater than that between the project and other parts of the organization. Project members move from project to project, taking their experience with them, but they often have few opportunities to exchange ideas and information with those carrying out similar roles on other projects. Organizations that are more functionally orientated, in which different disciplines are grouped together, tend to be better able to manage the accumula-tion of specialist expertise. Engineers in the same discipline are able to share their experience of working on different projects. Functions effectively take the form of knowledge silos, but this means that there is typically a lower level of interaction with other functions, encouraging problems with project integration.

Many of the companies that participated in the survey have experimented with different styles of project organization, but they seem to experience some difficulty in arriving at a conclusive position on this. This is well illustrated by an aerospace and defence firm, which has fluctuated between functionally and project-orientated approaches several times over the past ten years. As an unintended consequence of this see-sawing of approaches, one of this company's project managers suggested that even though new arrangements were put in place the previous style of organization would persist for a time because people would continue to keep in touch with colleagues with whom they previously worked closely. He described this as a kind of 'shadow organization' existing behind the formal organizational structure. Without conscious design there are intense interactions within both projects and functions.

Other companies have made more purposeful attempts to mix the benefits of project-orientated and functionally orientated structures, with varying success. A producer of rail systems has attempted to promote both project integration and the development of functional expertise by moving staff between projects and functions on a periodic basis. Ideally, people work within a dedicated project team for the duration of the project and they are then reassigned to work within functional areas so that they can communicate their experiences and gain insights into developments within their discipline. However, this rarely happens in practice because time pressures and resource constraints mean that there is a strong impetus to move people onto new projects as quickly as possible. Several of the survey companies are interested in encouraging communities of practice as a way of overcoming the problems with dedicated project teams. These are informal groups of people, such as project managers or electrical engineers, who participate in the same activity but who do not normally have the opportunity to communicate their experiences to others who have similar interests.

Important influences on the style of project organization are the size of projects and the demands for specialist expertise. Where companies are simultaneously involved in a series of small projects it does not make sense to tie staff to a particular project. Instead, employees will typically work across a range of projects. This creates issues around how resources are allocated between projects and the priority given to different streams of work. For some employees with highly specialized skills for which there is a strong demand it may be necessary to share their input across several projects or have them work only for a limited phase of a project. Acoustics engineers at an aircraft engine manufacturer occupy such a role. These 'travelling experts' can act as channels for communicating between projects. By moving between projects they are able to keep less mobile project team members apprised of what is happening on other projects.

Project staffing

Approaches to project staffing both influence and are influenced by the relative priority assigned to codification processes with regard to more socially embedded and context-dependent knowledge practices. Where it is considered possible to codify and decontextualize knowledge away from specific project contexts there is less emphasis on ensuring continuity in staffing between projects. However, if the experience built up by project teams is viewed as distributed, collective and context sensitive, then it will be seen as important to keep at least a core of project members together through different projects. Opinions on this issue differed quite widely among interview respondents. For many project managers, continuity in staffing is an ideal that it is not always practical to achieve. Depending on project timing, people with the relevant experience may not be available. There were nevertheless some cases where moving core teams between similar projects had been achieved.

There were also companies that did not necessarily see continuity in staffing between projects as desirable. The business development manager at a surveyed firm suggested that 'it is not necessarily the case that you need to have the same people working project after project, whether it is possible or not. Here we use the term "positive regrouping" to describe our approach to setting up new teams. It means allocating people in an intelligent way focusing on a core of people'. This same manager also offered the following comment referring to the need to capture, codify and distribute project-related information: 'It is the only way the company can survive – you have to take the knowledge out of the people'. While keeping the same team of people working together may promote the transfer of experience between projects, there is the danger that they will become less creative and innovative because they lack an influx of new ideas (Janis, 1974).

Conclusions

Project-based organizations developing complex products constitute particularly interesting phenomena to be investigated by students of organizational knowledge and learning. So far, the extent to which larger samples of such organizations have been studied from an organizational learning perspective has been limited. This chapter has reported on a survey of fifty project-based organizations operating in a multitude of sectors and differing substantially in size.

The survey indicated a range of practices, procedures and mechanisms of varying formality and pervasiveness through which organizations were, both consciously and unintentionally, addressing the issue of learning between projects. This chapter reported on some preliminary attempts of analysing and organizing this empirical diversity. Using the concept of learning landscapes as one starting point for analysing inter-project learning, further interpretations were offered aiming at making sense of the heterogeneity exhibited in the organizations investigated. In particular, dimensions such as the technical complexity involved, the technical novelty of projects, the timing of projects, organizational size, project organization and project staffing have been stressed.

The results presented in this chapter are consistent with previous research. For instance, Bartezzaghi et al. (1997, p. 123) argued that 'there are some meta-capabilities at higher levels, which are progressively refined, experience after experience, and remain valid even when dealing with radical changes'. This consistency would point to further investigation of the concept of meta-capabilities or meta-models in understanding interproject learning in project-based firms. The concept of meta-capabilities, which owes more than a little to the work of Bateson (1972), is also congruent with the notion of frames and scripts (e.g. Minsky, 1975; Schank and Childers, 1984). Frames can be thought of as stereotypical models of certain sorts of general situation, precise instances of which may vary widely in their actual detail. The idea is that there are few situations that are completely new. Scripts are general strategies for action guided by some understanding of the range of things that might be expected to happen under such situations and the responses that are appropriate. Thus, for example, a group of engineers coming together to discuss an engineering problem that none of them have encountered in this exact form before, depending on how experienced they are, will probably share some common understanding of what such problem-solving situations involve and the range of practices that they are likely to encounter. They are also likely to behave in ways that they know from previous experience have the potential to solve the problem, even though the solution may not be readily at hand. These background assumptions form the general framework out of which specific solutions can be improvised. It is because scripts, unlike totally rigid procedures, are flexible that such improvisation is possible.

However, there are instances where established meta-models, frames or scripts are themselves inappropriate for the situation at hand. Problems will occur if the, often implicit, assumptions guiding action prove to be unfounded. For instance, it may be that not all the engineers in the previous example are equally familiar with such problem-solving situations or they may fail to appreciate that the problem they are trying to solve is so radical as to make it unsusceptible to established approaches. The problem is that existing frames or mental models can become so embedded that it is extremely difficult to identify how far they are consistent with previously unencountered situations. Several researchers have suggested that the tendency to try to relate every new problem to past experience may limit the range of solutions that are thought to be feasible, or even that are recognized (e.g. Argyris and Schön, 1978; Levinthal and March, 1993; Bain, 1998; Snyder and Cummings, 1998). In addition, while it is tempting to associate learning with positive growth and change, this is not always the case. Previously learned approaches may become inappropriate and it is for this reason that some authors refer to the need for 'unlearning' as well as learning (e.g. Hedberg, 1981; Fiol and Lyles, 1985). As a consequence, it should not be taken for granted that interproject learning is necessarily a good thing. This very much depends on the characteristics of learning and their influences on practice. The dangers of unreflexively repeating previous patterns of action, which are often reinforced by a perceived association with successful outcomes, mean that it is important to direct interpretative efforts at the assumptions and mental models upon which detailed processes of identifying and solving problems are built (Hedberg and Wolff, 2001). Unfortunately, project time pressures and the cult of immediacy hinder such reflexive practices, with the result that existing practices are simply reproduced.

References

Argyris, C. and Schön, D. A. (1978) *Organizational Learning: A Theory of Action Perspective*. Reading, MA: Addison-Wesley.

Ascher, H. (1965) *Cost Quality Relationships in the Air Frame Industry.* Santa Monica, CA: Rand Corporation.

Bain, A. (1998) Social defenses against organizational learning. *Human Relations* 51(3): 413–429.

Bartezzaghi, E., Corso, M. and Verganti, R. (1997) Continuous improvement and inter-project learning in new product development. *International Journal of Technology Management* 14: 116–138.

Bateson, G. (1972) *Steps to an Ecology of Mind.* New York: Ballantine.

DeFillippi, R. and Arthur, M. (1998) Paradox in project-based enterprise: the case of film making. *California Management Review* 40(2): 125–139.

Engeström, Y. (2000) Comment on Blackler et al. activity theory and the social construction of knowledge: a story of four umpires. *Organization* 7(2): 301–310.

Fiol, C. M. and Lyles, M. A. (1985) Organizational learning. *Academy of Management Review* 10: 803–813.

Grant, R. M. (1996) Prospering in dynamically-competitive environments: organizational capability as knowledge integration. *Organization Science* 7(4): 375–387.

Hedberg, B. (1981) How organizations learn and unlearn. In Nyström, F. and Starbuck, W. (eds) *Handbook of Organizational Design*, Vol. 1, *Adapting Organizations to their Environments.* New York: Oxford University Press, pp. 3–27.

Hedberg, B. and Wolff, R. (2001) Organizing, learning, and strategizing: from construction to discovery. In Dierkes, M., Berthoin Antal, A., Child, J. and Nonaka, I. (eds) *Handbook of Organizational Learning and Knowledge.* Oxford: Oxford University Press, pp. 535–556.

Hobday, M. (1998) Product complexity, innovation and industrial organisation. *Research Policy* 26: 689–710.

Janis, I. (1974) *Victims of Groupthink.* Boston, MA: Houghton Mifflin.

Levinthal, D. A. and March, J. G. (1993) The myopia of learning. *Strategic Management Journal* 14: 95–112.

Lindkvist, L., Söderlund, J. and Tell, F. (1998) Managing product development projects – on the significance of fountains and deadlines. *Organization Studies* 19(6): 931–951.

March, J. G., Sproull, L. S. and Tamuz, M. (1991) Learning from samples of one or fewer. *Organization Science* 2(1): 1–13.

Minsky, M. A. (1975) Framework for representing knowledge. In Winston, P. H. (ed.) *The Psychology of Computer Vision.* New York: McGraw-Hill, pp. 211–277.

Nelson, R. R. and Winter, S. G. (1982) *An Evolutionary Theory of Economic Change.* Cambridge, MA: Harvard University Press.

Prencipe, A. and Tell, F. (2001) Inter-project learning: processes and outcomes of knowledge codification in project-based firms. *Research Policy* 30: 1373–1394.

Schank, R. and Childers, P. (1984) *The Cognitive Computer: On Language, Learning and Artificial Intelligence*. Reading, MA: Addison-Wesley.

Snyder, W. M. and Cummings, T. G. (1998) Organizational learning disorders: conceptual model and intervention hypotheses. *Human Relations* 51(7): 873–895.

Söderlund, J. (2000) Time-limited and complex interaction – studies of industrial projects. Linköping Studies in Management and Economics, Dissertations, No. 42.

Tell, F. and Söderlund, J. (2001) Lärande mellan projekt. In Berggren, C. and Lindkvist, L. (eds) *Projekt: Organisation for målorientering och lärande*. Lund: Studentlitteratur.

Zollo, M. and Winter, S. G. (2002) Deliberate learning and the evolution of dynamic capabilities. *Organization Science*, 13(13): 339–351.

Chapter 11

Learning from project failure

Terry Williams, Fran Ackermann, Colin Eden and Susan Howick

Introduction

This final chapter describes the experiences of a team of management scientists helping a global manufacturing company to learn from its project management experiences, mainly from project failures. The team has been involved in detailed post-mortem analysis of a range of projects as part of work preparing claims by contractors against clients over the past eleven years, particularly delay and disruption (D&D) claims. The projects have been in a range of industries, including railway rolling-stock, aerospace, civil engineering and shipbuilding, and have been situated in Europe, Canada, the UK and the USA. The total value of all the claims has been around US $1.5 billion, all of which has been met with a significant degree of success through out-of-court settlements. A significant proportion of these claims has been with one particular global manufacturing company, and both the company and the team have been concerned to ensure that organizational learning is attained from the experiences, resulting in changes in project management practice.

The chapter initially looks at why learning from complex projects is usually difficult. It is argued that it is the systemic nature of complex projects that the reasons for their behaviour are not always apparent. Analysis that appreciates the systemic consequences of disruptions is crucial to organizational learning. This type of analysis facilitates the project team to appreciate the systemicity inherent in such projects. This appreciation, though, needs to be converted in changed practice which requires an infusion into the company culture. The chapter goes on to discuss how the authors' involvement with this specific company has facilitated this process, not only in increasing awareness and appreciation of project systemicity, but also in providing new management processes that attempt to identify at-risk projects in the very earliest stages.

This chapter does not include a separate traditional case study. This is because the chapter is the combination of a set of lessons about project behaviour drawn from a range of case studies.

Why is learning from projects difficult?

What is a 'complex' project? Simon (1982) describes a complex system as one in which 'the whole is more than the sum of the parts, not in an ultimate, metaphysical sense but in the important pragmatic sense that, given the properties of the parts and the laws of interaction, it is not a trivial matter to infer the properties of the whole'. This description of a complex system suggests that, when we come to look at the behaviour of complex projects, while we may know the effects and issues that impacted upon the project, and we may know the outcomes from the project, it is difficult to understand intuitively how the latter came from the former. Indeed, it is becoming increasingly recognized that analysing such projects using traditional project-management techniques, which are based around the ideas of decomposing the project into its constituent parts and rigidly maintaining a plan based on the decomposition, is insufficient and does not explain the outcomes (Koskela and Howell, 2002; Malgrati and Damiani, 2002; Williams, 2003a).

Understanding how complex projects behave under imperfect conditions has developed in recent years through a number of streams of modelling work. A key stream is represented by the authors of this chapter, carried out at Strathclyde University in Scotland. This team has been involved in post-mortem analysis of a range of complex projects over the past decade, mainly in preparing D&D claims. Two members of the team had already developed cognitive/causal mapping techniques, backed up by purpose-built software (Decision Explorer and Group Explorer; see www.banxia.com and www. phrontis.com, respectively) to elicit, understand and analyse the structure of complex systems of causality (Ackermann and Eden, 2004). These techniques were immediately appropriate to study causality in a project, and the use of system dynamics to produce quantitative results followed naturally. The methodology and techniques used on the first claim, on the Channel Tunnel 'Shuttle' train-wagons, are described in Ackermann et al. (1997), and the techniques have been further developed. The section following briefly describes the techniques.

The claims all entail a detailed analysis of the dynamic behaviour of large complex and disrupted projects. The team thus needed to be able to trace complex sets of causal links from actions taken by the parties through the dynamic behaviours set up within the project and, subsequently, to understand and quantify the resulting effects. It is only in this way that the effects of the disruptive actions taken by the client (and contractor) can be tracked through all the complex interacting parts of the project and thus the outcome of the project explained. The projects are all characterized by 'messiness': root causes of problems are often unclear, complex patterns of causality are unclear, and many of the effects observed are counterintuitive. This stream of work has therefore built up an understanding of project behaviour, providing explanations that derive from the systemic interrelated set of causal effects that determine the behaviour of projects.

This approach was important because the effects of disruptions in projects, which sometimes appear trivial, are not individual, isolated, influences; rather, they combine together in systemic structures. One way in which influences compound is sometimes called the portfolio effect, where effects combine to give an effect greater than the sum of their individual effects; for example, a succession of change orders (also referred to as variations) on a project can collide: as management try to deal with them, their effects can compound each other in unintended and unexpected ways. A second and more fundamental impact is the combination of effects into dynamic behaviour characterized by feedback loops. When effect A causes, exacerbates or promotes effect B, which causes, exacerbates or promotes effect C, and so on, this can be captured by traditional decomposition methods so long as the chain is not too complex or does not return and form a loop; however, where effect A leads to effect B leads to effect C leads back to effect A, this creates dynamic consequences driven by a feedback loop. Where these loops are positive (self-sustaining), each effect tends to increase itself and the project spirals towards increasing negative outcomes (vicious circles). Williams et al. (1995) describe typical examples of such loops for the Channel Tunnel Shuttle train-wagons analysis. It is well known that managers make decisions particularly poorly for problems involving feedback mechanisms (Sterman, 1989), and it is these loops that often produce the counterintuitive behaviour within projects, drawing some simple feedback-loop diagrams.

Perhaps the most important way in which such loops are set up and exacerbated derives from management responses to project perturbations; hence the sometimes counterintuitive effect of such actions. Eden et al. (2000) and Williams (2002) describe some of these effects, showing how feedback structures can be set up and how they can highly magnify small effects in a project. Particular actions are those taken to accelerate projects delayed because of responses to disruptions, such as increasing parallelism between activities, starting activities earlier than appropriate and increasing staffing levels beyond efficient levels. All such actions typically set up feedback loops and bring about unanticipated and often counterintuitive results. A key lesson here is that a major cause of feedback and thus of badly failed projects is management action taken to accelerate a time-constrained project after a delay and the prospect of failure have been noticed.

Another stream of work (the first to begin chronologically) has been carried out by Cooper and others at PA Consulting. They also use system dynamics to model the systemic relationships within a project, although their methodology appears not as clearly defined in the literature, nor does it appear to pay attention to the causal structuring aspect of analysis. This work began over twenty years ago (Cooper, 1980) and has analysed project behaviour in various domains. Cooper et al. (2002) point to a number of factors that inhibit successful post-project analysis, including 'the difficulty in determining the true causes of project performance'. They also discuss feedback structures as the root of the complexity, but point to three archetypal structures that underlie project dynamics: the rework cycle (including the discovery of unexpected rework), feed-back effects on productivity and work quality, and knock-on effects from upstream phases to downstream phases (Cooper, 1993; Lyneis et al., 2001). The Strathclyde team, in contrast, tends to start with the specificities of the project and partici-pants in it, with few a priori assumptions, rather than applica-tion of predefined project templates.

For complex projects, then, collecting project data is not usu-ally the problem; it is, rather, gaining causal understanding about what went wrong (or right) and why. Analysis needs to provide not only the easy lessons ('there was bad weather which delayed the whole project by two weeks'), but also the lessons that derive from these more complex, possibly non-intuitive behaviours of projects that may follow from the dis-ruption of bad weather ['we doubled our workforce on this project but it only yielded 5 per cent extra output', an example of Cooper's (1994) '$2000 hour']. Unless an elaborated under-standing of causality can be determined it is impossible to go beyond trite learning and prescriptions about how to manage better future projects. The outcome of large projects is generally messy and the history is unclear, and simple reflection does not provide lessons about project behaviour that is non-intuitive or counterintuitive, so structuring of causality and simulation modelling is necessary to establish, with any confidence, the chains of causality and their effects.

The need for learning lessons from projects in practice is well known. Kerzner (2000) places continuous learning and improvement as the highest level of project management maturity in an organization. Cooke-Davis (2002), from a major empirical study, finds one of the twelve key success factors in project-orientated organizations to be 'an effective means of "learning from experience" on projects, that combines explicit knowledge with tacit knowledge in a way that encourages people to learn and to embed that learning into continuous improvement of project management processes and practices'. But such reviews have so far had hardly any mention in many of the organizational maturity models – standards that meas-ure how mature a company is in applying project manage-ment (e.g. Cooke-Davies and Arzymanow, 2002) – although recent maturity standards work, reported in Schlichter (2001), requires a process to capture, store and disseminate lessons learned, and it is thought that the results of this work in the Project Management Institute (PMI) OPM3 standard (Project Management Institute, 2003) will also discuss postproject lessons learned. There are also some examples of postproject review processes in practice. Probably most well known is the Post Project Appraisal (PPA) Unit at BP (Gulliver, 1987), and Turner et al. (2000) mention systems used by Ericsson and ABB Ltd.

In practice, projects are often not reviewed at all. This can be for a variety of reasons, some of which are discussed in Williams (2003b), but a key reason is that these methods are not designed to take into account complexity and do not attempt to model or explain causality [e.g. Roth and Kleiner's (1998) 'Learning histories' record but do not analyse]. The standard methods simply do not provide the facility to understand what happened and thus to learn lessons. So how do we analyse a complex project and understand what happened and why? How do we sort through the 'mess' that results in practice and trace the complex structures of causality? And, how do we translate this learning into new practice? The next section describes the techniques used by the Strathclyde team in the post-mortem work, analysing actual projects to find the underlying causal structures and thus to learn the real lessons from the project experiences.

Using causal mapping to facilitate learning

Causal mapping has been used extensively to assist with a range of messy or complex situations, including strategic problem structuring (Eden and Ackermann, 2001) and strategy development (Eden and Ackermann, 1998). When taken in the context of system dynamics modelling experience it appeared to make sense to adopt it before the construction of the simulation model to quantify the impact of disruptions on project failure (Eden and Harris, 1976). Although used to model complex situations, it is important to note that this application of causal mapping was different to other more traditional uses in that it was predominantly forensic in focus (Ackermann and Eden, 2004). Mapping works through building up an extensive causal network (a large directed graph), comprising contributions (assertions, facts, options, events, issues, etc.) and their relationships, in the form of a 'means–end' structure. Thus, those involved in constructing the causal map are able not only to examine the consequences of particular actions, but also to tease out some of the detail explaining particular statements and consider the whole as well as the parts. The map, often referred to as a model, thus becomes an artefact capable of analysis and consideration, providing it is constructed using formal and consistent rules.

Facilitating its use, the technique can be used in a variety of modes ranging from the construction of individual maps (cognitive maps) generated during interviews with project participants, to computer-supported working with groups of project participants. Interviews provide the means for in-depth consideration and reflection of a single manager responsible for a particular part of the project. The resultant cognitive map depicts one perspective on a part of the project. This process of mapping through individual interviews also often acts as a cathartic experience for the interviewee, where those involved are better able to understand their own thinking and actions; that is, individual learning occurs. Group techniques provide the means for shared understanding, mutual questioning of how different viewpoints connect with each other, and the means for negotiating agreed understanding of the reasons for project outcomes. Using computer-based mapping software (Decision Explorer) enables visual interactive modelling (allowing for easy amendments both in terms of the content itself and what is displayed on a public screen), along with the ability to enable anonymous contributions, and ensure rapid and more complete capture of views, which include views that could not be easily expressed in a public forum. The software facilitates real-time and 'backroom' analysis of the resultant model.

The use of causal mapping on projects that have failed has enabled the authors to identify a number of ways in which mapping facilitates learning. These are as follows.

Appreciation of the complexity following disruptions

Maps built to reflect projects that have failed typically require over 2000 nodes within them to explain the nature of outcomes. This wealth of material provides three key benefits. The first follows from the ability to track multiple and extended ramifications of simple disruptions through to major consequential outcomes. The second surrounds the ability to understand the impact of interactions between different parts of, and responsibilities for, the project in its entirety. Thus, for example, engineers in one part of a project can appreciate the situation of those in other parts (in many large projects, there are different groups working on different aspects of the project, sometimes in different plants and countries), and the engineering function and manufacturing functions can understand how their apparently independent problematic situations have been self-generated and self-sustained. The third benefit follows from the ability to understand the impact of portfolios of disruptions, where individual items alone would probably not have resulted in difficulties, but their combinatorial effect results in massive disruptive consequences. For example, an engineer being asked to make changes to one part of the project is unaware that other engineers are being asked to make other changes that impact across to the other part of the project. As a result, the cross-impact creates unexpected rework (triggering the 'rework cycle' referred to above) and resources believed to be available for other work (if there were no multiple impacts and rework) are no longer available, resulting in managers mitigating the demand for earned value output, requesting overtime and so creating exhausted staff who are also demoralized through continually repeating the same work, resulting in lower productivity and so the need to take on extra staff. Multiple feedback loops can be traced as the last of these situations is analysed and illustrated through the causal model.

Ability to stand back and reflect on own decisions

Frequently, a feeling of guilt besets managers involved in projects that are considered to have 'failed'; they feel that they did not do their job properly and are less competent than they had presumed. As a result, they often become defensive and not open to exploring what went wrong and what could be done about avoiding experiencing the situation again. However, as noted above, as they begin a guided tour of the systemic consequences of impacts to the project and explore its complexity, they begin to realize that their job was extremely difficult and that, given the circumstances, they did a competent if not outstanding job. As a consequence, their defensiveness drops and they become more open to understanding what occurred and why, using their experiences and the model's ability to help them to reflect and so to learn effectively (Kolb, 1984).

Analysing the model

In addition to helping project participants to reflect on the complexity, analysis routines built into the mapping software Decision Explorer enable a number of additional insights to be detected. The first of these is the presence of the type of feedback discussed above. Typically several hundred less obvious feedback loops are discovered and analysis facilitates their discovery; more importantly, the most crucial aspects of these loops are determined. Feedback loops, if positive, cause escalatory behaviour (both virtuous and/or vicious depending on the point of view), or stable/controlled behaviour if the feedback loop is negative. When examining projects that have failed the analyses have revealed that these may contain anywhere up to 1000 vicious feedback loops, well beyond what any individual project manager or project participant could understand while working on the project. While project members may have sight of some of the elements that contribute towards escalatory feedback they rarely have a sense of its extensiveness. As stated above, here learning is gained through both appreciating that dynamic behaviour can span different disciplines and understanding the ramifications of various mitigating actions.

The analysis also enables the detection of central nodes, those that have had a major impact on the project outcome.

Often participants are surprised that events they thought had a significant impact on the project, when scrutinized in terms of their structural position, turn out to be relatively minor. Other events, initially seen as trivial, emerge as key. Detection of these central nodes can also provide valuable clues about the main triggers of the feedback behaviour.

Triangulating the causal map with more precise modelling forms

Notwithstanding the above benefits gained from mapping, further learning can be gained through examining the simulation model of the project using quantitative modelling techniques, namely system dynamics (continuous simulation modelling). Here the aggregated beliefs of those involved in the qualitative mapping process can be tested against the data held on record, data such as labour usage, levels of overtime, key times of low morale, productivity and project progress measures. The simulation model is formed from an 'influence diagram', which is generated by paring down the qualitative causal model to its disruption triggers and main dynamic and quantifiable components (variables). Once the model has been built, the data underpinning the original estimate are entered to determine whether the model behaves in a manner that is representative of the project as it was expected to unfold without disruptions.

This process of validating the original expectations is crucial because this model represents the stream of events that will be disrupted, and so is the benchmark for judging the consequences of the full portfolio of disruptions. The outcome of the model over simulated time is also expected to match the actual project behaviour over time. Often this leads to a challenging of core beliefs and assumptions about the causes of project behaviour. For example, there may be differences between the model and actual peaks of labour usage. In these circumstances it is usual to discover that crucial aspects of disruptive consequences have been missed from the qualitative model, for example, timelags in forecasting the extent of the project completion delay. Many of these missing aspects of understanding derive from postrationalization and the development of urban

myths about the management of the project. Thus, the continual comparison between simulation model outcomes and the
qualitative causal model enables continual refinement of both
until satisfactory triangulation occurs. This process of triangulation drives important learning about project management
weaknesses and strengths.

Alongside checking the structure of the causal model, building simulation models often generates the need to build
additional models examining particular project properties. A
common example of one such project property is the need to
understand and unpick the attributes of the learning curve
(Howick and Eden, 2004). Organizations usually adopt a learning curve that is historically based and appears sound.
However, these curves are disrupted in complex ways where
there is consequential movement of labour, new approaches to
tooling required, hiring of new and untrained labour, use of
overtime and significant design changes. These consequences
affect both personal and corporate learning rates and progress.
Typically, extended modelling of the learning processes reveals
inadequacies in the use of the learning curve to any project.

Another example is appreciating the extent and nature of
the impact of project acceleration. Traditionally, to meet the
deadlines, managers accelerate work; however, through scru-
tinizing the simulation model along with ancillary spreadsheet
models, this assumption may be demonstrated as fallible
(Howick and Eden, 2001).

Encouraging learning organization-wide

The learning from failed projects discussed above has been
largely centred on those directly involved in the specific projects. Here, attempts to translate the learning across the whole
organization are discussed. Two approaches to encouraging
learning on an organization-wide basis are presented: a management training tool and the development of a methodology
for assessing risk.

As mentioned previously, a significant proportion of the
claims that the Strathclyde team have worked on have been
for one particular global manufacturing company. Although

the outcome of these claims has been relatively successful, the team and the organization wanted to draw general lessons from the experiences to improve the company's project management processes across the whole of the organization. In addition, the experiences gained from detailed analysis of claim projects have provided the organization with unique learning opportunities that were regarded as potentially setting them aside from their competitors.

Project management simulation tool

A project management training tool was seen to be an advantageous method of disseminating the learning discussed above (Williams et al., 1996). The impact of feedback dynamics was regarded as one of the most significant aspects of learning that was required. Research into dynamic decision making shows that managers suffer from persistent misperceptions of feedback (Sterman, 1989; Paich and Sterman, 1993; Diehl and Sterman, 1995) and it has been argued that system dynamics can help to overcome these problems and offer a framework for conceptualizing complex business issues (Graham et al., 1992). In addition to this, the use of a simulation tool means that the delays between the user's decisions and their effects are shortened. The tool therefore makes it easier for the user to observe cause and effect relationships, which is an important step towards identifying feedback dynamics in the project. A simulation tool also provides a risk-free environment for users to investigate decision processes.

The simulation tool was designed and constructed by the Strathclyde team based on their experiences of analysing a number of large, complex projects. The tool simulates a complex multimillion dollar project. The purpose of the simulated project is to design and construct a generic, but identifiable, product for the company that recognizes the specific nature of all of the products built by the organization. As often occurs in reality, two simple and apparently manageable disruptions occur at the beginning of the project: the client takes longer than expected to approve designs and also makes more comments than expected on the submitted designs. The aim of the simulation is for a group of managers to seek to deliver the project on time and within budget, given penalties for late delivery. Each group makes managerial decisions, on a monthly basis, about, for example, staffing levels in each of engineering design, industrial engineering and manufacturing (by choosing to obtain extra staff from other projects, from overtime or by hiring new staff), taking shortcuts in design checks, undertaking work-arounds to accelerate progress, and changing the amount of pressure to increase work output that should be placed on staff over the month.

A complex system dynamics model, based on the claim models, forms the basis of the simulation tool. A user-friendly and professional-looking interface was built on top of the system dynamics model using Visual Basic. The interface contains several layers of typical management reports. At the highest level, the user can gain information on the project status as a whole. To gain more detailed information on different aspects of the project, the user can drill down the different levels. In this way, the user can attempt to form a logical understanding of why particular results have occurred, based on similar information provided in the real world. Once users have reviewed the management reports, they form decisions for the following month, which will then be implemented in the simulation. The updated management reports are then made available again.

An additional facility that is also available at the end of a simulated month is the ability to forecast the expected outturn of the project. This is carried out in two ways. First, a traditional earned value forecast is made using the methods recommended as good project management and implemented by the organization for real projects. This forecast assumes that the same level of productivity will be gained over the remainder of the project as has been achieved in the project to date. The second forecast is arrived at by simulating the remainder of the project with all currently generated feedback dynamics included. This second forecast attempts to project forward the impact of attempts already made to accelerate the project in response to forecast delays in delivery, and generally shows a larger overrun in the project than the first, but presents a more realistic picture than most project planning tools. The comparison between the two forecasts provides the foundation of discussions on the limitations of traditional project management tools and the importance of feedback dynamics.

Before progressing to decision making for the next simulated month, the facilitators lead a focused learning discussion around some of the issues that have arisen over the preceding simulated month situations. In doing so, they encourage users to consider the potential long-term consequences of each set of their decisions to mitigate the growing impact of the disruptions, as well as develop a better understanding of the impact of apparently trivial client delays and changes to the design. This enables cause and effect relationships to be formed from their experiences. Users are also encouraged to construct causal maps of the feedback loops developing from the aggregation of the identified cause and effect relationships. The developing causal maps help with changing the users' understanding of the feedback nature of disrupted projects. The process of building feedback loops also provides the important transfer of learning from the simulation to analogous projects (Bakken et al., 1992).

Over a period of seven years, several hundred presidents, vice-presidents, directors and project managers from around the UK used the simulation tool as a part of a series of senior management seminars. Those who attend the seminars always identify with the issues raised during the use of the tool as being similar to those they face during day-to-day contact with their large, complex projects. The company expects to continue using the simulation tool in conjunction with newly developed web-based interactive project management learning material. Participants will study the main issues surrounding the management of complex projects via the web-based material, before attending a seminar where they will be exposed to the simulation tool and focus on the more advanced issues of managing a complex project that are highlighted by using the simulation.

Enhancing the company's risk management processes

The second way in which the Strathclyde team has worked with the company in disseminating the experiences gained through the several project analyses is through providing new tools to enhance the company's risk management processes. The various project analyses had highlighted the importance of risk systemicity; that is, the interrelationship between risks, as opposed to treating them as independent (often implied with risk register lists). In addition, there were many aspects of disrupted projects that were never properly assessed as a part of their accepted risk identification process. The team and organization therefore wanted to increase awareness and appreciation of the systemic nature of risks, and force a wider view of risk assessment within and across projects throughout the organization. In order to do so, new management processes were required to attempt to identify at-risk projects in the very earliest stages.

Various tools and techniques were researched and developed for the company. The tool that has had the greatest impact on the company's risk management processes has been labelled the 'Risk Filter' (Ackermann et al., 2003). As traditional project risk registers used by the organization neither took account of the systemic interactions between risks nor assessed many external risks, the Risk Filter was developed to be used alongside such existing risk management techniques. The Risk Filter was designed to be used in the very early stages of the bid process and identifies the key areas within the risk system of a particular project where effort should be devoted to mitigation, or a contingency fund acknowledged. Those projects that dropped through the Risk Filter were to be those not requiring further research and evaluation along the broader dimensions of risk used in the Risk Filter.

The filter was designed using extensive research and analysis of the entire claim models, both causal maps and quantitative simulation models. This research indicated the nature of risk systemicity and identified the crucial risk factors not currently assessed by the organization. The Risk Filter emerged as an organization-specific questionnaire within which were embedded the systemic properties. As the individual risks were assessed independently the risk impact was determined by considering the whole portfolio of answers and their impact on each other. The overall risk impact was used to judge the extent to which the project required further risk management work (dropping through the filter), required further research, required risk assessors to meet in a designed risk management workshop, or suggested the project to be too risky for further bid evaluation. The Risk Filter is now used on all the company's projects, and is also used at several stages during the life of a project to aid in the risk assessment and management of each project.

Conclusions

Learning from project failure is shown here to be difficult and potentially expensive, but possible. In this case the learning became possible because the cost of analysis of failure was borne by the need for developing forensic models to support litigation. In addition, the particular nature of the models (causal mapping and linked system dynamics simulation) enhanced the potential for focused learning. In many instances such potential for learning is lost as the focus remains on litigation only. In the examples provided in this chapter, the organization exploited the link between the use of academics to aid litigation modelling and their professional focus on learning. This link also made it easier to encourage learning by project staff specifically involved in failed projects as the litigation modelling progressed (the first part of this chapter), and also to consider the development of new processes and training tools (the latter part of the chapter).

References

Ackermann, F. and Eden, C. (2004) Using causal mapping: individual and group; traditional and new. In Pidd, M. (ed.) *Systems Modelling: Theory and Practice*. Chichester: Wiley, pp. 127–145.

Ackermann, F., Eden, C. and Williams, T. (1997) Modelling for litigation: mixing qualitative and quantitative approaches. *Interfaces* 27(2): 48–65.

Ackermann, F., Eden, C., Williams, T., Howick, S. and Gill, K. (2003) Systemic risk assessment: a case study. Working Paper 2003/1. Glasgow: University of Strathclyde, Department of Management Science.

Bakken, B., Gould, J. and Kin, D. (1992) Experimentation in learning organisations: a management flight simulator approach. *European Journal of Operational Research* 59: 167–182.

Cooke-Davis, T. (2002) The 'real' success factors on projects. *International Journal of Project Management* 20(3): 185–190.

Cooke-Davies, T. and Arzymanow, A. (2002) The maturity of project management in different industries. *IRNOP 5: Fifth International Conference of the International Research Network of Organizing by Projects*, Renesse, The Netherlands, May. East Horsley: EuroProjex.

Cooper, K. G. (1980) Naval ship production: a claim settled and a framework built. *Interfaces* 10 (6): 20–36.

Cooper, K. G. (1993) The rework cycle: benchmarks for the project manager. *Project Management Journal* 24(1): 17–21.

Cooper, K. G. (1994) The $2000 hour: how managers influence project performance through the rework cycle. *Project Management Journal* 25(1): 11–24.

Cooper, K. G., Lyneis, J. M. and Bryant, B. J. (2002) Learning to learn, from past to future. *International Journal of Project Management* 20(3): 213–219.

Diehl, E. and Sterman, J. D. (1995) Effects of feedback complexity on dynamic decision making. *Organisational Behavior and Human Decision Processes* 62: 198–215.

Eden, C. and Ackermann, F. (1998) *Making Strategy: The Journey of Strategic Management*. London: Sage.

Eden, C. and Ackermann, F. (2001) SODA – the principles. In Rosenhead, J. and Mingers, J. (eds) *Rational Analysis in a Problematic World Revisited*. London: Wiley, pp. 21–42.

Eden, C. and Harris, J. (1976) *Management Decision and Decision Analysis*. London: Macmillan.

Eden, C. L., Williams, T. M., Ackermann, F. A. and Howick, S. (2000) On the nature of disruption and delay (D&D) in major projects. *Journal of the Operational Research Society* 51(3): 291–300.

Graham, A. K., Morecroft, J. D. W., Senge, P. M. and Sterman J. D. (1992) Model-supported case studies for management education. *European Journal for Operational Research* 59: 151–166.

Gulliver, F. R. (1987) Post-project appraisals pay. *Harvard Business Review* (March–April): 128–131.

Howick, S. and Eden, C. (2001) The impact of disruption and delay when compressing large projects: going for incentives? *Journal of the Operational Research Society* 52: 26–34.

Howick, S. and Eden, C. (2004) Managing learning in disrupted projects: in the nature of corporate and personal learning. Working Paper 2004/02. Glasgow: University of Strathclyde, Department of Management Science.

Kerzner, H. (2000) *Applied Project Management: Best Practices on Implementation*. New York: Wiley.

Kolb, D. A. (1984) *Experiential Learning*. Englewood Cliffs, NJ: Prentice-Hall.

Koskela, L. and Howell, G. (2002) The underlying theory of project management is obsolete. *Proceedings of PMI (Project Management Institute) Research Conference.* Seattle, PA: Project Management Institute, pp. 293–300.

Lyneis, J. M., Cooper, K. G. and Els, S. A. (2001) Strategic management of complex projects: a case study using system dynamics. *System Dynamics Review* 17: 237–260.

Malgrati, A. and Damiani, M. (2002) Rethinking the new project management framework: new epistemology, new insights. *Proceedings of PMI (Project Management Institute) Research Conference.* Seattle, PA: Project Management Institute, pp. 371–380.

Paich, M. and Sterman, J. D. (1993) Boom, bust, and failures to learn in experimental markets. *Management Science* 39: 1439–1458.

Project Management Institute (2003) *Organizational Project Management Maturity Model (OPM3) Overview.* Seattle, PA: Project Management Institute.

Roth, G. and Kleiner, A. (1998) Developing organisational memory through learning histories. *Organisational Dynamics* (Autumn): 43–59.

Schlichter, J. (2001) PMI's organizational project management maturity model: emerging standards. *Proceedings of PMI 2001, PMI's Annual Symposium.* Upper Darby, PA: Project Management Institute.

Simon, H. A. (1982) *Sciences of the Artificial*, 2nd edn. Cambridge, MA: MIT Press.

Sterman, J. D. (1989) Modeling of managerial behavior: misperceptions of feedback in a dynamic decision making experiment. *Management Science* 35: 321–339.

Turner, J. R., Keegan, A. and Crawford, L. (2000) Learning by experience in the project-based organization. *Proceedings of the PMI Research Conference.* Paris, PA: Project Management Institute.

Williams, T. M. (2002) *Modelling Complex Projects.* London: Wiley.

Williams, T. M. (2003a) The contribution of mathematical modelling to the practice of project management. *IMA Journal of Management Mathematics* 14(1): 3–30.

Williams, T. M. (2003b) Learning from projects. *Journal of the Operational Research Society* 54(5): 443–451.

Williams, T. M., Eden C. L., Ackermann, F. R. and Tait, A. (1995) Vicious circles of parallelism. *International Journal of Project Management* 13(3): 151–155.

Williams, T. M., Howick, S., Eden, C. and Ackermann, F. (1996) Modelling the management of complex projects: industry/university collaboration. Presented at the *UnIG '96 International Conference on Technology Management:* University/Industry/Government Collaboration, Istanbul, June, pp. 157–161.

Index